Hiking

Acadia National Park

Help Us Keep This Guide Up to Date

Every effort has been made by the authors and editors to make this guide as accurate and useful as possible. However, many things can change after a guide is published—trails are rerouted, regulations change, techniques evolve, facilities come under new managment, etc.

We would love to hear from you concerning your experiences with this guide and how you feel it could be improved and kept up to date. While we may not be able to respond to all comments and suggestions, we'll take them to heart and we'll also make certain to share them with the authors. Please send your comments and suggestions to the following address:

The Globe Pequot Press
Reader Response/Editorial Department
P.O. Box 480
Guilford, CT 06437

Or you may e-mail us at:

editorial@globe-pequot.com

Thanks for your input, and happy travels!

*A***FALCON**GUIDE®

Hiking

Acadia National Park

Dolores Kong and Dan Ring

FALCON®

GUILFORD, CONNECTICUT

AN IMPRINT OF THE GLOBE PEQUOT PRESS

Library of Congress Cataloging-in-Publication Data

Kong, Dolores.
    Hiking Acadia National Park / by Dolores Kong and Dan Ring.— 1st ed.
        p. cm.
    Includes index.
    ISBN 1-56044-923-3
    1. Hiking—Maine—Acadia National Park—Guidebooks. 2. Trails—Maine— Acadia National Park—Guidebooks. 3. Acadia National Park (Me.)—Guidebooks. I. Ring, Dan (Daniel) II. Title.

GV199.42.M22 A324 2001
917.41'450444—dc21

                             2001023941

Contents

Acknowledgments

For showing us a side of Acadia that most people don't see, and for being so generous with their time, we'd like to thank Jim Vekasi, Gary Stellpflug, Chris Barter, Wayne Barter, John Cousins, Deb Wade, David Kari, Kristen Britain, and the rest of the Acadia National Park staff; Margie Coffin, landscape architect for the National Park Service's Olmsted Center for Landscape Preservation; and Marla Major, associate conservation director for Friends of Acadia. Thank you for helping us to make this guide as accurate as possible. We'd also like to thank our friends Dianne Dumanoski and Carlo Obligato, Carol Stocker, and Robert Mussey for sharing with us their love of nature and history.

Map Legend

Interstate	(95)
US Highway	(1)
State or other principal road	(3) (233)
Paved road	
Park Loop Road	
Unpaved road, graded	
Unpaved road, poor	
Park carriage road	
Trailhead	○
Main trail	
Secondary trail	
Lakes/Waterways	
River/Stream	
Wetlands	
Park boundary	
Acadia National Park	

Campground	▲
Cabins/Buildings	■
Peak	1,000 ft.
Gate	•—•
Bridge	
Visitor center/ Ranger station	
Picnic area	᚛
Parking area	(P)
City/Town	○
Boat landing	
Boat route	
Lighthouse	
Hike number	15
Map orientation	N
Scale	0 0.5 1 Miles

Overview Map

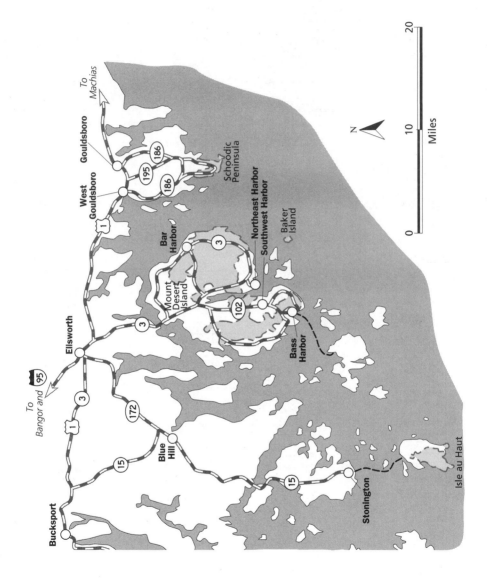

Introduction

There's nowhere else like Maine's Acadia National Park, where you can see the surf crash on pink granite cliffs or the fog roll in over Frenchman Bay, where you can walk moderate ridge trails to spectacular mountaintop views of the ocean, or scale cliffs on iron rungs and ladders.

With 120 miles of hiking trails and 45 miles of carriage roads throughout its approximately 40,000 acres, Acadia provides a wealth of opportunity to experience the many aspects of nature, for visitors of all fitness levels and abilities. Beginners can get dramatic views on easy trails such as the Ocean Path and the Cadillac Summit Loop, and the more experienced hikers will enjoy the Beehive Trail and other strenuous cliff climbs.

Even before Acadia was established as the first national park in the East in 1916, people were attracted by what the area had to offer. Native Americans, European settlers, nineteenth-century artists such as Thomas Cole and Frederic Church, and the Rockefellers, the Vanderbilts, and the Carnegies all came here lured by the beauty and the mystery, or the natural resources. In fact, the extensive trail system includes Native American paths, old roads, and trails built by local village improvement associations near the turn of the twentieth century.

To preserve this history, in 1999 Acadia National Park, the National Park Service's Olmsted Center for Landscape Preservation, and Friends of Acadia began a major planning project for trail management, maintenance, and reconstruction. The project, estimated to take at least ten years to complete, is being funded by a $4 million commitment from Acadia National Park and $9 million in private matching funds raised by Friends of Acadia.

Acadia's trail system has been nominated for the National Register of Historic Places, and funding for trail maintenance comes from a variety of sources, including millions of dollars from private donors and visitor fees. Federal officials announced in 1999 that Acadia will become the first national park with trails maintained by a private endowment, Acadia Trails Forever, raised in partnership with Friends of Acadia.

The 45 miles of carriage roads in Acadia are equally historic, constructed by Mount Desert Island summer resident John D. Rockefeller Jr., beginning in 1911. Although the carriage roads are suitable for hiking, they are also used by bicyclists and horseback riders, and are not described in this guide.

From open mountain ridge trails to lush forest paths, from oceanside strolls to cliff climbs, Acadia offers them all. The most famous of Acadia views—toward Frenchman Bay, the Porcupine Islands, and Bar Harbor—come from any number of trails that go up Champlain, Dorr, or Cadillac, the three easternmost mountains on Mount Desert Island and closest to the bay. But there are equally stunning views from hikes up the mountains to the west, Penobscot and Sargent, for instance, or Acadia Mountain.

Most of the park's trails are located on Mount Desert Island, within a short ride from Bar Harbor, the island's main town. But there are also trails worth exploring on Isle au Haut—reachable only by mail boat from Stonington—and on Schoodic Peninsula—the only part of the park on the mainland. There is no backpacking allowed in the park, except a limited amount on Isle au Haut to designated campsites at lean-to shelters only with a special use permit obtained ahead of time. There is no camping on trails allowed anywhere in the park.

Most of Acadia's trails are only a few miles long, but some of them are extremely challenging, with iron rungs and ladders bolted into vertical rock faces, or intricately laid stone steps, to make the paths passable. Some trails go along open ledges and can be difficult to navigate when wet or icy. Don't let the relatively short length of the trails or the relatively low elevation of the mountains lull you into complacency.

Some of the cliff trails may be closed during peregrine falcon breeding season from spring to late summer. If you are hiking this time of year, check with park officials before climbing the Precipice Trail, the Jordan Cliffs Trail, or the Valley Cove section of the Flying Mountain Trail. In Acadia you also need to be careful during wet or stormy weather. Trails along exposed mountain ridges can get slick when wet. Even casual walkers along the rocky shore must exercise caution.

NATURAL HISTORY

With nearly 300 species of birds, mammals such as white-tailed deer, red foxes, and coyotes, and habitats that range from mountaintop to seaside, Acadia National Park offers plenty of opportunities to enjoy nature.

In parts of the park, you may still see reminders of a huge fire that swept through much of Mount Desert Island in 1947. To learn more, visit the Wild Gardens of Acadia and the Nature Center at the Sieur de Monts entrance to the park, on Maine Highway 3 south of Bar Harbor. There is also a display along the Park Loop Road south of Hulls Cove Visitor Center that describes the great fire of 1947.

THREATENED AND ENDANGERED SPECIES

Acadia National Park features two magnificent birds that were only recently removed from the federal endangered species list—the bald eagle and the peregrine falcon. But the park continues to protect the birds, particularly the peregrine falcon. During the falcons' breeding season from spring to late summer, the park may close certain cliff trails to protect the chicks. The park also has rare yellow lady's slippers and other vegetation.

GEOLOGY

Glaciers, rivers, the ocean, the movement of tectonic plates, and volcanic activity all helped shape Acadia over the millennia. The result: pink granite cliffs, black bands of basaltic rock known as dikes, the fjord called Somes Sound, and Acadia's many mountains. At the top of Cadillac Mountain, you can learn more about the geology from the displays along the Cadillac Summit Loop Trail.

Low tide along Schoodic Peninsula makes a tranquil Acadia scene.

HUMAN HISTORY

Thousands of years before European settlers set eyes on the Maine coast, Native Americans canoed, fished, and made a life here. Some of their paths are part of Acadia's historic trail system, and their culture and heritage are celebrated and preserved at the Abbe Museum, located at the Sieur de Monts entrance to the park.

The museum, founded by Dr. Robert Abbe, a pioneer of the medical use of radium, expects to open a year-round facility in 2001 in downtown Bar Harbor, besides maintaining its seasonal museum at the Sieur de Monts Spring area.

In 1604, Samuel Champlain, navigator for French explorer Pierre Dugua Sieur de Mons, gave this area the name l'Isle des Monts Desert—or Island of Barren Mountains. This part of Acadia's history lives on in such landmarks as Sieur de Monts Spring and Champlain Mountain.

George B. Dorr, a park founder and its first superintendent, is remembered with Dorr Mountain, which towers over the land he first bought and preserved, around Sieur de Monts Spring.

A path leads to Sieur de Monts Spring and the sweet waters of Acadia.

How to Use This Guide

Covering nearly all 120 miles of the hiking trails in Acadia National Park, this guide is divided geographically into four parts: Mount Desert Island east of Somes Sound, Mount Desert Island west of Somes Sound, Isle au Haut, and the Schoodic Peninsula. Trails that extend beyond park boundaries are outside the scope of this book, but they are referred to in the text of some hikes. For example, in the description for Jesup Path, a reference is made to the Great Meadow Loop, a village connector trail built by Friends of Acadia in 1999 and 2000, linking Bar Harbor to the park.

Each section of this guide starts with an introduction providing an overview of the hikes and some of the highlights in that area. Various hikes up the same mountain are grouped together, allowing an easy comparison based on difficulty or length of the trail.

Each hike chapter is numbered and begins with an at-a-glance section featuring highlights, type of hike, total distance, difficulty, directions to the trailhead, parking and trailhead facilities, key mileage points, and other information. Each chapter includes a trail map, an elevation graph, and a hike description. A hike may also have an options section.

The **Highlights** section describes the views and terrain and notes any special features, such as if it's a less-traveled trail, or if it's closed during peregrine falcon breeding season.

The **Type of hike** outlines whether it's a loop or an out-and-back hike.

The **Total distance** gives the mileage. Keep in mind that while we did our best to record accurate mileages, the distances are only approximate both in the hike narrative and on the map.

The **Difficulty** rating for each hike—easy, moderate, or strenuous—is based on our walking each trail and assessing the terrain and elevation gain. Easy trails are those that are basically flat and well graded and are suitable for families with young children or adults not seeking rigorous exercise. Moderate trails have some elevation gain and rough footing. Strenuous trails have either steep ascents or iron rungs and ladders, and should be hiked only by those unafraid of heights.

The **Parking and trailhead facilities** section lets you know if parking is available and lists facilities such as chemical toilet, restrooms, phone, restaurant, and so on.

The **Key points** section describes cumulative mileage, key trail junctions, and prominent trail features. The trailhead is listed as the first key point, usually at mileage 0.0. But sometimes the starting mileage reflects the distance that must be traveled on another trail first, before the trailhead for the hike being described is reached. **The hike** details the terrain, the scenery, and other special aspects of the trail. And the **Options** section summarizes alternative loops, additional mileage, and different return routes than what's described for the official hike.

5

Backcountry Safety and Hazards

BEING PREPARED

Although Acadia is one of the most visited national parks and its backcountry is never too far from civilization, don't let that lull you into a false sense of security. Visitors to Acadia have been injured in falls while hiking along trails. The hazards here are not from bears or mountain lions as may be the case out West, but from hiking accidents. To minimize the risk of injury, wear proper clothing and footwear, know your limits, watch the weather, and mind your step.

The mountains are relatively low here, but the exposed ridges can still be dangerous during stormy weather. If rain starts falling, head for shelter, being careful not to slip on the wet granite. When hiking along the coast, watch out for storm waves, especially in spring and fall.

HAZARDS

Ticks that transmit Lyme disease and other biting insects. To minimize the risk of Lyme disease, wear long pants and tuck them into your socks. After the hike, check for ticks. Insect repellent should also be taken along on the hike in case mosquitoes and blackflies are a problem.

Poison ivy. Wearing long pants as well as a long-sleeved shirt is a good way to prevent contact with poison ivy, but perhaps the best way is to learn how to spot and avoid the plant, which has distinctive leaves in groups of three.

Heat exhaustion. To prevent heat exhaustion, drink plenty of water if you're hiking on a hot day. Don't wait until you feel thirsty.

Hypothermia. To prevent hypothermia, wear layers of wool or a synthetic like fleece or polypropylene, all of which continue to insulate when wet. Avoid wearing cotton because it does not insulate when wet. Take along a top layer that is water and wind resistant. The best prevention, however, is to avoid hiking in cold, wet weather.

Giardia. Do not drink the water you may encounter on the trails, or you may risk diarrhea and dehydration from a microbe called *Giardia lamblia*. Take your own supply of drinking water and carry it in a daypack.

And finally, follow some simple rules of etiquette while hiking. If crossing a carriage road to continue on a trail, look both ways and give any horseback riders or bicyclists the right-of-way. Allow faster hikers to pass on the trail, and let slower hikers know of your presence before you pass on the left. Do not kick or throw loose stones. Although there are hazards to hiking in Acadia as elsewhere, some commonsense measures will make your

Rushing water continues to shape Acadia.

trip safe and enjoyable. For further reading, refer to Falcon Publishing's *Wild Country Companion* and *Wilderness First Aid.*

SEASONS AND WEATHER

July and August are the most popular months in Acadia, but hiking here is possible from late April through early to mid-November. In fact, late spring and early to midfall offer some of the best hiking, with plenty of solitude. You will be able to take advantage of offseason rates for lodging and practically have the trails to yourself. If you wait until fall, you can hike some of the trails that may have been closed from spring to late summer during the peregrine falcon breeding season.

In the summer, temperatures reach 70 to 80 degrees F, and fog may be common. In spring and fall, the highs reach 50 to 60 degrees F; in winter, highs are about 30 degrees F, and lows may be below zero. Snow falls occasionally, with as much as 60 inches possible some winters. But as in all New England, weather can change suddenly. Be prepared no matter what season you are hiking. To get up-to-date weather, check www.weather.com or weather.gov. You can also refer to Falcon's *Reading Weather.*

TRIP ESSENTIALS

Maps

We have provided maps that are suitable for most hikes, but the distances are only approximate. You can purchase the USGS Acadia National Park and Vicinity Map before hiking in the park.

Mount Desert Island

A good jumping-off point for any hiking trip to Acadia is the seasonal Hulls Cove Visitor Center on Maine Highway 3, just northwest of Bar Harbor on Mount Desert Island. There, you can watch a free film about the park and get updated trail conditions and other information. There is a well-stocked bookstore run by Eastern National at the visitor center. After October 31, you can get visitor information from the park headquarters on ME 233, west of Bar Harbor.

The park entrance fee is $10 per vehicle for a seven-day pass. From late June to Labor Day there is a free Island Explorer shuttle bus between points on Mount Desert Island and the park. See the appendix for information on the Island Explorer.

Park regulations permit fires and camping only in designated sites. Pets must be leashed and attended, and they are not allowed on ladder trails, beaches, inside public buildings, or on ranger programs. Do not feed the wildlife. Visitors are prohibited from collecting plants, animals, rocks, and other natural or historic features.

Most of the Acadia backcountry on Mount Desert Island is never far from civilization, with gas, groceries, lodging, and restaurants in Bar Harbor, Northeast Harbor, Southwest Harbor, and other towns. And on the Park Loop Road, close to many trails, is the Jordan Pond House, famous for its popovers

Ocean ducks known as common eiders are often seen frolicking off the rocky coast.

and afternoon tea, and its view of the twin peaks known as the Bubbles.

The Jordan Pond House restaurant and gift shop are open mid-May to October, 11:30 A.M. to 8 P.M., and until 9 P.M. from late June to early September.

Aside from wearing proper footwear and clothing, and carrying drinking water and insect repellent, the most planning you will need to do for a hiking trip on Mount Desert Island is to make sure you have accommodations, especially during the summer.

There are plenty of private campgrounds, motels, and hotels on the island, but they often get booked up. There is a Thompson Island Information Center on ME 3 as you cross from the mainland to Mount Desert Island, if you need to check for lodging. See the appendix for local chamber of commerce numbers, addresses, and websites.

Acadia offers two campgrounds on Mount Desert Island, Blackwoods and Seawall campgrounds. Blackwoods Campground, south of Bar Harbor on ME 3, is open year-round, with reservations required only from mid-June through mid-September. Call (800) 365-2267 or go to the Internet, http://reservations.nps.gov, to reserve a site. Seawall Campground, open only from late May to the end of September on a first-come, first-served basis, is off ME 102A, south of Southwest Harbor. Campsites are $18 per night in season, with lower rates during the off-season and for walk-in sites.

Schoodic Peninsula

A hiking trip to Schoodic Peninsula requires little preparation other than making sure you have accommodations. This less visited part of the park, nearly 50 miles from Bar Harbor, is close to the towns of Winter Harbor, Birch Harbor, and Gouldsboro, where there are some accommodations and services. There is no overnight camping in this part of the park.

Isle au Haut

To visit Isle au Haut, reachable only by mail boat from Stonington, nearly 65 miles from Bar Harbor, you'll need to make the most preparations. Stonington offers some groceries and restaurants if you forget to pack a lunch, and it has lodging and bike rentals.

For a day trip here, you'll need to know the mail boat schedule and pack a picnic lunch. To check the boat schedule, contact the Isle au Haut Co. (207) 367-5193. There's a limit on the number of visitors allowed per day on the island, so it's best to get to the mail boat early.

There are no snack stands at Duck Harbor Landing, where most visitors to Isle au Haut get off, only a small grocery store with limited hours 5 miles away at the town landing. Take your own sandwiches and drinks and carry your own trash out. The only backpacking allowed in Acadia is on Isle au Haut between May 15 and October 15, and it's limited to getting you to and from the mail boat to designated campsites at lean-to shelters at Duck Harbor Campground. You need a special use permit. There is no camping allowed along the trails.

From mid-June through early September, Monday through Saturday, the mail boat lands at Duck Harbor, making it a very short backpack. The rest of the time, the boat goes only to the town landing, which is about a 5-mile backpack away from the campground.

To apply for a special use permit for one of the five lean-to shelters at Duck Harbor Campground, you must either make a reservation request in person at the year-round park headquarters on ME 233 or get a reservation request form and return it by mail, postmarked April 1 or later, to Acadia National Park, P.O. Box 177, Bar Harbor, ME 04609, attention Isle au Haut Reservations. Telephone requests are not accepted, although you can call (207) 288-3338 to get a reservation request form sent to you. At the time this guide went to publication, the fee is $25 for up to three nights at the height of the season, or up to five nights before June 15 and after September 15. You must have your special use permit with you when you land on Isle au Haut.

No pets are allowed overnight at Duck Harbor Campground, although they are allowed on day hiking trips. The campground has no trash disposal. Facilities include fire rings, picnic tables, pit toilets, and a hand pump for water. Isle au Haut has no private campgrounds.

Zero Impact

To keep Acadia as natural and unspoiled as possible, follow these zero-impact principles suggested by the park service and the Leave No Trace program, managed by LNT Inc., a Boulder, Colorado–based nonprofit organization:

- Plan ahead and prepare.

- Travel on durable surfaces and stay on trails. Walk in the center of the path, to prevent trail widening and erosion.

- Dispose of waste properly. Pack it in, pack it out, and dispose of human waste in a hole 6 inches deep and at least 100 feet from water or trails.

- Leave what you find. Don't remove such natural objects as stones, flowers, starfish, or antlers.

- Minimize campfire impacts.

- Respect wildlife. Do not feed wildlife because they can starve in winter, get hit by cars, or become pests.

- Be considerate of other visitors.

- Leash pets. Keeping pets on leashes no longer than 6 feet protects pets and wildlife, and is proper trail etiquette.

Authors' Favorite Hikes

EASY DAY HIKES	1 Bar Island Trail
	8 Sand Beach and Great Head Trail
	9 Ocean Path
	27 Cadillac Summit Loop Trail
	36 Jordan Pond Shore Trail, eastern half
	62 Beech Cliff Trail
	79 Wonderland Trail
MODERATE DAY HIKES	3 Beachcroft Trail
	4 Bear Brook Trail
	10 Gorham Mountain Trail
	25 Cadillac Mountain South Ridge Trail
	33 Day Mountain Trail
	38 Bubble Rock Trail
	44 Penobscot Mountain Trail
	47 Sargent Mountain South Ridge Trail
	54 Parkman Mountain Trail
	57 Acadia Mountain Trail
	61 Flying Mountain Trail
	84 Cliff Trail, Isle au Haut
STRENUOUS DAY HIKES	2 Precipice Trail
	6 Beehive Trail
	45 Jordan Cliffs Trail
	50 Giant Slide Trail
	63 Beech Cliff Ladder Trail
	82 Duck Harbor Mountain Trail, Isle au Haut

Mount Desert Island, East of Somes Sound

Most of Acadia National Park's trails, the main Park Loop Road, and many of the best views are on the eastern half of Mount Desert Island. From the summit of Cadillac Mountain, the highest on the Atlantic coast, you can see Bar Harbor, Frenchman Bay, and the Porcupine Islands, one of Acadia's best-known vistas. A summit road takes you to the top, or you can hike up one of the mountain's several trails. You can get even closer-up views of the ocean from such lower peaks as Dorr, Champlain, and Gorham mountains, such easy to moderate trails as Ocean Path and Sand Beach and Great Head Trail, and challenging cliff climbs like the Beehive and Precipice trails. This part of the park also features the Jordan Pond House, famous for its afternoon tea and popovers, and its view of the distinctive mountains called the Bubbles. A series of trails leaves from here, ranging from a pond loop to long routes up Penobscot and Sargent mountains. Another major jumping-off point for trails in this part of the park is at the Sieur de Monts entrance on Maine Highway 3, south of Bar Harbor. The Wild Gardens of Acadia, the Nature Center, and the Abbe Museum are also located here, and you can spend hours learning about the Native American and natural history of the area. The westernmost peaks in this section of the park include Norumbega, Parkman, Sargent, and Penobscot mountains. The views from these open summits range from Somes Sound to the west, the Cranberry Isles to the south, and Cadillac Mountain to the east.

Mount Desert Island, East of Somes Sound

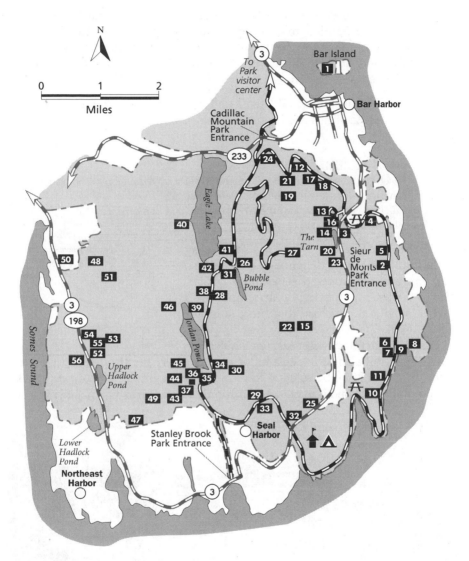

1 Bar Island Trail

Highlights: Low-tide walk to rocky island off Bar Harbor.
Type of hike: Day hike; out-and-back.
Total distance: 1.4 miles.
Difficulty: Easy.

Finding the trailhead: From Maine Highway 3 outside park visitor center, head south 2.5 miles, toward downtown Bar Harbor. At the first intersection after the College of the Atlantic, turn left (east) onto West Street. The trail, visible only at low tide, leaves off Bridge Street, the first left from West Street on the edge of downtown.

Parking and trailhead facilities: Limited on-street parking can be found on West Street; facilities are in town.

Key points:
- 0.0 Bar Island Trailhead.
- 0.3 Reach the shore of Bar Island; head northeast up a gravel road behind a gate.
- 0.5 Junction; bear left (northeast) at a trail sign.
- 0.6 Junction; bear right (southeast) up to the island summit.
- 0.7 Island summit.

The hike: The Bar Island Trail is a short, easy jaunt within shouting distance of Bar Harbor, but you feel transported to another world. That's the beauty of being on an island, even such a small one so close to a busy summer resort town.

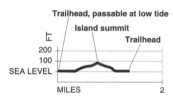

Easy enough for the least seasoned hiker, the Bar Island Trail also provides a bit of risk to satisfy the thrill-seeking adventurer—it can only be traveled at low tide, when a gravel bar connecting Bar Harbor and the island is exposed. "Caution!" a sign warns you once you reach

Only at low tide is the trail to Bar Island visible.

Bar Island Trail

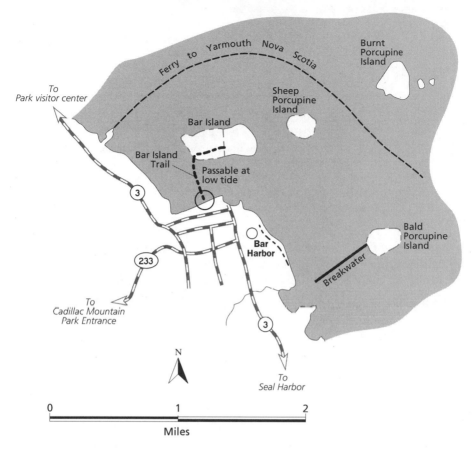

the island's rocky shores. "Safe crossing is $1\frac{1}{2}$ hours on either side of low tide. Check tide chart for daily tide time! Caution!" For your convenience, a tide chart is posted.

First described in 1867, the trail was reopened by the National Park Service in the 1990s. The island is still partly privately owned.

From the foot of Bridge Street in Bar Harbor, walk northwest across the gravel bar, reaching the island in 0.3 mile. Some of the resort town's historic summer "cottages"—really mansions—are visible along Bar Harbor's shoreline to the left (southwest) as you cross the gravel bar.

Once you reach Bar Island, head northeast up the gravel road behind the gate. The trail soon levels off at a grassy field. At 0.5 mile, bear left (northeast) at a trail sign pointing into the woods toward Bar Island summit. At 0.6 mile, bear right (southeast) at the fork, up a rocky knob. At 0.7 mile, you reach the summit, with its old wooden flagpole and views toward Bar Harbor.

From here you can hear the town's church bells, see the fishing and recreational boats along the harbor, and take in the smells of the sea and the views of the mountains. Return the way you came.

Options: Instead of taking the gravel road inland toward the summit, you can walk along the rocky shores on the western side of Bar Island, making it as long or as short a hike as you like.

2 Precipice Trail

Highlights: Dramatic and strenuous cliff climb to top of Champlain Mountain. May be closed during peregrine falcon breeding season, from spring through late summer.

Type of hike: Day hike; loop.

Total distance: 0.8 mile one way, or 2.3 to 3.1 miles to do a loop.

Difficulty: Strenuous.

Finding the trailhead: Enter the park at the Sieur de Monts entrance, 2 miles south of downtown Bar Harbor on Maine Highway 3. Turn right (south) on the one-way Park Loop Road. The trailhead is 2 miles from the entrance, on the right, at the Precipice Trail parking area.

Parking and trailhead facilities: Park at the Precipice Trail parking area; there are no facilities.

Key points:
- 0.0 Precipice Trailhead.
- 0.3 Junction with the East Face Trail. Bear left to continue up Precipice.
- 0.8 Champlain Mountain summit and junction with the Bear Brook Trail.
- 2.3 Return to the trailhead via the Bear Brook Trail and the East Face Trail.
- 3.1 Or return to the trailhead via the Bear Brook Trail and the Park Loop Road.

The hike: One of the steepest and most dramatic climbs in Acadia, the Precipice Trail ascends 930 feet in 0.8 mile, taking you by cliffs where peregrine falcons have begun breeding again and providing you with a bird's-eye view of the coast. But be aware that the trail is usually closed from spring to late summer during falcon breeding season to protect the still-threatened birds, so plan your climb accordingly.

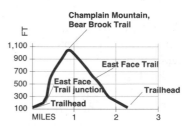

If you happen to hike when the trail is closed, you may still be able to get a look at peregrine falcons or other raptors soaring above the Precipice. A park service employee regularly sets up a high-powered scope in the Precipice parking area for people to look through when the trail is closed.

At the start of the trail, a big yellow sign warns: "The Precipice is maintained as a nontechnical climbing route, not a hiking trail. Attempt this route only if you are physically fit, wearing proper footwear, and have experience in climbing near exposed cliffs and heights. Allow three hours for a round-trip climb. Avoid this route during inclement weather or darkness. Stay on

Precipice Trail

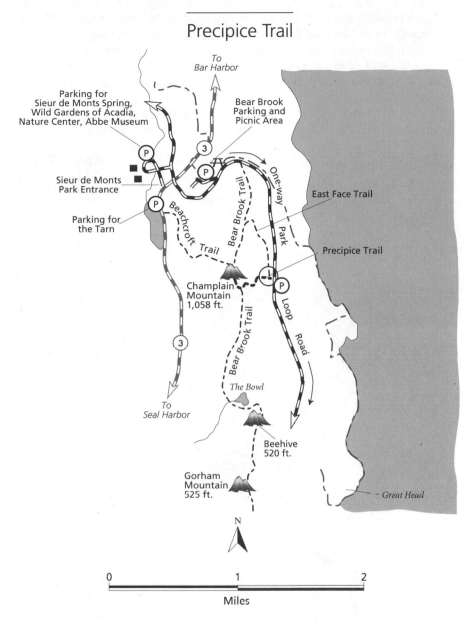

To
Bar Harbor

Parking for
Sieur de Monts Spring,
Wild Gardens of Acadia,
Nature Center, Abbe Museum

Bear Brook
Parking and
Picnic Area

P

3

P

Sieur de Monts
Park Entrance

East Face Trail

P

Beachcroft Trail

Bear Brook Trail

One-way

Park

Precipice Trail

Parking for
the Tarn

Champlain
Mountain
1,058 ft.

P

Bear Brook Trail

Loop Road

3

The Bowl

To
Seal Harbor

Beehive
520 ft.

Gorham
Mountain
525 ft.

Great Head

N

0   1   2

Miles

trail and do not throw or dislodge rocks onto hikers below. Persons have re-
ceived serious injuries and others have died on this mountain side!" And as
if to drive home the warning and test your fitness and nerve, the trail soon
brings you to the first rock face requiring a climb up iron rungs.

At 0.3 mile, the trail reaches a junction with the East Face Trail, which
leads north-northwest toward the ridge of Champlain Mountain. Bear left
(southwest) at this junction to continue up the Precipice Trail.

Continue up the Precipice on switchbacks. The trail soon levels off slightly, but don't let that mislead you into thinking you're near the top. Next

begins the really precipitous climb up scores of metal rungs and even a five-rung ladder bolted into the rock face. Strategically placed wood bridges help you across otherwise impassable crevices in the narrow, exposed rock ledge. Nearing the end of the steepest climb, a sign warns that it's easier to go up the Precipice Trail than down it and recommends a descent via the Bear Brook Trail 10 minutes ahead.

The rest of the trail is a more gradual hike up a rocky ledge of Champlain Mountain, with a final set of three iron rungs up one last rock face. At 0.8

A long series of iron rungs and a ladder help you up the Precipice Trail.

mile, reach the 1,058-foot summit of Champlain Mountain and the junction with the Bear Brook Trail. The peak provides the closest mountaintop views of Porcupine Islands and the rest of Frenchman Bay in all of Acadia. To descend as recommended by the trail warning sign, turn right (north) on the Bear Brook Trail.

The easiest descent is straight down the Bear Brook Trail for 1.1 miles to the Park Loop Road. Turn right (southeast) on the Park Loop Road and walk 1.2 miles back to the Precipice Trail parking area. This makes an approximately 3.1-mile loop. You can also take the Bear Brook Trail only 0.7 mile north, then turn right (east) on the East Face Trail and loop directly back to the Precipice Trail parking area. Even though this route eliminates the need to walk on the Park Loop Road, it is a more difficult way back. This makes a 2.3-mile loop.

3 Beachcroft Trail

Highlights: Intricately laid stone steps along much of the way lead to open views along Huguenot Head and Champlain Mountain.
Type of hike: Day hike; out-and-back.
Total distance: 2.4 miles.
Difficulty: Moderate, then strenuous.

Finding the trailhead: From downtown Bar Harbor, head south on Maine Highway 3 for 2 miles and pass the park's Sieur de Monts entrance by 0.2 mile. The parking lot is just north of the Tarn. The trailhead is on the left side of ME 3, diagonally across the road from the parking lot.

Parking and trailhead facilities: Park at the Tarn parking lot on the right (west) side of ME 3; there are no facilities.

Key points:
  0.0   Beachcroft Trailhead.
  0.6   Shoulder of Huguenot Head.
  1.2   Champlain Mountain summit.

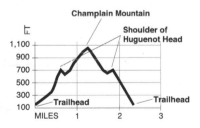

The hike: The Beachcroft Trail climbs to the shoulder of Huguenot Head at an average 100-foot elevation gain each tenth mile, but remarkably, it sometimes feels like a walk along a garden path. The gradual switchbacks and neatly laid stepping stones turn what would otherwise be a vertical scramble into a more gentle ascent.

Adding to the wonder are the constant open views north toward Frenchman Bay, west toward Dorr Mountain and east toward the summit of

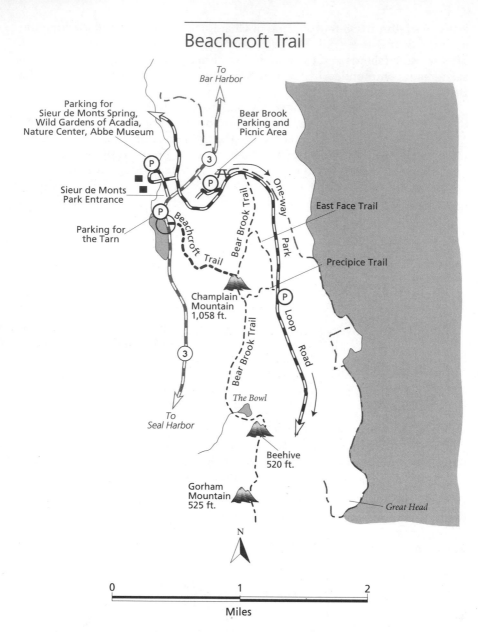

To
Bar Harbor

Parking for
Sieur de Monts Spring,
Wild Gardens of Acadia,
Nature Center, Abbe Museum

Bear Brook
Parking and
Picnic Area

Sieur de Monts
Park Entrance

Parking for
the Tarn

Beachcroft Trail

Bear Brook Trail

One-way

Park

East Face Trail

Precipice Trail

Champlain
Mountain
1,058 ft.

Bear Brook Trail

Loop
Road

The Bowl

To
Seal Harbor

Beehive
520 ft.

Gorham
Mountain
525 ft.

Great Head

N

0	1	2

Miles

Champlain Mountain, where the trail is heading. The dome-shaped Huguenot Head, visible from Bar Harbor, has been a popular destination for more than a century. The Beachcroft Trail, built and rebuilt in the late 1800s and early 1900s, was named after the estate of a Bar Harbor summer resident who financed construction. It consists of hundreds of hand-hewn stepping stones and countless switchbacks.

From the trailhead, ascend the switchbacks and stone steps, catching your breath on the plentiful level sections along the way. Near the shoulder of Huguenot Head, the trail widens and levels off. It circles around to the other side at 0.6 mile, just below the head's summit. The trail then dips into a gully before it begins the strenuous ascent up the sheer west face of Champlain Mountain. The moderate part of the trail is over. Carefully pick your steps and follow the cairns up the rock face. You reach the open Champlain summit at 1.2 miles. Return the way you came.

Options: Climb only to the shoulder of Huguenot Head for a shorter, easier climb of 1.2 miles round trip, while still getting most of the views.

4 Bear Brook Trail

Highlights: Expansive views from summit of Champlain Mountain and all along the open ridge.
Type of hike: Day hike; out-and-back.
Total distance: 2.2 miles, summit and back, or 5.2 miles, trail's end and back.
Difficulty: Moderate.

Finding the trailhead: Enter the park at the Sieur de Monts entrance, 2 miles south of downtown Bar Harbor on Maine Highway 3. Turn right (south) on one-way Park Loop Road. The trailhead is 0.8 mile from the entrance, on the right soon after the Bear Brook picnic area.

Parking and trailhead facilities: There is a small parking area on the left, across the road just beyond the trailhead, but no facilities.

Key points:
0.0 Bear Brook Trailhead.
0.4 Junction with the East Face Trail.
1.1 Champlain Mountain summit; junction with the Precipice Trail.
2.6 The Bowl.

The hike: One early morning when we hiked the Bear Brook Trail, we saw a blanket of fog roll in to Frenchman Bay, enveloping the Porcupine Islands in the space of a few minutes. Amazingly, the

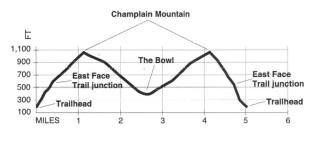

ridgetop trail continued to be bathed in sunshine as the foghorns sounded their warning below.

Contrasts like these are possible only in places like Acadia, where the mountains meet the sea. The Bear Brook Trail goes along the great ridge that's closest to the ocean in the park, providing spectacular views from Frenchman Bay to Great Head as it climbs Champlain Mountain and descends to

Bear Brook Trail

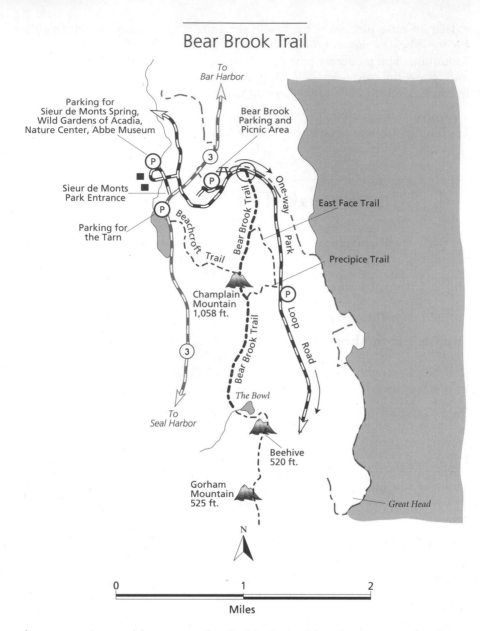

To
Bar Harbor

Parking for
Sieur de Monts Spring,
Wild Gardens of Acadia,
Nature Center, Abbe Museum

Bear Brook
Parking and
Picnic Area

(P)

(3)

(P)

Sieur de Monts
Park Entrance

(P)

East Face Trail

Parking for
the Tarn

(P)

Bear Brook Trail

One-Way

Park

Beachcroft Trail

Precipice Trail

(P)

Champlain
Mountain
1,058 ft.

Bear Brook Trail

Loop

(3)

Road

The Bowl

To
Seal Harbor

Beehive
520 ft.

Gorham
Mountain
525 ft.

Great Head

N

0   1   2

Miles

the mountain pond known as the Bowl. It provides the most moderate access of all the trails up Champlain's summit.

From the trailhead, head south and start ascending through a birch grove and up a stone-and-log stairway. You can hear the sound of a power plant almost all the way to the summit.

The trail levels off a bit at 0.2 mile and then ascends more steeply up some stone steps. You reach a junction with the East Face Trail at 0.4 mile. Continue straight (south) and climb a sheer pink granite face. Follow blue blazes as you near the summit.

Champlain Mountain's 1,058-foot summit is reached at 1.1 miles, offering the closest mountaintop views of the Porcupine Islands in all of Acadia. Many people turn around here at the summit, for a round-trip hike of 2.2 miles.

For the hardy hiker looking for more mileage and views, however, the Bear Brook Trail descends the ridge for another 1½ miles, offering views of Sand Beach, Great Head, the Beehive, the Bowl, and Gorham Mountain. Carefully follow the blue blazes. The trail ends at the Bowl at 2.6 miles. Return the way you came, for a round trip of 5.2 miles.

Options: In late summer—after the peregrine falcon chicks that have been hatching every year along the cliffs of Champlain Mountain mature and fly off—you can do a strenuous loop by adding on the East Face and Precipice trails. Even though the loop adds on less than 0.5 mile to the total distance to Champlain summit and back, it is very difficult because of the near-vertical ascent up the Precipice, with iron rungs for handholds and footholds. At the junction with the East Face Trail at 0.4 mile from the Bear Brook Trailhead, bear left (southeast) and descend for 0.5 mile along Champlain's rocky east face.

At the Precipice Trail junction, bear right and climb steeply for another 0.5 mile to the summit of Champlain. Return by turning right (north) and head down the ridge back to the Bear Brook Trailhead.

While the summit of Champlain Mountain is under sunny skies, the islands below are fogged in.

5 East Face Trail

Highlights: Steep climb to 360-degree views up the precipitous east face of Champlain Mountain.
Type of hike: Day hike; out-and-back.
Total distance: 2.2 miles.
Difficulty: Strenuous.

Finding the trailhead: Enter the park at the Sieur de Monts entrance, 2 miles south of downtown Bar Harbor on Maine Highway 3. Turn right (south) on the one-way Park Loop Road. From the entrance, the trailhead is 1.6 miles on the right.

Parking and trailhead facilities: Park along the Park Loop Road; there are no facilities.

Key points:
- 0.0 East Face Trailhead.
- 0.2 Junction; bear right.
- 0.5 Junction with the Bear Brook Trail; turn left.
- 1.1 Champlain Mountain summit, return the way you came.

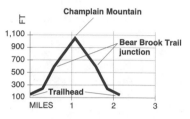

The hike: If the nearby Precipice Trail is closed for peregrine falcon breeding season, the East Face Trail provides an almost as precipitous alternative up Champlain Mountain. From the Park Loop Road, the trail immediately starts its steep ascent. At 0.2 mile, bear right at a junction and circle up the rugged east face. At 0.5 mile, reach a junction with the Bear Brook Trail, on the north ridge of Champlain. Turn left on the Bear Brook Trail and climb the open ridge with great views. Reach the 1,058-foot summit at 1.1 miles.

Champlain is the closest mountain in Acadia to Frenchman Bay. You almost feel as if you're right on top of the Porcupine Islands here. To the west are Dorr and Cadillac mountains, while across the bay to the east is Schoodic Peninsula, the only section of Acadia that's part of the mainland. To the south is the Gulf of Maine. Return the way you came.

Options: Rather than going back down the steep East Face Trail, you can stay straight on the Bear Brook Trail all the way north to the Park Loop Road. Then turn right and walk along the loop road, reaching the East Face Trailhead in another 0.8 mile.

East Face Trail

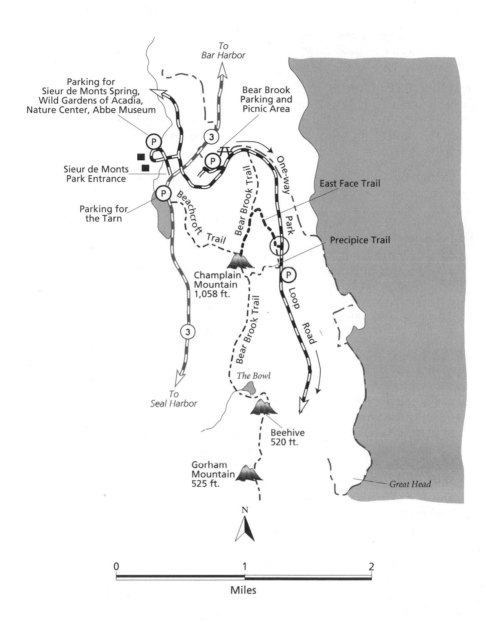

Parking for
Sieur de Monts Spring,
Wild Gardens of Acadia,
Nature Center, Abbe Museum

Sieur de Monts
Park Entrance

Parking for
the Tarn

*To
Bar Harbor*

Bear Brook
Parking and
Picnic Area

3

One-way

Bear Brook Trail

Beachcroft Trail

East Face Trail

Precipice Trail

Champlain
Mountain
1,058 ft.

Bear Brook Trail

Loop Road

3

The Bowl

*To
Seal Harbor*

Beehive
520 ft.

Gorham
Mountain
525 ft.

Great Head

N

0   1   2
Miles

6 Beehive Trail

Highlights:	Nearly vertical climb up 520-foot Beehive using iron rungs, with spectacular close-up views of Sand Beach and Great Head.
Type of hike:	Day hike; loop.
Total distance:	1.8 miles.
Difficulty:	Strenuous.

Finding the trailhead: From the park visitor center, drive south on the Park Loop Road for 3 miles and turn left (east) at the sign to Sand Beach. Follow the one-way Park Loop Road for 5.5 miles, past the fee station to the beach. Take the Bowl Trail, across the road from the beach, for 0.2 mile to the Beehive Trailhead.

Parking and trailhead facilities: The Sand Beach parking lot is on the left (east) of the one-way Park Loop Road. There are seasonally open restrooms, a beach changing area, and a pay phone.

Key points:
- 0.0   Bowl Trailhead.
- 0.2   Beehive Trailhead; turn right (north) onto the Beehive Trail.
- 0.5   Beehive summit.
- 0.6   Junction with a spur to the Bowl Trail.
- 1.0   The Bowl; junction with the Bowl Trail.
- 1.8   Return to the trailhead, completing the loop.

The hike: The Beehive Trail is not for the faint of heart or weak of limb, nor for those afraid of heights or crowds. It features an almost perpendicular climb up iron rungs at its steepest and a Grand Central Station–like atmosphere at its busiest. So crowded is the narrow trail during the peak summer season that

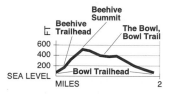

from a distance people climbing up and down it look like bees swarming around a hive.

The Beehive, a 520-foot-high granite dome overlooking Sand Beach, was named by nineteenth-century artist Frederic Church of the Hudson River School, for its jagged, glacially carved face. The trail up it was built in the early 1900s by the Bar Harbor Village Improvement Association.

From the Bowl Trailhead across from the Sand Beach parking lot, hike gradually up, reaching the junction with the Beehive Trail in 0.2 mile. You know you're there when you see this sign: "Caution: Trail Steep with Exposed Cliffs and Fixed Iron Rungs," which emphasizes the danger associated with climbing this trail.

Turn right (north) onto the Beehive Trail, swiftly climbing above the trees. Iron hand and foot rungs take you over the most difficult parts of the cliff face. Only one hiker can pass at a time in many spots, so there is often a

Beehive Trail

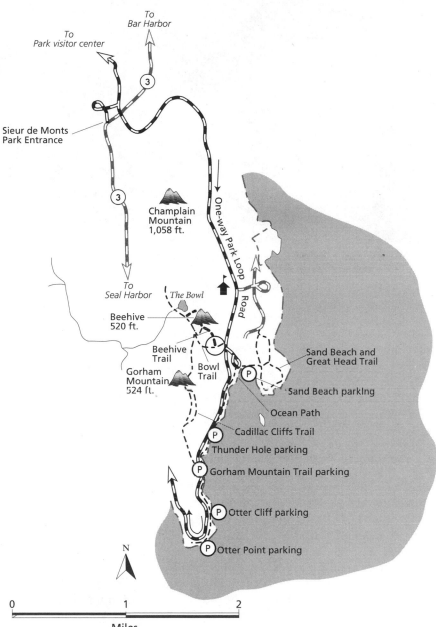

To
Bar Harbor

To
Park visitor center

3

Sieur de Monts
Park Entrance

3

Champlain
Mountain
1,058 ft.

One-way Park Loop Road

To
Seal Harbor

The Bowl

Beehive
520 ft.

Beehive
Trail

Bowl
Trail

Gorham
Mountain
524 ft.

Sand Beach and
Great Head Trail

P

Sand Beach parking

Ocean Path

P   Cadillac Cliffs Trail

Thunder Hole parking

P   Gorham Mountain Trail parking

P Otter Cliff parking

P Otter Point parking

N

0   1   2

Miles

The unique pink granite of Acadia gives the Beehive its distinctive look.

trail jam as people wait to climb up or down. If you're not too afraid of heights to look as you hike this precarious stretch, you can get magnificent bird's-eye views of Sand Beach and Great Head.

At 0.5 mile, you reach the top of the Beehive, where you can take in the panorama without having to worry about falling off the edge. The trail starts descending with a view of Otter Cliff to the south, and at 0.6 mile reaches a junction with a spur back down to the Bowl Trail. Continue straight on the Beehive Trail, and at 1 mile, reach the mountain pond known as the Bowl.

As with many of Acadia's precipitous trails with iron rungs, it's easier to go up the Beehive than to go down. So rather than descending the same precarious way, turn left at the Bowl, on to the Bowl Trail, and loop back less steeply to the park road for a total distance of 1.8 miles.

Options: There are two ways to avoid climbing the iron rungs while still getting the views from the top of the Beehive. Take the Bowl Trail straight for 0.8 mile to the Bowl. Turn right at the pond and follow the Beehive Trail for another 0.4 mile, first heading northeast along the Bowl's shore, and then southeast up to the top of the Beehive the back way. Return the same way for a round trip of 2.4 miles.

The alternative is to take the Bowl Trail straight past the official Beehive Trailhead at 0.2 mile, and turn right (northeast) at 0.5 mile, onto a 0.2-mile spur that takes you up the back side of the Beehive. Once you reach the ridge, bear right and attain the top of the Beehive in another 0.2 mile. Return the same way for an approximately 1.8-mile round trip.

7 Bowl Trail

Highlights: Mountain pond nestled behind the Beehive.
Type of hike: Day hike; out-and-back.
Total distance: 1.6 miles.
Difficulty: Moderate.

Finding the trailhead: From the park visitor center, drive south on the Park Loop Road for 3 miles and turn left (east) at the sign to Sand Beach. Follow the one-way Park Loop Road for 5.5 miles, past the fee station to the beach. The trailhead is across the road from the beach.

Parking and trailhead facilities: The Sand Beach parking lot is on the left (east) of the one-way Park Loop Road. There are seasonally open restrooms, a beach changing area, and a pay phone.

Key points:
- 0.0   Bowl Trailhead.
- 0.2   Junction with the Beehive Trail.
- 0.4   Junction with a spur trail to the Gorham Mountain Trail.
- 0.5   Junction with spur trail to the Beehive.
- 0.6   Junction with the Gorham Mountain Trail.
- 0.8   The Bowl; return the way you came.

The hike: Views of a great blue heron taking off low across the water's surface or a turkey vulture soaring high on thermals are among the rewards possible when you hike to the Bowl, a mountain pond at more than 400 feet elevation.

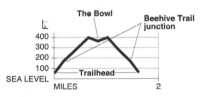

We were lucky and got both views in the same day along a section of the trail that skirts the shoreline. Hike in the early morning or late afternoon to improve your chances of such sightings.

The Bowl Trail climbs gradually, passing junctions with the Beehive Trailhead at 0.2 mile, a spur to the Gorham Mountain Trail at 0.4 mile, another spur to the Beehive at 0.5 mile, and the Gorham Mountain Trail at 0.6 mile. Next, the Bowl Trail heads up steeply through the woods, then down, arriving at 0.8 mile at the pond nestled high in the mountains. Return the way you came.

Options: If you're not afraid of heights, you can do a loop by first going up the 0.8-mile Beehive Trail, then down the Bowl Trail. At the Bowl, turn left (southwest) along the shore, and take the Bowl Trail back to your car.

Or add on another 1.2 miles round trip for spectacular views from 525-foot Gorham Mountain. At 0.4 mile from the Bowl Trailhead, turn left at the short spur to the Gorham Mountain Trail, and bear left again until the summit is reached in another 0.6 mile. Return the way you came.

Bowl Trail

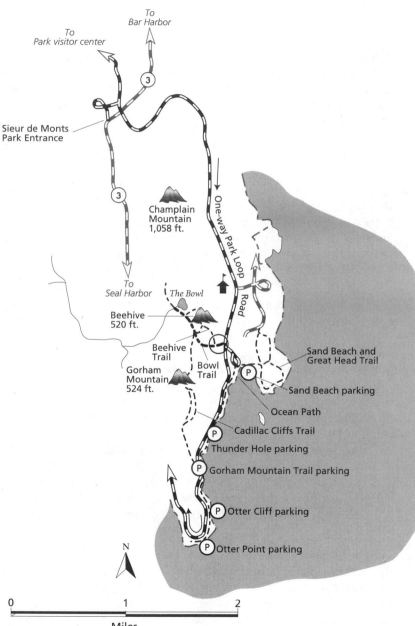

To
Park visitor center

To
Bar Harbor

3

Sieur de Monts
Park Entrance

3

Champlain
Mountain
1,058 ft.

One-way Park Loop Road

To
Seal Harbor

The Bowl

Beehive
520 ft.

Beehive
Trail

Bowl
Trail

Gorham
Mountain
524 ft.

Sand Beach and
Great Head Trail

P

Sand Beach parking

Ocean Path

P Cadillac Cliffs Trail

Thunder Hole parking

P Gorham Mountain Trail parking

P Otter Cliff parking

P Otter Point parking

N

0   1   2

Miles

8 Sand Beach and Great Head Trail

Highlights:	Acadia's only ocean beach, made of sand, tiny shell fragments, and quartz pink feldspar; grand views from Great Head.
Type of hike:	Day hike; loop.
Total distance:	1.4 miles.
Difficulty:	Moderate.

Finding the trailhead: From the park visitor center, drive south on the Park Loop Road for 3 miles and turn left (east) at the sign to Sand Beach. Follow the one-way Park Loop Road for 5.5 miles, past the fee station to the beach. The trailhead is down the stairs and on the far east end of the beach.

Parking and trailhead facilities: The Sand Beach parking lot is on the left (east) side of the one-way Park Loop Road. There are seasonally open restrooms, a beach changing area, and a pay phone.

Key points:
- 0.0 Great Head Trailhead; the east end of Sand Beach.
- 0.1 Bear right (southeast) at the top of the stairs.
- 0.2 Junction with a spur inland; bear right (south) along the shore.
- 0.5 South end of the Great Head peninsula.
- 0.8 Great Head summit.
- 1.1 Junction with a spur to Great Head ridge; bear left (southwest).
- 1.4 Great Head Trailhead.

The hike: Next to Sand Beach and jutting into the sea, the Great Head peninsula is in a perfect spot to break up lazy afternoons of lounging on the beach. With a relatively modest scramble up the rocky slope of Great Head, you

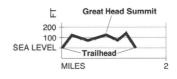

reach spectacular views of the beach you just left behind, the Beehive, Champlain Mountain, Otter Cliff, Egg Rock, and the Cranberry Isles. Also visible just off the tip of the peninsula is an unusual rock formation called Old Soaker.

The trail, built more than 150 years ago, was popular with artists and tourists beginning in the mid-1800s. A teahouse once stood on Great Head, and its ruins are still visible. A large millstone near the trailhead is another reminder of man's history here. Today, during the busy summer season, you may see boaters coming close to the Great Head cliffs, or rock climbers tackling the sheer face.

To get to the trailhead from the parking lot, head down the stairs to the beach and travel to the farthest, or easternmost, end. Cross a channel—best at low tide to keep your feet dry—to the Great Head Trailhead. At the trailhead, ascend the series of 41 steps, bordered by a split rail fence. At the top of the steps, turn right (southeast) and follow the blue blazes up the rocky

Sand Beach and Great Head Trail

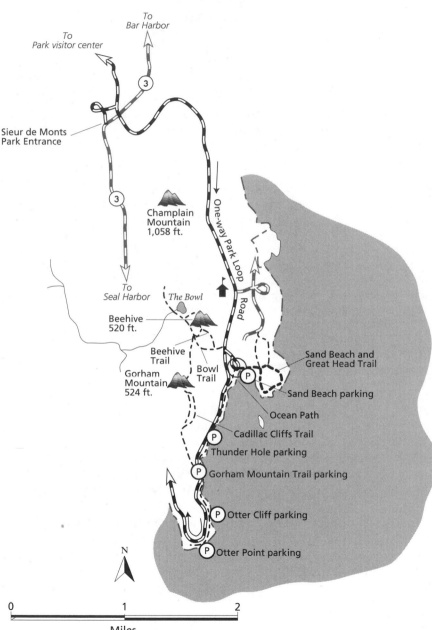

To
Bar Harbor

To
Park visitor center

3

Sieur de Monts
Park Entrance

3

Champlain
Mountain
1,058 ft.

One-way Park Loop Road

To
Seal Harbor

The Bowl

Beehive
520 ft.

Beehive
Trail

Bowl
Trail

Gorham
Mountain
524 ft.

Sand Beach and
Great Head Trail

P

Sand Beach parking

Ocean Path

Cadillac Cliffs Trail

P

Thunder Hole parking

P   Gorham Mountain Trail parking

P   Otter Cliff parking

P   Otter Point parking

N

0   1   2

Miles

ledges. Views of Sand Beach, the Beehive, and Champlain Mountain are immediately visible.

At the next trail junction at 0.2 mile, bear right (south) to head toward the tip of the peninsula, with views of rectangular Old Soaker nearby, and Otter Cliff and Cranberry Isles in the distance.

At 0.5 mile, the trail rounds the peninsula. At 0.8 mile it reaches the summit of Great Head, where there are views of Frenchman Bay and Egg Rock. At 1.1 miles, along a level section of the trail, is a junction in a birch grove. Turn left (southwest) and ascend gradually up Great Head ridge, with views of Champlain Mountain, the Beehive, and Gorham Mountain. At the last junction, bear right (northwest) to return to the trailhead and Sand Beach, for a loop hike of 1.4 miles.

Options: A longer loop is possible by adding on a path through the woods. At the trail junction in the birch grove, at 1.1 miles, head straight (northwest) instead of going left and up Great Head ridge. The trail soon comes out near the Schooner Head Road parking lot. Turn left (southwest) to continue on the woods trail for another 0.4 mile back to Sand Beach.

Looking back over Sand Beach from Great Head.

9 Ocean Path

Highlights: Thunder Hole; Otter Cliff; pink granite shoreline.
Type of hike: Day hike; out-and-back.
Total distance: 4 miles.
Difficulty: Easy.

Finding the trailhead: From the park visitor center, drive south on the Park Loop Road for 3 miles and turn left (east) at the sign to Sand Beach. Follow the one-way Park Loop Road for 5.5 miles past the fee station to the beach. The trailhead is on the right just before the stairs to the beach.

Parking and trailhead facilities: The Sand Beach parking lot is on the left (east) side of the one-way Park Loop Road. There are seasonally open restrooms, a beach changing area, and a pay phone.

Key points:
0.0   Ocean Path Trailhead.
1.0   Thunder Hole.
1.3   Gorham Mountain Trailhead, across the Park Loop Road.
1.8   Otter Cliff.
2.0   Otter Point.
4.0   Return the same way you came.

The hike: The sounds of the ocean and the views of rocky cliffs and pink granite shore-line are never far from Ocean Path. At Thunder Hole, halfway along the path, when the conditions

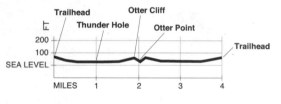

are just right, the surf crashes through rocky chasms with a thunderous roar. And at Otter Point at trail's end, the sound of a ringing buoy fills the air.

Rock climbers can be seen scaling Otter Cliff, one of the best rock climbing areas in the eastern United States, while picnickers and sun worshipers can be found enjoying themselves on the flat pink granite slabs that dot the shore here.

First used as a buckboard road in the 1870s, Ocean Path and Ocean Drive were rebuilt in the 1930s by the Civilian Conservation Corps, with funding assistance from John D. Rockefeller Jr.

Because of its ease and accessibility, Ocean Path can be crowded during the height of the tourist season. The best time to walk it is either very early or very late on a summer's day, or in the spring or fall as we have.

Ocean Path Trailhead is on the right just before the stairs to Sand Beach. Follow the gravel path past the changing rooms and restrooms, up a series of stairs, then left (south) when you reach a secondary parking area. The easy trail takes you southwest along the shore, paralleling the Ocean Drive section of the Park Loop Road.

Ocean Path

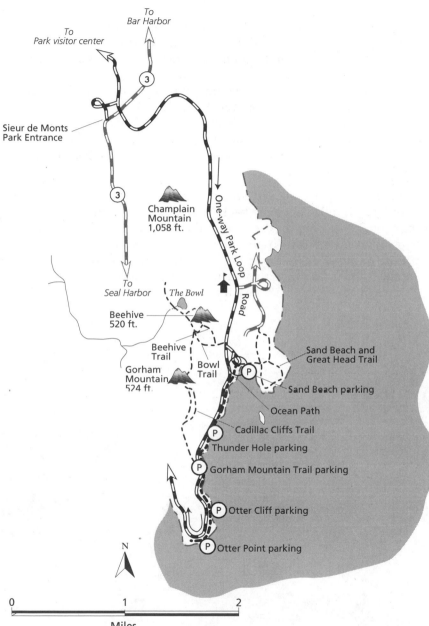

To Bar Harbor

To Park visitor center

3

Sieur de Monts Park Entrance

3

Champlain Mountain 1,058 ft.

One-way Park Loop Road

To Seal Harbor

The Bowl

Beehive 520 ft.

Beehive Trail

Gorham Mountain 524 ft.

Bowl Trail

Sand Beach and Great Head Trail

P

Sand Beach parking

Ocean Path

P Cadillac Cliffs Trail

Thunder Hole parking

P Gorham Mountain Trail parking

P Otter Cliff parking

P Otter Point parking

N

0   1   2
Miles

You reach popular Thunder Hole in 1 mile. Many casual visitors driving through the park on a calm summer day often stop here and cause a traffic jam but go away disappointed. It turns out that the best time to experience the power of Thunder Hole is right after a storm, when the surf crashes violently through the chasm, pushing trapped air against the rock and creating a reverberating boom.

At 1.3 miles, you'll pass a short series of stairs on the right, which lead you across the Park Loop Road to the Gorham Mountain Trailhead. All along the path, the pink granite shoreline attracts picnickers and bird watchers.

The path's only noticeable elevation gain comes as it rises through the woods toward Otter Cliff, reached in 1.8 miles. On the approach you can see rock climbers scaling the rock face or waiting at the top of the cliff for their turn. A series of stairs leads down on the left to the rock climber's registration board. The path ends at the parking lot at Otter Point, at 2 miles. Return the way you came.

Options: Leave one car at Sand Beach parking lot, then drive to Otter Point to do the trail 2 miles one way back to Sand Beach. Or make a moderate 3.4-mile loop by adding on the Gorham Mountain and Bowl trails. At 1.3 miles from the Ocean Path Trailhead, take the stairs leading across the Park Loop Road to the Gorham Mountain Trailhead. Head north on the Gorham Mountain Trail for 1.5 miles, then turn right and head east on the Bowl Trail for 0.6 mile, back to the Sand Beach parking lot.

Ocean Path brings you by huge pink granite slabs and views of Gorham Mountain, the Beehive, Sand Beach, and Great Head.

When the free Island Explorer bus shuttle is operating from late June through Labor Day, leave a car at Otter Point, hike one way to Thunder Hole or Sand Beach, and catch the shuttle back to the car.

10 Gorham Mountain Trail

<table>
<tr><td>Highlights:</td><td>Views of Great Head, Sand Beach, Otter Cliff, Champlain Mountain, and the Beehive; spur to Cadillac Cliffs and ancient sea cave.</td></tr>
<tr><td>Type of hike:</td><td>Day hike; out-and-back.</td></tr>
<tr><td>Total distance:</td><td>3 miles.</td></tr>
<tr><td>Difficulty:</td><td>Moderate.</td></tr>
</table>

Finding the trailhead: From the park visitor center, drive south on the Park Loop Road for 3 miles and turn left (east) at the sign to Sand Beach. Follow the one-way Park Loop Road for 7 miles, passing the fee station, Sand Beach, and Thunder Hole to the Gorham Mountain sign.

Parking and trailhead facilities: The Gorham Mountain parking lot is on the right (west) side of the one-way Park Loop Road; there are no facilities.

Key points:
- 0.0   Gorham Mountain Trailhead.
- 0.2   Junction with the southern end of the Cadillac Cliffs Trail.
- 0.5   Junction with the northern end of the Cadillac Cliffs Trail.
- 0.9   Gorham Mountain summit.
- 1.4   Junction with a spur trail to the Bowl Trail.
- 1.5   Trail ends at the Bowl Trail.

The hike: The Gorham Mountain Trail provides some of the most rewarding views in Acadia for relatively modest effort, featuring nearly uninterrupted ridgetop panoramas of everything from Great Head and Sand Beach to the Beehive. It is part of the great ridge that runs north all the way to Champlain Mountain and is closest to the ocean of all Acadia's mountain ridges.

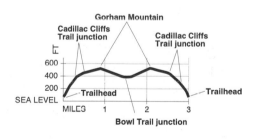

An additional bonus is a 0.5-mile spur trail to the once-submerged Cadillac Cliffs and ancient sea cave, demonstrating the powerful geologic forces that helped shape Mount Desert Island.

From the Gorham Mountain parking lot, climb gradually up open ledges, heading north. At 0.2 mile, the Cadillac Cliffs Trail leads to the right (northeast) paralleling and then rejoining the Gorham Mountain Trail. If you're

Gorham Mountain Trail

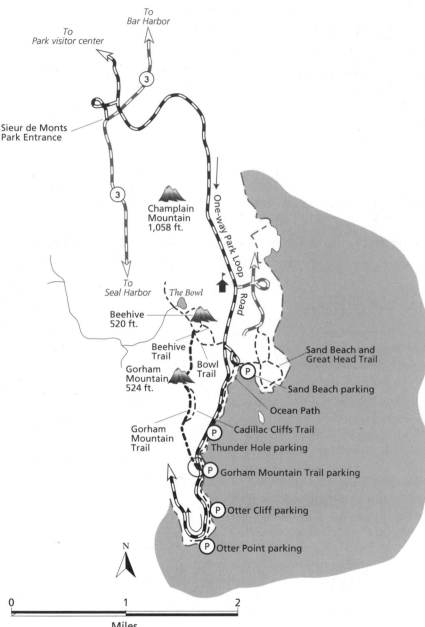

To
Bar Harbor

To
Park visitor center

③

Sieur de Monts
Park Entrance

③

Champlain
Mountain
1,058 ft.

One-way Park Loop Road

To
Seal Harbor

The Bowl

Beehive
520 ft.

Beehive
Trail

Bowl
Trail

Gorham
Mountain
524 ft.

Sand Beach and
Great Head Trail

Ⓟ

Sand Beach parking

Ocean Path

Gorham
Mountain
Trail

Ⓟ Cadillac Cliffs Trail

Thunder Hole parking

Ⓟ Gorham Mountain Trail parking

Ⓟ Otter Cliff parking

Ⓟ Otter Point parking

N

0   1   2

Miles

inclined to add the Cadillac Cliffs spur, it's best to do the ascent rather than the descent because of the iron rungs and steep rock face along the way.

Continue on the Gorham Mountain Trail as it moderately ascends the ridge. Pass the junction with the northern end of the Cadillac Cliffs Trail at 0.5 mile. All along here are views to the south of Otter Cliff; to the east, of Great Head and Sand Beach; and to the north, of the Beehive and Champlain Mountain. Visible in the distance at various points are Frenchman Bay and Egg Rock.

At 0.9 mile, you reach the summit of Gorham Mountain, elevation 525 feet. Many hikers turn around here, but the trail does continue north down the ridge, passing the junction at 1.4 miles with a spur to the Bowl Trail and ending officially at the Bowl Trail at 1.5 miles. Return the way you came, adding on Cadillac Cliffs if you choose.

Options: For a 3.4-mile loop that takes Ocean Path back, take Gorham Mountain Trail to its end at the Bowl Trail. Turn right (southeast) onto the Bowl Trail and travel 0.6 mile toward the Park Loop Road and Sand Beach. Cross the road and the Sand Beach parking lot to the Ocean Path Trailhead, on the right just before the stairs to the beach. Follow the path past the changing rooms and restrooms, up a series of stairs, then left (south) when you reach a secondary parking area. Follow the very easy gravel path that parallels the ocean and the Park Loop Road, and reach the Gorham Mountain Trailhead parking lot in another 1.3 miles.

Sand Beach, Great Head, and the rocky little island known as Old Soaker, as seen from the Gorham Mountain Trail.

11 Cadillac Cliffs Trail

Highlights: Ancient sea cliffs and sea cave.
Type of hike: Day hike; loop in combination with Gorham Mountain Trail.
Total distance: 1.2 miles.
Difficulty: Strenuous.

Finding the trailhead: From the park visitor center, drive south on the Park Loop Road for 3 miles and turn left (east) at the sign to Sand Beach. Follow the one-way Park Loop Road for 7 miles, passing the fee station, Sand Beach, and Thunder Hole to the Gorham Mountain sign. Take the Gorham Mountain Trail 0.2 mile to the Cadillac Cliffs Trailhead.

Parking and trailhead facilities: The Gorham Mountain parking lot is on the right (west) side of the one-way Park Loop Road; there are no facilities.

Key points:
- 0.0 Gorham Mountain Trailhead.
- 0.2 Cadillac Cliffs Trailhead; bear right (northeast) onto the Cadillac Cliffs Trail.
- 0.6 Cliffs and an ancient sea cave.
- 0.7 Junction with the Gorham Mountain Trail; turn left (south).
- 1.2 Gorham Mountain Trailhead.

The hike: The sea washes against the shore hundreds of feet below the pink Cadillac Cliffs, but these rock formations were once submerged below the ocean's surface. As the Cadillac Cliffs Trail winds through huge rock slabs perched against each other and skirts the base of the cliffs and an ancient sea cave, it provides a reminder of nature's powerful forces.

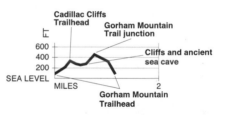

A spur off the Gorham Mountain Trail, the Cadillac Cliffs Trail can be done as the first half of a loop or the second half. Hiking the cliffs first brings you to the interesting rock formations more quickly. To do the cliffs first, hike in 0.2 mile from the Gorham Mountain Trailhead and bear right (northeast) onto the Cadillac Cliffs Trail at a plaque commemorating trailblazer Waldron Bates.

You'll soon go under two huge rock slabs perched against each other. Shortly, the towering cliffs and old sea cave loom on the left, at 0.6 mile. A path has been worn through the woods at the base of the cliffs, but the official trail takes you along one of the pinkish rock ledges right along the mouth of the sea cave. Cross the short wooden boardwalk to get off the ledge. The cliffs are their most impressive when you look back after getting off the ledge. The layers of smooth pink granite look like giant blocks stacked neatly on top of each other.

Cadillac Cliffs Trail

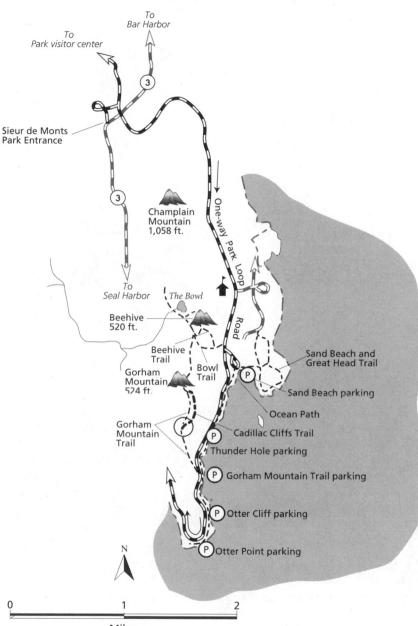

To
Bar Harbor

To
Park visitor center

3

Sieur de Monts
Park Entrance

3

Champlain
Mountain
1,058 ft.

One-way Park Loop

To
Seal Harbor

The Bowl

Beehive
520 ft.

Beehive
Trail

Bowl
Trail

Gorham
Mountain
524 ft.

Road

Sand Beach and
Great Head Trail

Sand Beach parking

P

Ocean Path

Gorham
Mountain
Trail

P

Cadillac Cliffs Trail

P

Thunder Hole parking

P

Gorham Mountain Trail parking

P

Otter Cliff parking

P

Otter Point parking

N

0   1   2

Miles

Powerful geological forces have pushed these ancient sea cliffs far from the ocean.

At 0.7 mile, the trail brings you up a series of iron rungs, to rejoin the Gorham Mountain Trail. Turn left (southeast) on the ridge trail, and descend open ledges to return to the parking lot.

Options: To do the Cadillac Cliffs Trail as the second half of the loop, skip the first junction with the Cadillac Cliffs Trail and turn right (southeast) at the second junction, at 0.5 mile from the Gorham Mountain Trailhead. This will take you down steeply to the cliffs. Follow the Cadillac Cliffs Trail back to the Gorham Mountain Trail, closing the loop. Turn left and return to the parking lot, for a total hike distance of 1.2 miles.

Or add on the 525-foot Gorham Mountain summit with its grand vistas, by heading north up the Gorham Mountain Trail 0.4 mile beyond the second junction with the Cadillac Cliffs Trail. Including the Cadillac Cliffs spur, the total distance is 2 miles.

12 Dorr Mountain North Ridge Trail

Highlights:	Summits of Kebo and Dorr mountains along largely open ridge; great views atop Dorr.
Type of hike:	Day hike; out-and-back.
Total distance:	4 miles.
Difficulty:	Moderate.

Finding the trailhead: From the park visitor center, drive south on the Park Loop Road for 3 miles and turn left (east) at the sign to Sand Beach. Follow the one-way Park Loop Road for 1 mile. The trailhead is on the right, across from a series of huge boulders lining the road, and just before a rock outcropping as the road starts to curve to the right.

Parking and trailhead facilities: Limited parking is along the side of the road at the trailhead; there are no facilities.

Key points:
- 0.0 Dorr Mountain North Ridge Trailhead.
- 0.3 Kebo Mountain summit.
- 1.2 Junction with the Hemlock Trail.
- 1.9 Junction with the Cadillac-Dorr Trail.
- 2.0 Dorr Mountain summit.

The hike: The short climb up and views atop the 470-foot Kebo Mountain at the start of the Dorr Mountain

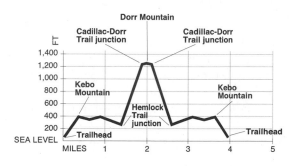

Dorr Mountain North Ridge Trail

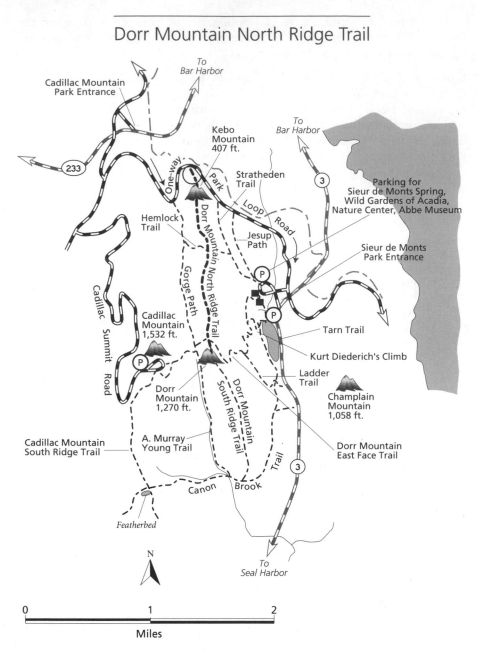

North Ridge Trail are just a preview of the hike and vistas to come. The trail begins with a series of seven small stone steps, then climbs steeply up rocky knobs and more stone steps, providing views beginning at 0.1 mile, all the way to Kebo at 0.3 mile. To the northeast are Frenchman Bay and the Porcupine Islands, with Cadillac Mountain's north ridge to the west and Dorr Mountain, where the trail is heading, to the south. Hikers content with Kebo Mountain's views can turn around here, for only a 0.6-mile round trip.

The North Ridge Trail continues up and down more rocky knobs lined with low sweet blueberry bushes and offers more tantalizing views through pitch pines. It descends to a junction with the Hemlock Trail at 1.2 miles. Leveling off briefly, the trail then starts a short steep climb up rock-strewn woods. Birches and striped maple (also known as moosewood because its shoots are a favorite food of moose) dominate here.

The North Ridge Trail then ascends to pitch pine territory and above tree-line, going occasionally up smooth rock faces. The views that were first hinted at atop low Kebo Mountain open up dramatically here, high on Dorr Mountain's rocky north ridge.

At 1.9 miles, reach a junction with the Cadillac-Dorr Trail, also called the Dorr Mountain Notch Trail, which heads down precipitously to the west 0.2 mile to the gorge between Cadillac and Dorr. From there, ambitious hikers can climb another steep 0.4 mile to the top of Cadillac, Acadia's highest mountain.

Continuing on the North Ridge Trail, you'll see two sets of blue blazes near the summit. The blazes on the right lead directly up to the 1,270-foot Dorr Mountain, at 2 miles. The blue blazes on the left point to a short side loop overlooking dramatic views of Frenchman Bay and Champlain Mountain. At the summit, the magnificent vistas of mountains and sea are a fitting tribute to George B. Dorr, who loved the area so much he helped found Acadia, and for whom the mountain is named. Return the way you came.

Options: Loops with a bit more mileage and more steep descents are possible, by heading down either east or west from Dorr Mountain summit. For

Views of Porcupine Islands from Kebo Mountain are just a preview of the vistas from Dorr.

an approximately 4.6-mile loop, adding on a strenuously steep descent of the gorge between Cadillac and Dorr, head back north from the summit 0.1 mile, to the junction with the Cadillac-Dorr Trail. Descend steeply 0.1 mile, left (west) until you reach the gorge. Turn right (north) on the Gorge Path, for 0.9 mile, to a junction with the Hemlock Trail. Turn right (east) onto the Hemlock Trail for 0.3 mile, and then turn left (north) at the junction with the Dorr Mountain North Ridge Trail. Return to trailhead parking area in another 1.2 miles.

For an approximately 5.4-mile loop down the steep east face of Dorr, continue south from the summit for 0.1 mile, and turn left (east) down the Dorr Mountain East Face Trail, toward Sieur de Monts Spring. In 0.5 mile, reach the junction with the Ladder Trail. Bear left (north) to continue on the Dorr Mountain East Face Trail toward the spring. Pass Kurt Diederich's Climb on the right in another 0.5 mile, and reach the spring at 1.5 miles from the summit. Turn left at the springs area onto the well-graded Jesup Path, heading north-northwest. In 0.1 mile beyond the spring, bear left at a four-way intersection, onto the Stratheden Trail. Follow this trail about 0.3 mile to a junction with the Hemlock Trail. Turn left (west) on the Hemlock Trail for 0.2 mile, to a junction with the Dorr Mountain North Ridge Trail. Turn right (north) and return along the Dorr Mountain North Ridge Trail another 1.2 miles back to the parking area.

13 Dorr Mountain East Face Trail (Emery Path)

Highlights: Steep climb up hundreds of stone steps to spectacular views atop 1,270-foot Dorr Mountain.
Type of hike: Day hike; out-and-back.
Total distance: 3 miles.
Difficulty: Moderate to strenuous.

Finding the trailhead: Enter the park at the Sieur de Monts entrance, 2 miles south of downtown Bar Harbor on Maine Highway 3, and turn into the Wild Gardens of Acadia, Nature Center, and Abbe Museum parking lot. Head left (south) behind the Nature Center, toward Sieur de Monts Spring. Turn right (west) at the domed springhouse, to the trailhead.

Parking and trailhead facilities: Park at the Wild Gardens of Acadia, Nature Center, and Abbe Museum parking lot, or the nearby Tarn parking lot to the south on ME 3. Restrooms and drinking fountains are open seasonally at the gardens, nature center, and museum area.

Key points:
0.0   Dorr Mountain East Face Trailhead.
0.5   Junction with Kurt Diederich's Climb.

Dorr Mountain East Face Trail (Emery Path)

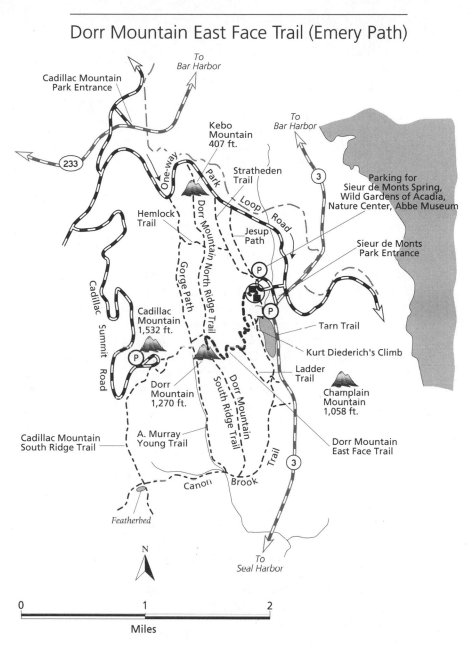

1.0 Junction with Ladder Trail; bear right up to the summit.
1.5 Dorr Mountain summit.

The hike: Like a stairway to heaven, this trail's hundreds of granite steps take you along switchbacks and the base of sheer rock walls, to the grand views atop Dorr Mountain. You have to admire the handiwork that went into constructing the stairs, as well as the mountaintop vistas. The trail begins behind the spring named after a French explorer, Pierre Dugua Sieur de Mons, whose navigator Samuel Champlain gave the name l'Isle des Monts Desert—Island of Barren Mountains—to this area. The trail is also known as Emery Path.

George B. Dorr, a founder of Acadia National Park, bought the spring in 1909 from owners of a failed commercial springwater business and donated it and the surrounding land as a foundation for the park.

The trail, one of three stone-stepped paths up the rugged east side of Dorr Mountain, soon brings you to a view of Huguenot Head, the domelike shoulder of Champlain Mountain, southeast across the valley. At the next switchback to the right, you'll notice a change in the color of the stone steps, from gray to pink, as a result of the different mineral content.

You will soon see the Porcupine Islands and Bar Harbor to the northeast and a full view of the Huguenot Head and the higher Champlain Mountain behind it to the southeast. In the most amazing architectural feat on the trail, the stone steps wind around like a spiral staircase through a huge rock crevice.

Reach a plateau, where there are some low-lying blueberry bushes, and the junction with Kurt Diederich's Climb at 0.5 mile. Continue up on switchbacks, reaching a junction with the Ladder Trail at 1 mile. Bear right (northwest) and climb steadily up the rest of the way, reaching the open summit of Dorr Mountain at 1.5 miles. Among the views from the 1,270-foot summit are Porcupine Islands and Bar Harbor to the northeast; Champlain Mountain and Huguenot Head to the east; Cranberry Isles and Gulf of Maine to the south; and Cadillac Mountain to the west. Return the way you came.

Options: On the return, you can descend via the Ladder Trail or Kurt Diederich's Climb and circle back to the Sieur de Monts Spring or Tarn parking area. To take the 0.4-mile-long Ladder Trail, descend the summit the way you came up, 0.5 mile back to the three-way junction with the Ladder Trail. Turn right and descend the Ladder Trail. At the bottom, turn left on the Tarn Trail, and take it to the four-way intersection at the north end of the pond. Go straight, following signs to Sieur de Monts Spring. (If you parked at the Tarn lot, turn right at the four-way intersection to return to that parking area.) The round trip is approximately 3.2 miles.

To take the 0.4-mile Kurt Diederich's Climb, descend the summit the way you came up, 1 mile back to the junction with Diederich's Climb. Turn right (southeast) to descend Diederich's Climb. At the bottom, turn left at the four-way intersection to return to the Sieur de Monts Spring parking area, or go straight to return to the Tarn parking area. The round trip is approximately 3.2 miles.

In an amazing architectural feat, stone steps wind through a rock crevice.

14 Kurt Diederich's Climb

Highlights:	Steep-stepped climb up sheer east face of Dorr Mountain, providing access to views from open summit.
Type of hike:	Day hike; out-and-back.
Total distance:	2.8 miles, plus 0.1 mile to reach trailhead.
Difficulty:	Moderate.

Finding the trailhead: Drive south of downtown Bar Harbor on Maine Highway 3 a little more than 2 miles, just past the Sieur de Monts park entrance to the Tarn parking lot on the right (west). Follow a dirt path at the south end of the parking area. Turn right at the end of a split rail fence, following another dirt path to a junction. Cross over the outlet of the Tarn on a series of rocks to the left. Do not follow the sign that points right to Sieur de Monts Spring. Reach the trailhead in 0.1 mile, at the four-way intersection. Go straight ahead up stone steps.

Parking and trailhead facilities: Park at the Tarn parking lot. There are no facilities at the trailhead, but restrooms and drinking fountains are available seasonally at Sieur de Monts Spring area, 0.3 mile north of the Tarn parking area along a woods path.

Key points:

0.0 Kurt Diederich's Climb Trailhead, reached after 0.1 mile on trail from the Tarn parking lot.

0.4 Junction with the Dorr Mountain East Face Trail; turn left.

1.4 Dorr Mountain summit.

2.8 Return the same way you came.

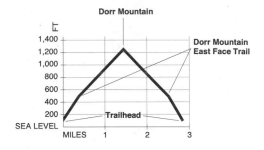

The hike: Arguably the most difficult way to access the summit of Dorr Mountain, Kurt Diederich's Climb takes you up 450 feet in only 0.4 mile, averaging more than 100 feet of elevation gain for each 0.1 mile, to the junction with the Dorr Mountain East Face Trail. By contrast, the rest of the way up to the summit, 1 mile more on the East Face Trail, averages only 72 feet elevation gain for each 0.1 mile.

Built in the early 1900s as a memorial path and one of three trails up Dorr Mountain's steep east face, Kurt Diederich's Climb brings you up via stone steps and switchbacks. The trail technically ends at 0.4 mile, at the junction with the Dorr Mountain East Face Trail, but turn left (south) at this junction to continue to the Dorr Mountain summit. Reach the 1,270-foot peak and its spectacular views of ocean and mountains at 1.4 miles. Return the way you came.

Kurt Diederich's Climb

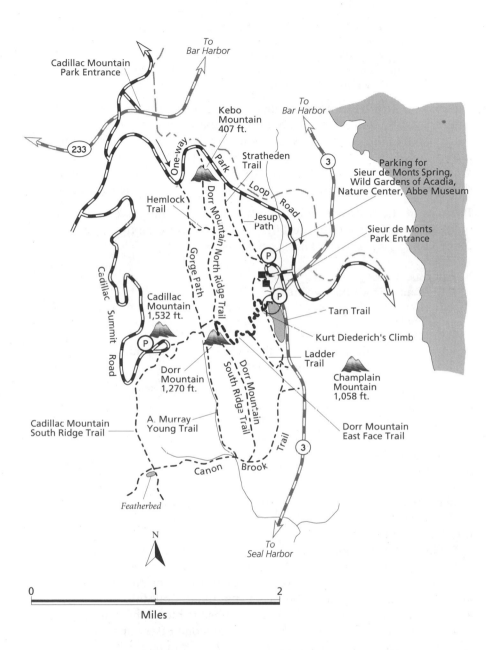

15 Dorr Mountain South Ridge Trail

Highlights: Relatively little-traveled route up Dorr Mountain, with open ridge views.
Type of hike: Day hike; out-and-back.
Total distance: 5.2 miles, including 1.2 miles to reach trailhead.
Difficulty: Moderate.

Finding the trailhead: Drive south of downtown Bar Harbor on Maine Highway 3 nearly 3 miles, past the Sieur de Monts park entrance and the Tarn parking lot, to the second gravel pullout south of the mountain pond. There is also a paved pullout on the east side of ME 3 here. Follow the Canon Brook Trail 1.2 miles, bearing left at the first junction, then turn right (north) at the second junction, where the Dorr Mountain South Ridge Trail begins.

Parking and trailhead facilities: Park at the second gravel pullout on the west side of ME 3 south of the Tarn, or paved pullout on the east side of ME 3, for Canon Brook Trail. There are no facilities.

Key points:
- 0.0 Canon Brook parking area.
- 1.2 Dorr Mountain South Ridge Trailhead, reached via the Canon Brook Trail.
- 2.6 Dorr Mountain summit.
- 4.0 Return to the junction with the Canon Brook Trail; turn left.
- 5.2 Return to the Canon Brook parking area.

The hike: The hardest Dorr Mountain trailhead to reach because of the need to hike in 1.2 miles on the Canon Brook Trail first, the South Ridge Trail is a relatively little-traveled route to the 1,270-foot summit.

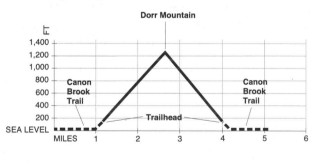

The trail heads north from the Canon Brook Trail, beginning with a relatively level stretch through the woods. Then comes a steep ascent up open rock face. Carefully follow the blue blazes and small cairns up the pink granite. Soon you'll begin getting views of Champlain Mountain to the right (east) and Cadillac to the left (west). Otter Cove is visible to the southeast.

As with many of Acadia's ridge trails, this one offers open vistas almost all the way up. At 1.4 miles, reach Dorr Mountain summit, with its views all around, stretching from Frenchman Bay to the east and Cadillac Mountain to the west, the Porcupine Islands to the north and the Gulf of Maine to the south. Return the way you came.

Dorr Mountain South Ridge Trail

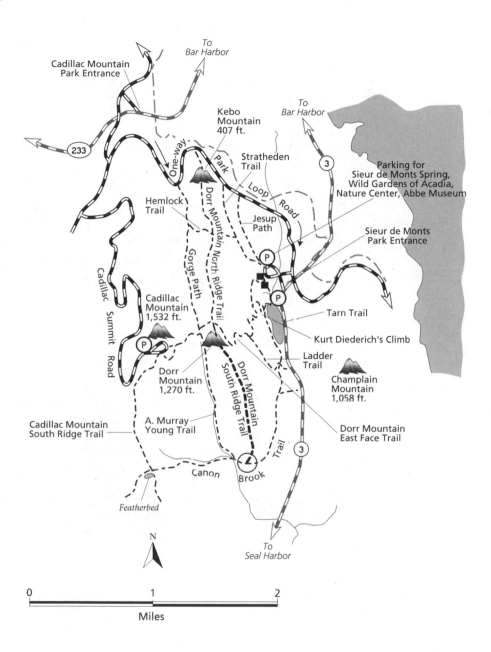

To Bar Harbor

Cadillac Mountain Park Entrance

To Bar Harbor

233

Kebo Mountain 407 ft.

Stratheden Trail

One-way

Park

Loop

Road

Parking for Sieur de Monts Spring, Wild Gardens of Acadia, Nature Center, Abbe Museum

Hemlock Trail

Jesup Path

Sieur de Monts Park Entrance

Cadillac Mountain 1,532 ft.

Cadillac Summit Road

Dorr Mountain North Ridge Trail

Gorge Path

3

P

P

Tarn Trail

Kurt Diederich's Climb

Dorr Mountain 1,270 ft.

Dorr Mountain South Ridge Trail

Ladder Trail

Champlain Mountain 1,058 ft.

Cadillac Mountain South Ridge Trail

A. Murray Young Trail

Dorr Mountain East Face Trail

Canon

Brook

Trail

3

Featherbed

To Seal Harbor

N

0   1   2
Miles

To get to the Dorr Mountain South Ridge Trailhead, you've got to pass views like this of Huguenot Head on the Canon Brook Trail.

Options: To do an approximately 3.1-mile loop, continue north on the ridge beyond the Dorr Mountain summit, and head right (east) down the Dorr Mountain East Face Trail for 0.4 mile. Then bear right at the junction with the strenuous Ladder Trail, descending another 0.4 mile. Turn right at the base of the Ladder Trail, and travel 0.2 mile. Then turn left at the next junction, returning back to the Canon Brook Trail parking area in another 0.3 mile.

16 Tarn Trail (Kane Path)

> **Highlights:** Walk along mountain pond, with views of Dorr Mountain and Huguenot Head and access to Dorr Mountain trails and Sieur de Monts Spring area.
> **Type of hike:** Day hike; out-and-back.
> **Total distance:** 2 miles.
> **Difficulty:** Easy to moderate.

Finding the trailhead: Drive south of downtown Bar Harbor on Maine Highway 3 a little more than 2 miles, just past the Sieur de Monts park entrance to the Tarn parking lot on the right (west). Follow a dirt path at the south end of the parking area. Turn right at the end of a split rail fence, following another dirt path to a junction. Cross over the outlet of the Tarn on a series of rocks to the left to begin the hike. Do not follow the sign that points right to the Sieur de Monts Spring.

Parking and trailhead facilities: Park at the Tarn parking lot. There are no facilities at the trailhead, but restrooms and drinking fountains are available seasonally at the Sieur de Monts Spring area, 0.3 mile north of the Tarn parking lot along a woods path.

Key points:
- 0.0 Tarn Trailhead.
- 0.1 Junction with the Jesup Path and Kurt Diederich's Climb; bear left.
- 0.8 Junction with the Ladder Trail.
- 1.0 Junction with the Canon Brook Trail.

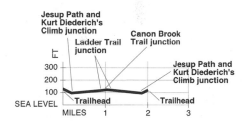

The hike: Rather than just driving by the Tarn on ME 3, take this trail to get a better appreciation of the mountain pond in the gorge between Dorr Mountain and Huguenot Head. Also known as Kane Path—"In Memory of John Innes Kane, a man of kindness who found his happiness in giving others pleasure," according to a 1913 plaque—the trail starts at the north end of the Tarn.

At 0.1 mile, you'll come to a four-way intersection, with Jesup Path leading right to the Sieur de Monts Spring and Kurt Diederich's Climb leading straight ahead up stone steps toward Dorr Mountain. Turn left (south) to follow the Tarn Trail along the west shore of the pond. Huguenot Head to the left (east) and Dorr Mountain to the right (west) soon come into view. You may also hear the traffic whizzing by on ME 3 across the pond.

Much of this part of the trail is on the flat surfaces of huge granite slabs, along the base of a Dorr Mountain rock slide. Some of the granite is pink, mirroring the pink of the rock slide on Huguenot Head across the gorge. Although the trail is fairly level, there is some rock hopping involved. The best

Tarn Trail (Kane Path)

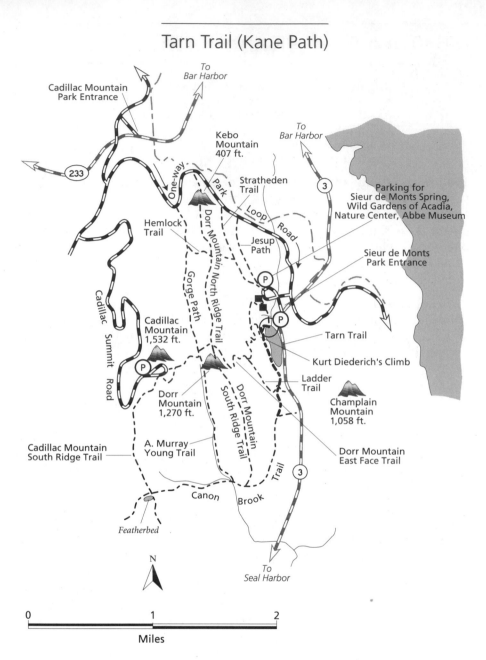

views are along the Tarn, so don't make the mistake of failing to notice them along the way. We once met an unappreciative hiker here who asked, "Does this trail go anywhere?"

At 0.8 mile, after passing the south end of the Tarn, the trail reaches a junction with the Ladder Trail, which heads steeply up Dorr Mountain. Continue on what has now become an easy wood path, reaching trail's end at 1 mile, at a junction with the Canon Brook Trail. Return the way you came.

Options: For a rugged loop up Dorr Mountain, take the Tarn Trail to the Ladder Trail. Turn right (west) and climb steeply on the 0.4-mile-long Ladder Trail to a three-way intersection with the Dorr Mountain East Face Trail. Bear left up 0.6 mile to the summit. Descend the way you came, back to the three-way intersection, but bear left (north) to continue on the Dorr Mountain East Face Trail rather than right to return on the Ladder Trail. At the next intersection, turn right (southeast) to descend the ridge via the steep 0.4-mile Kurt Diederich's Climb. At the bottom, go straight at the four-way intersection to return to the Tarn parking area. The round trip is approximately 3.2 miles.

Or you can descend all the way along the Dorr Mountain East Face Trail and visit the Sieur de Monts Spring, Wild Gardens of Acadia, Nature Center, and Abbe Museum. Bear left at each of the two intersections on the way down the ridge to the spring area. At the bottom, turn right (south) on Jesup Path, to return to Tarn parking, for a 3.6-mile loop.

17 Stratheden Trail

Highlights:	Well-graded woods walk connecting Park Loop Road to Sieur de Monts Spring area.
Type of hike:	Day hike; out-and-back.
Total distance:	2.2 miles.
Difficulty:	Easy.

Finding the trailhead: From the park visitor center, drive south on the Park Loop Road for 3 miles and turn left (east) at the sign to Sand Beach. Follow the one-way Park Loop Road for 1.4 miles, or 0.4 mile beyond the Dorr Mountain North Ridge Trailhead. The Stratheden Trailhead is on the right.

Parking and trailhead facilities: There is a small gravel pullout on the right of the one-way Park Loop Road, at the trailhead, but no facilities.

Key points:
- 0.0   Stratheden Trailhead.
- 0.7   Junction with the Hemlock Trail; go straight (southeast).
- 1.0   Junction with the Jesup Path; turn right (south).
- 1.1   Sieur de Monts Spring area.

The hike: Originally part of a century-old system of trails connecting downtown Bar Harbor to Sieur de Monts Spring and what had yet to become Acadia, the Stratheden Trail was reopened by the National Park Service in 1990. An easy, well-graded woods walk, the trail starts in a forest of birch trees and striped maple, also known as moosewood because its tender shoots are a favorite food of moose. You can spend countless hours exploring the Sieur de Monts Spring area, with the

Stratheden Trail

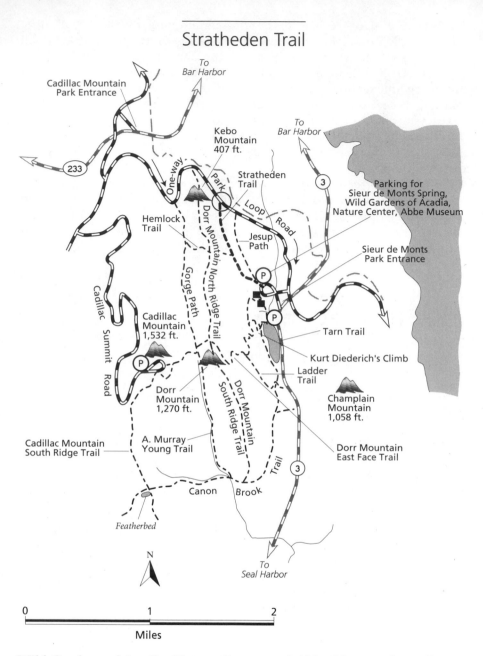

Wild Gardens of Acadia, Nature Center, and Abbe Museum here. Return the way you came.

Options: Form an easy loop of 2.2 miles by returning from the spring area on the Jesup Path. On the way back from the spring area, go straight at the first junction to follow Jesup Path 0.7 mile to the Park Loop Road, rather than left to continue on the Stratheden Trail. Turn left on the Park Loop Road to walk back 0.3 mile to your car.

18 Jesup Path
(Great Meadow Loop)

Highlights: Woods and field walk by the Great Meadow, Sieur de Monts Spring, Wild Gardens of Acadia, Nature Center, Abbe Museum, and the Tarn.
Type of hike: Day hike; out-and-back.
Total distance: 2 miles.
Difficulty: Easy.

Finding the trailhead: From the park visitor center, drive south on the Park Loop Road for 3 miles and turn left (east) at the sign to Sand Beach. Follow the one-way Park Loop Road for 1.7 miles. The trailhead is on the right soon after a road comes in on the left.

Parking and trailhead facilities: There is a small gravel pullout at the right of the one-way Park Loop Road, but no facilities.

Key points:

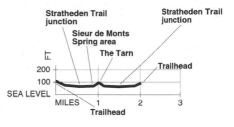

0.0	Jesup Path Trailhead.
0.1	Great Meadow.
0.3	Junction with an old gravel road; go straight (southeast).
0.7	Junction with the Stratheden Trail; go straight (south).
0.8	Sieur de Monts Spring area.
1.0	The Tarn.

The hike: Created nearly 100 years ago as part of a garden path that connected to downtown Bar Harbor, Jesup Path leads from the Park Loop Road to the Sieur de Monts Spring area and the mountain pond known as the Tarn, within park boundaries. As of fall 2000, through the efforts of Friends of Acadia, Jesup Path has been extended beyond the park's borders, as part of the Great Meadow Loop that reconnects Acadia to the outskirts of Bar Harbor.

Trails outside the park are beyond the scope of this guide, but this new part of the trail can be picked up on Cromwell Harbor Road, south of Bar Harbor and west of Maine Highway 3. Contact Friends of Acadia for more information.

From the trailhead on the Park Loop Road, the well-graded path heads south and soon skirts the Great Meadow. Views from this open marsh include Huguenot Head and Champlain Mountain to the left (southeast) and Dorr Mountain to the right (southwest). A series of plank bridges takes you over the wet spots. Take insect repellent during mosquito season.

In 0.3 mile, cross the old road at the four-way intersection, and go straight (southeast) across another plank bridge and into the woods. The trail then goes over a long series of log bridges. At 0.7 mile, come to another four-way intersection, a junction with the Stratheden Trail. Cross over the old gravel road and continue straight (south). In 0.8 mile, Jesup Path reaches the Sieur

Jesup Path (Great Meadow Loop)

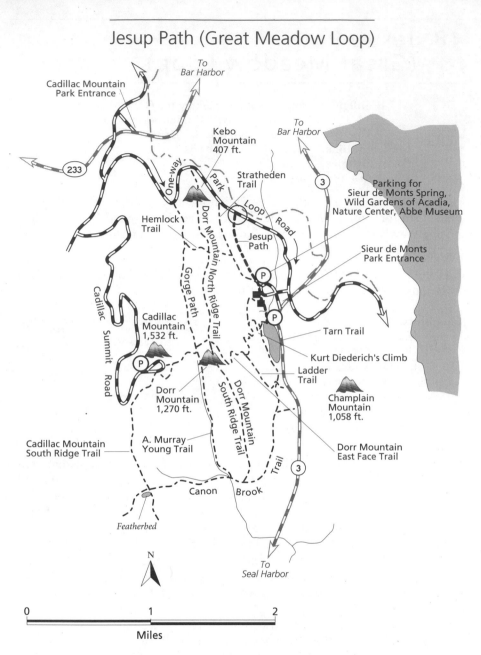

de Monts Spring area, featuring the Wild Gardens of Acadia, Nature Center, and Abbe Museum, and the spring itself, where hours can be spent learning about the flora and history of the park.

Continue on the trail, cross another plank bridge, and reach the Tarn at 1 mile in the gorge between Huguenot Head and Dorr Mountain. A plaque at this end of the trail reads, "In Memory of Morris K. and Maria DeWitt Jesup, Lovers of this Island, 1918." Return the way you came, for 2 miles round trip.

The Wild Gardens of Acadia is just one of the sights to see on the Jesup Path.

Options: For an easy loop of just a little more than 2.5 miles, follow the Jesup Path as described above, but on the return from the Sieur de Monts Spring, bear left at the first four-way intersection and follow the Stratheden Trail to the loop road. Turn right on the loop road and reach your destination after another 0.3 mile.

19 Hemlock Trail

Highlights:	Woods walk; important connector for Dorr Mountain loop.
Type of hike:	Day hike; out-and-back or part of loop up Dorr Mountain.
Total distance:	2 miles, including 0.5 mile to reach trailhead, or part of 3.2-mile loop.
Difficulty:	Easy to moderate.

Finding the trailhead: From the park visitor center, drive south on the Park Loop Road for 3 miles and turn left (east) at the sign to Sand Beach. Follow the one-way Park Loop Road for 0.8 mile. The Gorge Path Trailhead is on the right, just after the road crosses a stone bridge. The Hemlock Trailhead is 0.5 mile in on Gorge Path.

Parking and trailhead facilities: Park in a small gravel parking area for the Gorge Path on the right side of the one-way loop road, right after a stone bridge and trailhead; there are no facilities.

Hemlock Trail

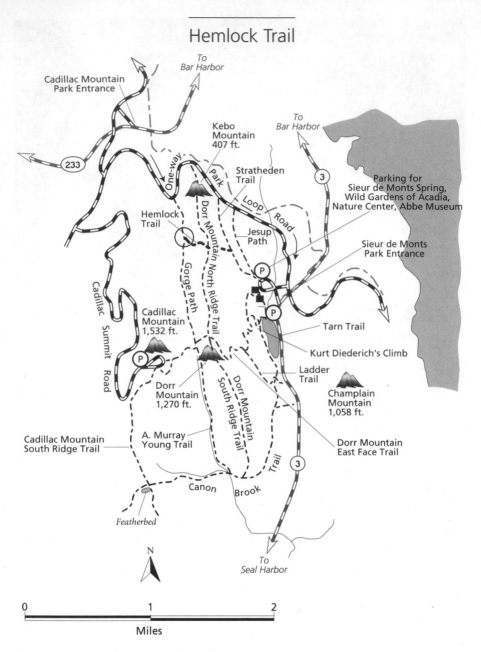

0   1   2

Miles

Key points:

0.5   Hemlock Trailhead, reached after 0.5 mile on the Gorge Path.

0.7   Cross an old woods path and creek bed.

0.8   Junction with the Dorr Mountain North Ridge Trail.

1.0   Junction with the Stratheden Trail.

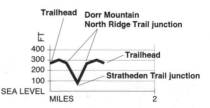

The hike: A major shortcut connector trail for a loop up Dorr Mountain, the Hemlock Trail turns what would otherwise be a 4.1-mile round trip—up the Gorge Path and down Dorr Mountain North Ridge Trail, including a half-mile walk back to the car on the Park Loop Road—into a 3.2-mile loop hike. It can also be used to access the Sieur de Monts Spring area, via the Stratheden Trail and Jesup Path.

The trail dates back more than 100 years, to the days of walking paths connecting downtown Bar Harbor to what was yet to become Acadia National Park. It even appears to still show evidence of the great fire of 1947 that destroyed much of the eastern side of Mount Desert Island, with a prominent burned-out tree hollow along the trail, just west of its junction with the Dorr Mountain North Ridge Trail.

To get to the Hemlock Trail, hike south on the Gorge Path for 0.5 mile, and turn left (east-southeast) at the Hemlock Trailhead. The Hemlock Trail is flat and well graded, and lined with plenty of birches, until it crosses an old woods path and creek bed at 0.7; then it gets very rocky.

At 0.8 mile, reach the junction with the Dorr Mountain North Ridge Trail. From here, you can continue straight (southeast) on the Hemlock Trail until it reaches the Stratheden Trail at 1 mile, ending with a clamber down a steep rock face. Return the way you came for a 2-mile round trip, or turn right and follow the Stratheden Trail and Jesup Path to reach the Sieur de Monts Spring area in an additional 0.4 mile.

But to do the approximately 3.2-mile moderate-to-strenuous loop incorporating the 1,270-foot Dorr Mountain summit, turn right off the Hemlock Trail at 0.3 mile, and head south-southwest on the Dorr Mountain North Ridge Trail. Ascend the ridge 0.8 mile to the summit. From the summit, backtrack 0.1 mile north on the ridge trail to pick up the Cadillac-Dorr Trail and descend steeply west for 0.1 mile into the gorge between the two mountains. Turn right and head north on Gorge Path for 1.4 miles to complete the loop back to your car.

---

20 Ladder Trail

Highlights:	Iron ladders and stone steps up to spectacular views on Dorr Mountain.
Type of hike:	Day hike; out-and-back.
Total distance:	1.8 miles.
Difficulty:	Strenuous.

Finding the trailhead: Drive south of downtown Bar Harbor on Maine Highway 3 2.6 miles, past the Sieur de Monts park entrance and the Tarn parking lot, to the first gravel pullout south of the mountain pond. The trailhead is on the west side of ME 3.

Parking and trailhead facilities: Park at first gravel pullout on the west side of ME 3 south of the Tarn; there are no facilities.

Ladder Trail

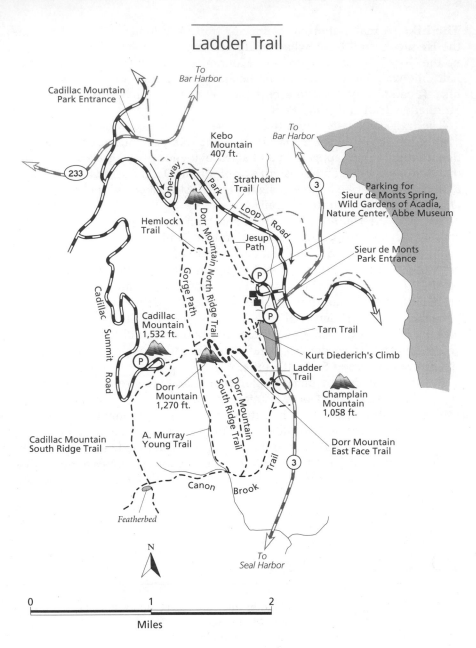

Key points:

- 0.0   Ladder Trailhead; junction with the Tarn Trail.
- 0.4   Junction with the Dorr Mountain East Face Trail; bear left.
- 0.8   Junction with the Dorr Mountain North Ridge Trail; bear left.
- 0.9   Dorr Mountain summit.

The hike: Alternating between iron ladders and stone steps, the Ladder Trail is one of the most challenging ways up Dorr Mountain, via the precipitous east face. From the gorge between Dorr and Champlain mountains, just south of the Tarn, the Ladder Trail immediately rises to the west up stone steps and switchbacks. You soon get views of the Porcupine Islands to the northeast. The trail takes you by a huge granite slab, and then through a cavelike crevice with low-hanging juniper.

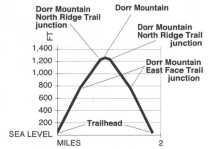

Soon, you'll reach the first iron ladder, a creaky but secure 10-step structure with four handrails to help you up. Then there's a 5-step ladder with two handrails bolted into the rock face. The trail next takes you among cavelike boulders, some with strange, triangular rock overhangs. One such overhang looks like a giant fish head. A 6-rung ladder takes you left and up to the top of the giant rock formations that just towered over you below. You'll pass one more giant rock face to your left, and a sprightly birch to your right—the kind of birch that makes a good swing for a kid, if the tree weren't growing on a precipitous mountain face. The trail continues on scores of granite stairs.

At 0.4 mile, reach a junction with the Dorr Mountain East Face Trail. Bear left to continue up to the summit. The ascent moderates here, and the trail begins taking you along the smooth rock faces typical of so many of Acadia's mountain ridges. You'll begin to get views of the Tarn below, as well as of Champlain Mountain, Frenchman Bay, and the Porcupines farther to the east and northeast. The trail environment alternates between open ridge and scrub oak and pitch pine, then climbs steeply to the summit. At 0.8 mile, at a junction with the Dorr Mountain North Ridge Trail, bear left on the ridge and attain the 1,270-foot peak at 0.9 mile. As we heard some hikers up Dorr say during one of our climbs, the views from here are "the best yet." Return the way you came.

The hulk of Huguenot Head dominates the view from the top of the Ladder Trail.

Options: For a 3.4-mile loop, head south from Dorr Mountain on the 1.4-mile-long Dorr Mountain South Ridge Trail. Turn left at the junction with the Canon Brook Trail and follow the path toward the Tarn for 1.1 miles. Stay straight past the turnoff to the Canon Brook Trail parking area, and turn right at the next junction to return to the Ladder Trail parking area.

21 Gorge Path

Highlights:	Up steep gorge between Cadillac and Dorr mountains, ending atop Cadillac.
Type of hike:	Day hike; out-and-back.
Total distance:	3.6 miles.
Difficulty:	Strenuous.

Finding the trailhead: From the park visitor center, drive south on the Park Loop Road for 3 miles and turn left (east) at the sign to Sand Beach. Follow the one-way Park Loop Road for 0.8 mile. The trailhead is on the right, just after the road crosses a stone bridge.

Parking and trailhead facilities: Park in a small gravel parking area on the right side of the one-way loop road, right after a stone bridge and trailhead. There are no facilities at the trailhead, but the gift shop and rest rooms are open in season at Cadillac summit.

Key points:

- 0.0 Gorge Path Trailhead.
- 0.5 Junction with the Hemlock Trail.
- 1.4 Junction with the Cadillac-Dorr Trail.
- 1.8 Cadillac Mountain summit; junction with the Cadillac Summit Loop Trail.

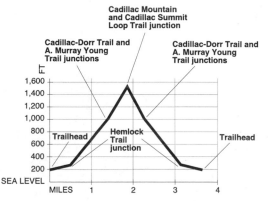

The hike: Rising from the wet and wooded depths of the ravine between Cadillac and Dorr mountains to the spectacular views of the highest peak in Acadia, Gorge Path provides the best contrast between dark forest and open summit of all the trails up Cadillac. First described in the 1870s as a path that allows "youth and enthusiasm . . . to find scope for their ambition," Gorge Path is still a challenge for the most ambitious hiker today.

Heading south from the trailhead, descend stone steps and hop over rocks to the other side of a creek, then quickly cross back over on a log bridge. In 0.1 mile, the path ascends steeply up a rock face, providing the first views of Cadillac to the right (west) and Dorr to the left (east).

Gorge Path

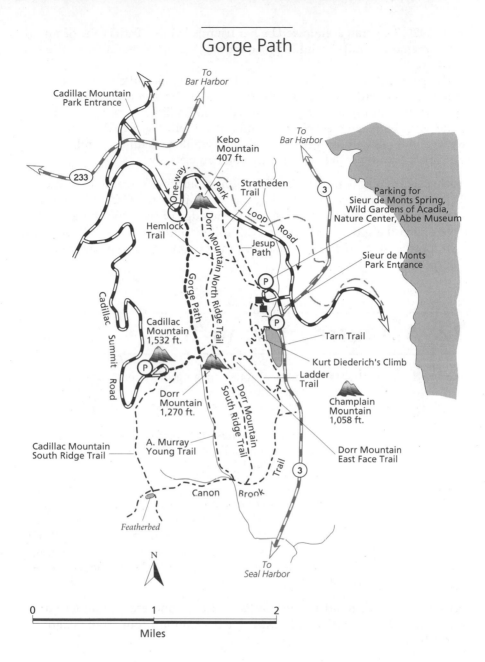

Follow the blue blazes (faint at times) and cairns up and over rock faces and across creek beds. Pass a junction at 0.5 mile with the Hemlock Trail, which heads to the left toward the Dorr Mountain North Ridge Trail and the Sieur de Monts Spring area. As the path steepens, roughly paralleling the creek that runs down the ravine, the gorge between Cadillac and Dorr narrows and the creek forms small waterfalls and cascades.

At one of these cascades set into a cliff on the Cadillac Mountain side of the gorge is a plaque: "In loving memory of Lilian Endicott Francklyn,

1891–1928. This trail is endowed by her friends." Gorge Path is one of a number of memorial trails sprinkled throughout Acadia, a reminder of the history here.

The path then crosses the creek a few more times and climbs steeply up a long series of stone steps, until it rises above the creek, at 1.0 mile. Leveling off, the path reaches a junction with the Cadillac-Dorr Trail at the top of the gorge between the two mountains, at 1.4 miles. Gorge Path turns right (west) and finally climbs precipitously up Cadillac Mountain, ending at the summit at 1.8 miles. Return the way you came.

Options: To do a loop that is slightly longer and more scenic than returning the same way, head north from the summit on the Cadillac Mountain North Ridge Trail, which leads right off the edge of the summit parking lot across from the gift shop. Descend 2.2 miles to the Park Loop Road. Turn right (northeast) on the road and walk 1 mile to return to your car, for a total round trip of 5 miles.

22 A. Murray Young Trail

Highlights: Less-traveled trail up gorge between Cadillac and Dorr mountains.

Type of hike: Day hike; out-and-back, or part of loop up Cadillac or Dorr Mountain.

Total distance: 5.2 miles, including 1.3 miles to reach trailhead; or 6-mile loop up Cadillac Mountain; or 5.3-mile loop up Dorr Mountain.

Difficulty: Moderate to strenuous.

Finding the trailhead: Drive south of downtown Bar Harbor on Maine Highway 3 nearly 3 miles, past the Sieur de Monts park entrance and the Tarn parking lot, to the second gravel pullout south of the mountain pond. Follow the Canon Brook Trail 1.3 miles, bearing left at the first junction, straight at the second junction, then turn right (north) at the third junction, where the A. Murray Young Trail begins.

Parking and trailhead facilities: Park at a second gravel pullout on the west side of ME 3 south of the Tarn, for the Canon Brook Trail. There are no facilities.

Key points:
- 0.0 Canon Brook Trail parking area.
- 1.3 A. Murray Young Trailhead, reached via the Canon Brook Trail.
- 2.6 Junction with the Gorge Path and Cadillac-Dorr Trail. Cadillac Mountain is to the left up a 0.4-mile spur; Dorr Mountain is to the right up a 0.2-mile spur.
- 3.9 Return to the junction with the Canon Brook Trail.
- 5.2 Return to the Canon Brook parking area.

A. Murray Young Trail

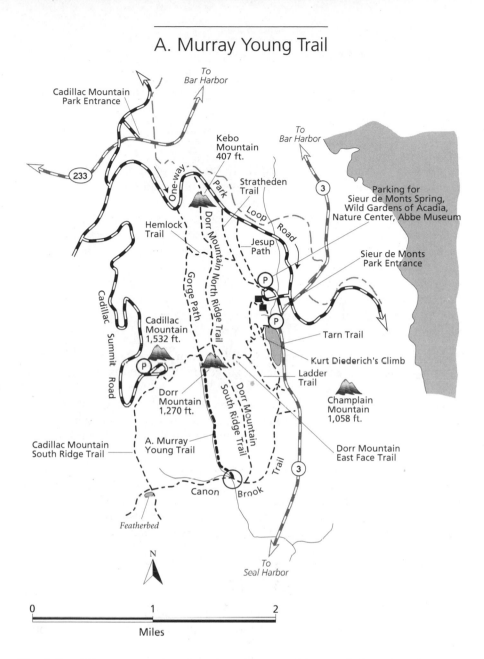

The hike: There are no spectacular vistas on this wooded trail, unless you tag on the short but steep climbs up to either Cadillac or Dorr Mountain at the end. Hard to get to because of the 1.3 miles required in on the Canon Brook Trail, the A. Murray Young Trail gives you the chance of making it up most of the way to Cadillac or Dorr without crowds of other hikers. You'll likely have plenty of company, however, if you hike up either summit.

The trail heads north from the Canon Brook Trail, crossing from one side of the creek that drains from the mountains to the other. At one such

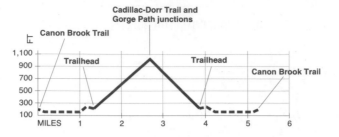

crossing near the start, a plaque reads, "In Memory of Andrew Murray Young, who loved this island where God has given of his beauty with a lavish hand."

Occasionally, the trail goes along flat stones laid in garden-path style and up stone steps. Ascending steadily, it passes some nice cascades two-thirds of the way up. After you reach the top of the creek, the trail gets rocky and steep, staying that way for the last quarter mile or so. At 2.6 miles from the start, the trail officially ends at a four-way intersection at the top of the gorge, at a junction with the Gorge Path and the Cadillac-Dorr Trail.

A steep 0.4-mile climb to the left (west) takes you up Cadillac, while an equally steep 0.2-mile climb to the right (east) takes you up Dorr. Return the way you came.

Options: To do a 6-mile loop up Cadillac, turn left at the four-way inter-section at trail's end at the top of the gorge and ascend very steeply the 0.4 mile to the summit. Descend via the Cadillac Mountain South Ridge Trail, reached across the summit parking lot and to the left of the gift shop. At the four-way intersection at the Featherbed, a mountain pond reached in 1.2 miles from the summit, turn left (east) onto the Canon Brook Trail, and follow it 1.8 miles back to the Canon Brook parking area.

To do a 5.3-mile loop up Dorr Mountain, turn right at the four-way in-tersection at trail's end at the top of the gorge and ascend the steep 0.2 mile to the summit. Turn right (south) and descend via the 1.3-mile Dorr Moun-tain South Ridge Trail. At the junction with the Canon Brook Trail, turn left (east) to return in another 1.2 miles to the Canon Brook parking area.

23 Canon Brook Trail

Highlights: Skirt Dorr Mountain up Cadillac ridge to a peaceful mountain pond.
Type of hike: Day hike; out-and-back.
Total distance: 3.6 miles.
Difficulty: Moderate to strenuous.

Finding the trailhead: Drive south of downtown Bar Harbor on Maine High-way 3 nearly 3 miles, past Sieur de Monts park entrance and the Tarn park-ing lot, to the second gravel pullout south of the mountain pond. There is also a paved pullout on the east side of ME 3 here. The trailhead is on the west side of ME 3.

Canon Brook Trail

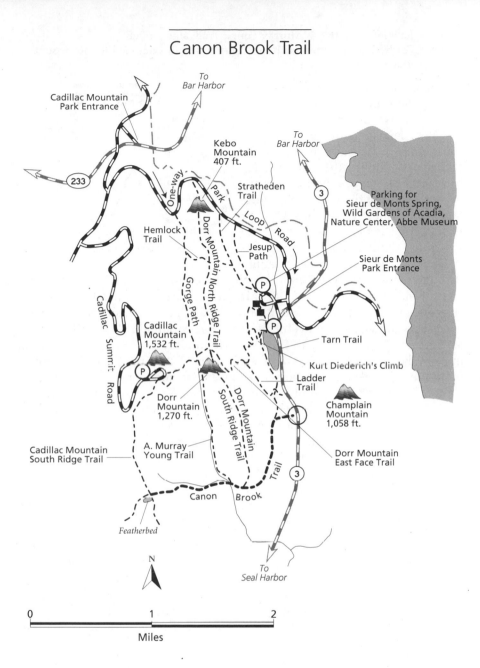

Parking and trailhead facilities: Park at the second gravel pullout south of the Tarn, on the west side of ME 3, or the paved pullout on the east side of ME 3; there are no facilities.

Key points:
- 0.0   Canon Brook Trailhead.
- 0.3   Junction with the Tarn Trail; turn left.
- 1.2   Junction with the Dorr Mountain South Ridge Trail; stay straight.

1.3   Junction with the A. Murray Young Trail; stay straight.

1.8   Featherbed; junction with the Pond Trail and Cadillac Mountain South Ridge Trail.

The hike: The relatively flat eastern half of the Canon Brook Trail may have been part of a pre–Revolutionary War carriage trail, but once it starts circling west and skirts the base of Dorr Mountain, the terrain gets rougher. The steepest part comes as the trail goes up the Cadillac Mountain south ridge, paralleling Canon Brook. That is also where the best views are, along the sheer rock faces.

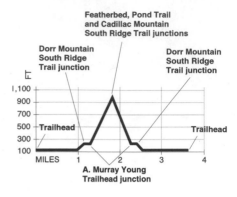

The trail begins with an easy jaunt through the woods. At 0.3 mile, reach a junction with the Tarn Trail at the base of the sheer east face of Dorr Mountain. Turn left to head south on the relatively level part of the Canon Brook Trail. Soon the trail veers west and starts ascending as it rounds the base of Dorr Mountain. The trail levels off as it nears the junction with the Dorr Mountain South Ridge Trail coming in from the right, at 1.2 miles. At 1.3 miles, the A. Murray Young Trail comes in on the right, from the gorge between Cadillac and Dorr mountains. Cross Canon Brook and start climbing steeply to the left up stone stairs. Then go up along a cascade, crossing from one side of it to the other. As you go up the sheer rock face with water coming down it, you get views of Champlain, the Beehive, and Otter Cliff behind you to the east.

The trail next heads into the woods, leveling off as you skirt a marsh. Stone stairs take you up one more time. At 1.8 miles, reach the Featherbed, where you can sit on log benches and take in the views around the mountain pond, or see a turkey vulture soar on the thermals as we did one beautiful morning. Return the way you came.

Options: To add on the Cadillac Mountain summit, from the Featherbed, turn right (north) on the Cadillac Mountain South Ridge Trail for another 1.2 miles to the 1,532-foot summit. Just before the summit road, turn right and parallel the road to the peak, which will be mobbed with cars and people during the height of the season. Return the way you came.

To do a challenging 4.6-mile loop, from the Featherbed, head north on the Cadillac Mountain South Ridge Trail to the Cadillac summit. Then head 0.6 mile east, steeply down the gorge separating Cadillac and Dorr mountains, and then steeply up Dorr. From the summit of Dorr, head south along the ridge a little way to pick up the Dorr Mountain East Face Trail. Descend along the East Face Trail for 0.5 mile, then turn right at the junction with the Ladder Trail. At the base of the Ladder Trail, turn right at the junction with the Tarn Trail and travel 0.2 mile. Turn left at the next junction to return to the Canon Brook Trail parking area in another 0.3 mile.

Hikers enjoy the view along the Canon Brook Trail.

24 Cadillac Mountain North Ridge Trail

Highlights: Views of Frenchman Bay, Bar Harbor, and Porcupine Islands on open ascent to highest mountain on Atlantic coast.
Type of hike: Day hike; out-and-back.
Total distance: 4.4 miles.
Difficulty: Moderate.

Finding the trailhead: From the park visitor center, drive south on the Park Loop Road for 3 miles and turn left (east) at the sign to Sand Beach. Follow the one-way Park Loop Road for 0.3 mile. The trailhead is on the right (south) side of the loop road.

Parking and trailhead facilities: Limited parking is along the side of the one-way Park Loop Road near the trailhead. There are no facilities at the trailhead, but the gift shop and restrooms are open in season at the summit.

Key points:
   0.0   Cadillac Mountain North Ridge Trailhead.
   0.6   Trail nears the Cadillac Summit Road.
   1.1   Steep climb up a series of more than 100 stone steps.
   1.3   Trail nears the summit road again, but follow the blue blazes to the left.
   2.2   Cadillac Mountain summit; junction with the Cadillac Summit Loop Trail.

The hike: The Cadillac Mountain North Ridge Trail follows old Native American footpaths and a former buckboard road up spectacular 1,532-foot Cadillac Mountain, the highest point on the Atlantic coast. Like many of the ridge trails in Acadia, this one is along exposed granite

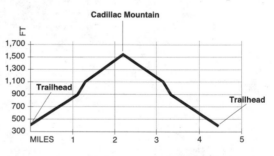

ledges much of the way, offering grand views of land and sea. Here the views include Bar Harbor, Frenchman Bay, and a series of distinctive rocky islands, beginning with Bar Island and extending into the bay with the Porcupines.

This is one of the oldest trails on Mount Desert Island. Recreational hikers ascended the mountain as early as the 1850s, when there was a survey station on the peak. In the late 1800s, a large hotel graced the summit. In the 1920s and 1930s, the trail was rerouted to accommodate the Cadillac Summit Road.

If you hike during the summer, be prepared for crowds at the summit and the sound and smell of cars on the way up. Motorists can drive up Cadillac, and the trail comes close to the summit road in two places.

Cadillac Mountain North Ridge Trail

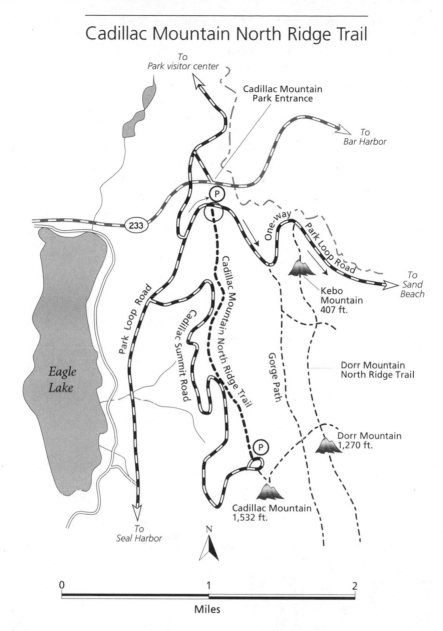

The blue-blazed trail begins across from the parking area with a series of four stone steps. Immediately, there are views of Bar Harbor and the islands to the left and behind you, or north and northeast. At 0.1 mile, the trail turns sharp right, dipping down into a cool grove of birches and evergreens.

Rising moderately, the southward-bound trail offers views of the low-lying Kebo Mountain to the left (east), Eagle Lake to the southwest, and Cadillac Mountain to the south-southeast. The trail levels off briefly, then begins rising again, offering clear views of Cadillac and the neighboring 1,270-foot Dorr Mountain.

At 0.6 mile, the trail comes close to the summit road, paralleling it to the east through the woods. At 1.1 miles, it begins climbing steeply through a birch forest up a series of more than 100 stone steps. The steps offer a natural resting spot, as we discovered. In this stretch of woods, we heard the distinctive song of the chickadee.

You clear treeline at 1.2 miles. Even though the trail has already offered glimpses of Bar Harbor and Frenchman Bay, the expansive view here is even more breathtaking. At 1.3 miles, the trail comes within view of the summit road, at a point where it looks like a Stonehenge of sorts with its border of huge granite rocks. This is a tricky spot. Do not follow a well-worn footpath to the road. Instead, stay to the left, away from the road, and follow the blue blazes.

The trail soon turns sharply left near a scenic road turnout and leaves the road behind. For the final assault up the pink granite of Cadillac Mountain, follow the cairns that mark the trail. At 2.2 miles, reach the summit parking area and the expansive views of Cadillac, including not only Frenchman Bay and Bar Harbor, but also Dorr Mountain and the Gulf of Maine to the east and the Beehive and Otter Cliff to the southeast.

You can take the easy 0.3-mile Cadillac Summit Loop Trail and learn about the geology of Mount Desert Island. The gift shop and restrooms at the summit are open in season. Return the way you came.

Options: This trail can also be done as a one-way, 2.2-mile hike, with one car at the trailhead and another at the Cadillac summit parking area. To get

Expansive views of Bar Harbor, Bar Island and the Porcupine Islands from atop the north ridge of Cadillac.

to the summit road from the park visitor center, head south on the Park Loop Road, but go straight past the Sand Beach sign rather than turn left. Take your next left onto the Cadillac Mountain summit road.

You can also do an approximately 4.8-mile loop, including a short walk on the Park Loop Road at the end, back to your car. From the Cadillac Summit Loop Trail, descend steeply east on Gorge Path, toward Dorr Mountain. Reach the gorge between the two mountains in 0.4 mile, then turn left (north) on Gorge Path and descend to the Park Loop Road in another 1.4 miles. Turn left on the loop road and reach your car in another 0.8 mile.

25 Cadillac Mountain South Ridge Trail

Highlights:	Fine views along Cadillac ridge and summit; spur trail to Eagles Crag; restful mountain pond called the Featherbed.
Type of hike:	Day hike; out-and-back.
Total distance:	7 miles.
Difficulty:	Moderate.

Finding the trailhead: From downtown Bar Harbor, head south 5 miles on Maine Highway 3 toward Seal Harbor. The trailhead is on the right, after the Blackwoods Campground entrance.

Parking and trailhead facilities: Park at a gravel pullout on the right (north) side of ME 3. There are no facilities at the trailhead, but the gift shop and restrooms are open in season at the summit.

Key points:

- 0.0 Cadillac Mountain South Ridge Trailhead.
- 0.8 Junction with the south end of the Eagles Crag Trail, 0.3-mile spur to cliffs.
- 1.0 Junction with the north end of the Eagles Crag Trail.
- 2.3 Featherbed; junction with the Canon Brook and Pond trails.
- 3.0 Junction with the Cadillac West Face Trail.
- 3.2 Near Cadillac Summit Road; turn right (northeast).
- 3.5 Cadillac Mountain summit.

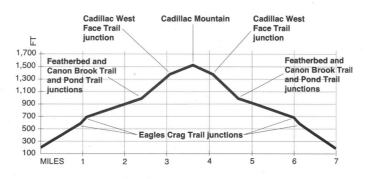

Cadillac Mountain South Ridge Trail

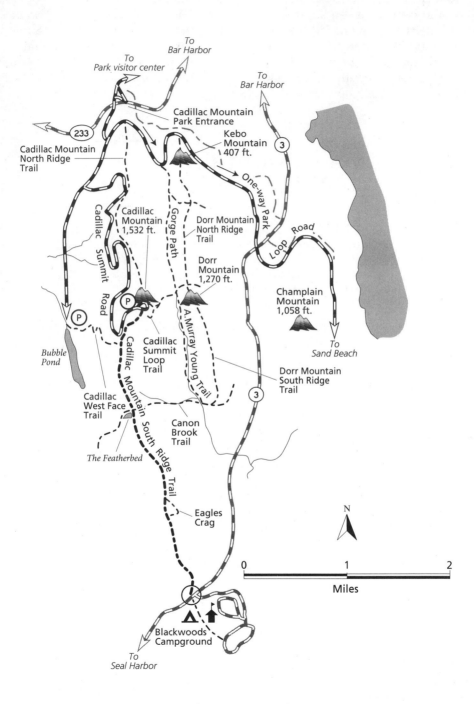

The hike: One of the longest trails in Acadia, the Cadillac Mountain South Ridge Trail provides open vistas for much of its length, while also offering the chance to see raptors soar at Eagles Crag or to rest at a peaceful mountain pond called the Featherbed.

Like the Cadillac Mountain North Ridge Trail, the South Ridge Trail is a gradual climb, but it has the advantage of not coming close to the Cadillac Summit Road until near the end. The trail, which can also be picked up via an extension from the Blackwoods Campground, begins by going over a few log bridges and ascending gradually.

At 0.8 mile, it reaches the junction with the south end of the 0.3-mile spur to Eagles Crag. The panorama from the top of Eagles Crag extends south and southeast to the Cranberry Isles and Otter Point, and north and northeast to Frenchman Bay, Huguenot Head, Champlain Mountain, and the Beehive. The Eagles Crag spur rejoins Cadillac's south ridge at the main trail's 1-mile mark. From now until Cadillac's summit, the trail offers open views along the way.

At 2.3 miles, reach the Featherbed, a perfect spot to rest and have lunch. Hand-hewn wooden benches here offer a place to sit and take in the views around the small mountain pond, listen to the bird song, and watch for wildlife. Here the Canon Brook Trail comes in from the east and the Pond Trail from the west.

Continue north, up a steep rocky crag, reaching the junction with the Cadillac West Face Trail at 3 miles. The views here are dramatic, with the Bubbles and Pemetic Mountain visible to the west, and the Cranberry Isles to the south. It is also a good place to see a sunset, because of its western exposure. Be prepared next for views of cars climbing the Cadillac Summit Road and people mobbing the mountaintop, if you're hiking during the peak summer season.

At 3.2 miles, as the trail nears the summit road and the Blue Hill overlook parking area, turn right before the road. Climb up a rock face using a conveniently placed iron rung and follow the trail as it basically parallels the summit road to the top. The trail goes on to a gravel road near the end, coming out at 3.5 miles at the summit parking area next to the gift shop. Cross the parking area and walk the short Cadillac Summit Loop Trail to get the best views and learn about the geology of Mount Desert Island. Return the way you came.

Options: For less ambitious hikers, there are two shorter options along the Cadillac Mountain South Ridge Trail. To do a 2.1-mile loop to Eagles Crag and back, head north from the trailhead 0.8 mile and bear right on to the southern end of the 0.3-mile spur to Eagles Crag. Circle north along the cliffs and back to the main trail, turn left and head back south, returning to the Cadillac Mountain South Ridge Trailhead in another 1 mile.

For a 1.8-mile round trip from Cadillac Summit Road to the Featherbed, park your car at the Blue Hill overlook parking area, cross the summit road, and head down the Cadillac Mountain South Ridge Trail, reaching the peaceful mountain pond in 0.9 mile.

More ambitious hikers can do a total 8.3-mile hike by adding a long loop that includes Dorr Mountain. From the Cadillac Summit Loop Trail, head east down the Gorge Path and climb up Dorr Mountain, across the notch in 0.6 mile. Then head south 1.3 miles on the Dorr Mountain South Ridge Trail and west 0.6 mile on the Canon Brook Trail, circling back to the Featherbed. At the junction with the mountain pond, turn left (south) and return the 2.3 miles back to the Cadillac Mountain South Ridge Trailhead.

26 Cadillac West Face Trail

Highlights: Shortest but steepest route up Cadillac; chance of spectacular sunset at Sunset Point.
Type of hike: Day hike; out-and-back.
Total distance: 2.8 miles.
Difficulty: Strenuous.

Finding the trailhead: From the park visitor center, head south on the Park Loop Road for 5 miles, past the Cadillac Mountain entrance to the Bubble Pond parking lot (not the Bubble Rock parking lot farther south). Walk toward Bubble Pond and bear left; cross footbridge to the trailhead on the left.

Parking and trailhead facilities: Park at the Bubble Pond parking lot. The facilities here include a chemical toilet and a picnic table.

Key points:
0.0   Cadillac West Face Trailhead.
0.9   Junction with the Cadillac Mountain South Ridge Trail at Sunset Point; turn left.
1.4   Cadillac Mountain summit.

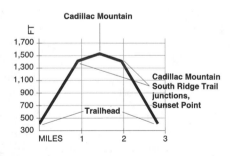

The hike: The Cadillac West Face Trail is the shortest approach to Acadia's highest mountain and therefore the steepest. Rising abruptly from Bubble Pond, the trail begins as a rocky path taking you up to a huge cedar grove. Bear to the left through the grove. Watch carefully for cairns marking the way, as it is easy to lose your way here. At one point, you need to hoist yourself up a difficult rock face. Watch for the blue blaze on the right.

Soon you get views of Bubble Pond down to your right (west) and Pemetic Mountain to the southwest. The rugged trail continues steeply up, and the views of Bubble Pond and Pemetic keep getting more expansive. After a series of switchbacks, you see your first glimpse of Eagle Lake to the northwest. Then you see Bar Island and the Porcupine Islands to the northeast

Cadillac West Face Trail

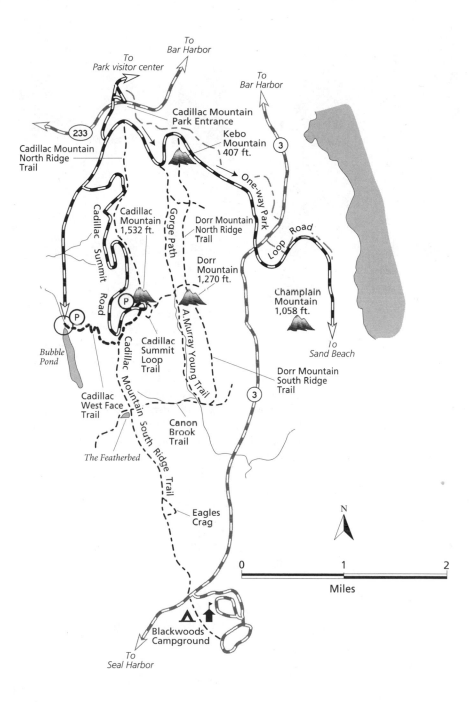

The Cadillac West Face Trail climbs steeply up from Bubble Pond, along the rough west face of Acadia's highest mountain, to the left.

and the Cranberry Isles to the south. The trail begins to moderate as you approach the ridge. A wide-open cliff face gives you the best views yet.

At 0.9 mile, reach Sunset Point and the junction with the Cadillac Mountain South Ridge Trail. This is a lovely place to see a sunset, but if that's your plan, it's best to hike to this point from the Cadillac Summit Road's nearby Blue Hill overlook parking area, rather than risk getting stuck on the steep West Face Trail after dark. To continue to the summit, turn left at Sunset Point and hike the rest of the way along the Cadillac Mountain South Ridge Trail. As the trail nears the summit road by the Blue Hill overlook, turn right and follow the trail as it parallels the road to the mountaintop parking lot. Reach the 1,532-foot peak at 1.4 miles, with its grand views of Bar Harbor, Frenchman Bay, and the surrounding mountains. But also be prepared for views of lots of cars and people if you hike this during the busy summer season. Return the way you came.

Options: To visit a peaceful mountain pond called the Featherbed on the way back down from Cadillac, follow the Cadillac Mountain South Ridge Trail straight past Sunset Point and the junction with the West Face Trail, reaching the pond with its log benches in another 0.7 mile. Turn right (west) onto the Pond Trail and follow it for 0.8 mile to a carriage road. Turn right on the carriage road and walk back 1.5 miles to the Bubble Pond parking area.

27 Cadillac Summit Loop Trail

Highlights: Spectacular views from Acadia's highest mountain; plaques with geological information.
Type of hike: Day hike; loop.
Total distance: 0.5 mile.
Difficulty: Easy.

Finding the trailhead: From the park visitor center, drive south on the Park Loop Road for 3.5 miles and turn left (east) at the sign for Cadillac Mountain. Ascend the winding summit road to the top. A paved walkway leaves from behind a large pink granite boulder with a memorial plaque.

Parking and trailhead facilities: Park at the summit parking area. The gift shop and restrooms are open in season. The walkway is partially wheelchair and baby-stroller accessible.

Key points:

0.0   Cadillac Summit Loop Trailhead.
0.5   Return to the trailhead, completing loop.

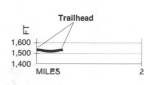

The hike: You gain a new appreciation for Cadillac Mountain on this trail, with plaques describing the geology of Mount Desert Island and the spectacular views from Acadia's highest summit, at 1,532 feet above sea level. The loop trail leaves from the eastern edge of the parking area, behind a large pink granite boulder with a plaque in memory of Stephen Tyng Mather, who laid the foundation for the National Park Service.

Walk the loop in a clockwise direction to follow the order of the descriptive plaques. The paved walkway, tinged to match the pink granite atop Cadillac, provides access to wheelchairs and baby strollers about halfway around the loop. You are also free to stray off the walkway and on to the mountain's pink granite ledges, but it is best to stay on the path or solid rock to avoid trampling vegetation, which leads to soil erosion.

Because of its grand vistas of Frenchman Bay, Porcupine Islands, and the other mountains of Acadia, as well as its easy accessibility, the loop trail can get very crowded in the summer. Early mornings and late afternoons are best, although the summit road is open one hour before sunrise for those wishing to catch the day's first rays and doesn't close until midnight, for those wanting to see starlit skies and the lights of Bar Harbor.

Options: Ambitious hikers can descend steeply from the loop trail into the gorge east of Cadillac and climb up the lower Dorr Mountain, which provides closer views of the ocean. The strenuous path connecting the two summits is 0.6 mile one way. Return the same way.

Cadillac Summit Loop Trail

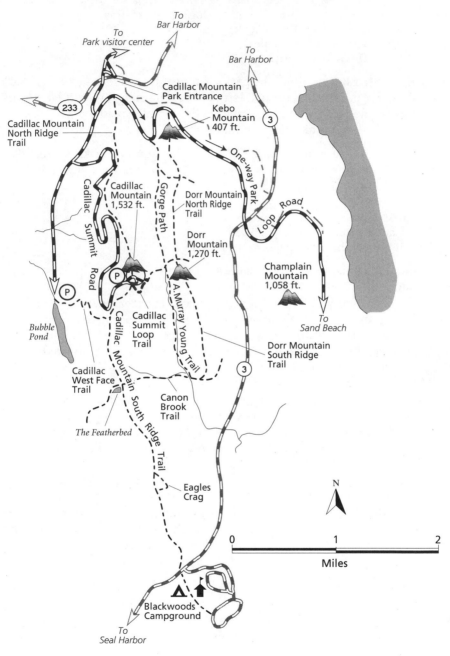

28 Bubbles-Pemetic Trail

Highlights: Log handrails, steps, and ladder; ravine; 360-degree views from atop Pemetic Mountain.
Type of hike: Day hike; out-and-back.
Total distance: 1.2 miles.
Difficulty: Strenuous.

Finding the trailhead: From the park visitor center, head south on the Park Loop Road for 6 miles, past the Cadillac Mountain entrance and the Bubble Pond parking lot. The trailhead is on the left (east) side of the loop road across from the Bubble Rock parking lot.

Parking and trailhead facilities: The Bubble Rock parking lot is on the right (west) side of the Park Loop Road. There are no facilities.

Key points:
- 0.0   Bubbles-Pemetic Trailhead.
- 0.1   Sharp right at the top of large boulders, before a giant cedar grove.
- 0.3   Ravine.
- 0.5   Junction with the Pemetic Northeast Face Trail; bear right (south).
- 0.6   Pemetic Mountain summit.

The hike: Retaining the name Native Americans used to call Mount Desert Island, Pemetic provides a 360-degree panorama from atop its 1,248-foot summit. To the north is Eagle Lake, and to the west, Jordan Pond and Penobscot Mountain. On the south are the Cranberry Isles, and Cadillac Mountain rises to the east.

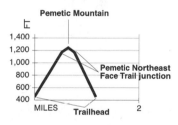

The Bubbles-Pemetic Trail was the last of the routes built up this scenic mountain in the 1920s. The others—Pemetic Mountain Trail, Pemetic Northeast Face Trail, Pemetic Southwest Trail—date from as early as the 1870s.

From the trailhead, cross a log bridge and take a sharp right up a pile of pink granite blocks following the cairns. In late May, blue marsh-violets bloom between the cracks in the pink granite along here, making for a colorful picture show.

At 0.1 mile, watch for another sharp right at the top of large boulders, just before a giant cedar grove. The trail zigzags. Follow the cairns and stone steps. At 0.2 mile, you'll come to a set of logs nailed into a rock face. Use them as handrails to help pull you up the increasingly steep trail.

You'll reach a ravine marked by a cryptic sign at 0.3 mile. One symbol appears to point you to the bottom of the ravine, and another steers you along the ledges overlooking the rocky chasm. We recommend the upland route that avoids the trail through the wet, rocky ravine (and a climb back up on a precariously perched log ladder).

Bubbles-Pemetic Trail

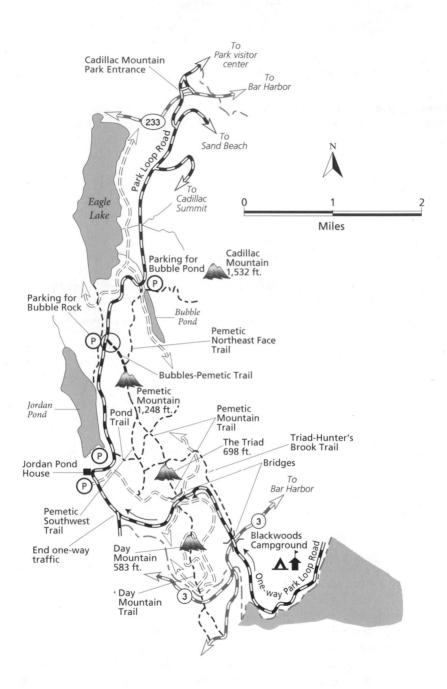

The mountaintop views on Pemetic are dramatic and ever changing.

At the top of the chasm, be sure to take a little spur trail to get a view of Eagle Lake to the north and the Bubbles to the west. Continue climbing along log-and-stone steps. The trail begins to level off; bear left and up at an open rock face. At 0.5 mile, you'll reach a junction with the Pemetic Northeast Face Trail. Bear right (south) and reach the summit at 0.6 mile for spectacular views across Bar Harbor of mountains and ocean. Return the way you came.

29 Pemetic Mountain Trail

Highlights: Less-traveled trail to Triad Summit and up cliffs and ridge to Pemetic's open peak.
Type of hike: Day hike; out-and-back.
Total distance: 3.6 miles.
Difficulty: Moderate to strenuous.

Finding the trailhead: From the Sieur de Monts entrance to the park, head south on the one-way Park Loop Road 8 miles, going under the Maine Highway 3 overpass, to the next overpass, where the Day Mountain carriage road goes over the Park Loop Road. Look for a wooden sign that says "Path to Carriage Road" on the right side just before the carriage road overpass. Take the path up. Pemetic Mountain Trailhead is diagonally left across the carriage road.

Pemetic Mountain Trail

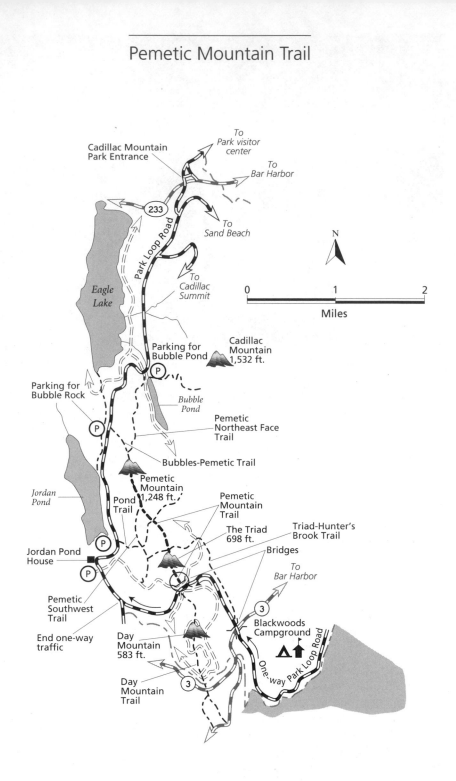

Cadillac Mountain
Park Entrance

To
Park visitor
center

To
Bar Harbor

233

Park Loop Road

To
Sand Beach

N

To
Cadillac
Summit

Eagle
Lake

0   1   2

Miles

Parking for
Bubble Pond

Cadillac
Mountain
1,532 ft.

P

Parking for
Bubble Rock

Bubble
Pond

Pemetic
Northeast Face
Trail

P

Bubbles-Pemetic Trail

Jordan
Pond

Pemetic
Mountain
1,248 ft.

Pond
Trail

Pemetic
Mountain
Trail

The Triad
698 ft.

Triad-Hunter's
Brook Trail

P

Bridges

Jordan Pond
House

P

To
Bar Harbor

3

Pemetic
Southwest
Trail

Blackwoods
Campground

End one-way
traffic

Day
Mountain
583 ft.

One-way Park Loop Road

3

Day
Mountain
Trail

Parking and trailhead facilities: Park on the gravel pullout along the Park Loop Road just before the Day Mountain carriage road overpass.

Key points:
- 0.0   Pemetic Mountain Trailhead.
- 0.3   Triad summit.
- 0.4   Junction with the eastern spur of the Triad-Hunter's Brook Trail coming in on the right; go straight and take the second right.
- 0.9   Junction with the Pond Trail.
- 1.1   Junction with the Pemetic Southwest Trail.
- 1.8   Pemetic Mountain summit.

The hike: Of the four trails up Pemetic, this is the longest, meandering up the Triad with its limited views first, before climbing up steep cliffs and open ridge to the spectacular views atop 1,248-foot Pemetic. It is also one of the harder trails up the peak to get to, making it one of the less-traveled routes.

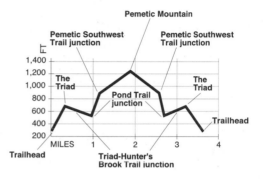

The start of the trail is a bit tricky, with blue blazes and cairns hard to find at first in the woods off the carriage road. A 0.3-mile climb brings you to the 698-foot summit of the Triad, with its limited views south to the Cranberry Isles. A plaque set in a rock just below the summit lists a former name of the path, "The Van Santvoord Trail."

At 0.4 mile, reach a junction with the eastern spur of the Triad-Hunter's Brook Trail coming in on the right. Go straight and take your next right to continue on the Pemetic Mountain Trail (the western spur of the Triad-Hunter's Brook Trail goes left here). Reach a four-way intersection with the Pond Trail at 0.9 mile. Go straight, and soon start the steep climb up the rocky cliffs of Pemetic. Again, the trail is tricky here. Watch for the blue blazes and cairns. There are some spots where the trail does go straight up cliffs and rock faces, hard as that may be to believe at first.

At 1.1 miles, attain the ridge at a junction with the Pemetic Southwest Trail, also known as the Pemetic West Cliff Trail. Continue straight up the open ridge, where you get hints of the panorama to come. Reach the summit with its 360-degree views at 1.8 miles. Eagle Lake is visible to the north, and Jordan Pond and Penobscot Mountain are to the west. South are the Cranberry Isles, and east is Cadillac Mountain. Return the way you came.

Options: You can loop back via the Pemetic Southwest Trail and Triad-Hunter's Brook Trail on the return from the Pemetic summit. On the descent, bear right at the first junction (southwest) onto the Pemetic Southwest Trail. Go straight through the next junction with the Pond Trail, then turn right (southwest) at the following junction with the Triad-Hunter's Brook Trail. Reach a carriage road in another 0.5 mile. Turn left at the carriage road, returning to the Pemetic Mountain Trailhead in another 0.7 mile. The loop is approximately 4.3 miles long.

30 Pemetic Southwest Trail (Pemetic West Cliff Trail)

Highlights:	Little-traveled trail to ridge of Pemetic Mountain from the southwest, providing access to the 1,248-foot summit.
Type of hike:	Day hike; out-and-back.
Total distance:	2.4 miles, plus 0.5 mile to reach trailhead.
Difficulty:	Moderate to strenuous.

Finding the trailhead: From the park visitor center, head south on the Park Loop Road for 7.6 miles, and turn right into the Jordan Pond parking lot (not the Jordan Pond House parking lot). Cross the Park Loop Road and take the Pond Trail 0.5 mile east to a junction with the Pemetic Southwest Trailhead. Turn left.

Parking and trailhead facilities: Park at the Jordan Pond parking lot. The restaurant, gift shop, and restrooms are open seasonally at the nearby Jordan Pond House.

Key points:
0.0 Pemetic Southwest Trailhead, reached after 0.5 mile on the Pond Trail.
0.5 Junction with the Pemetic Mountain Trail.
1.2 Pemetic Mountain summit.

The hike: This little-traveled trail, also known as Pemetic West Cliff Trail, provides an important link from the Jordan Pond area to Pemetic Mountain from the southwest. From the Pond Trail, the Pemetic Southwest Trail heads up the cliffs and rock faces of Pemetic, which can be slippery when wet.

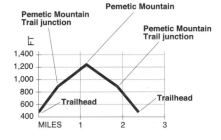

At 0.5 mile, reach a junction with the Pemetic Mountain Trail. Bear left up the ridge, attaining the summit of Pemetic Mountain at 1.2 miles. From the top, you get 360-degree views, with Cadillac to the northeast, Cranberry Isles to the south, Penobscot Mountain and Jordan Pond to the west, and Eagle Lake to the north. Return the way you came.

Options: You can loop back via the Pemetic Mountain Trail, over the 698-foot Triad with its limited views. On the descent from the Pemetic summit, bear left (southeast) at the junction with the Pemetic Mountain Trail rather than the right back onto the Pemetic Southwest Trail. Take the Pemetic Mountain Trail for another 1.1 miles over the Triad and down to a carriage road.

Pemetic Southwest Trail (Pemetic West Cliff Trail)

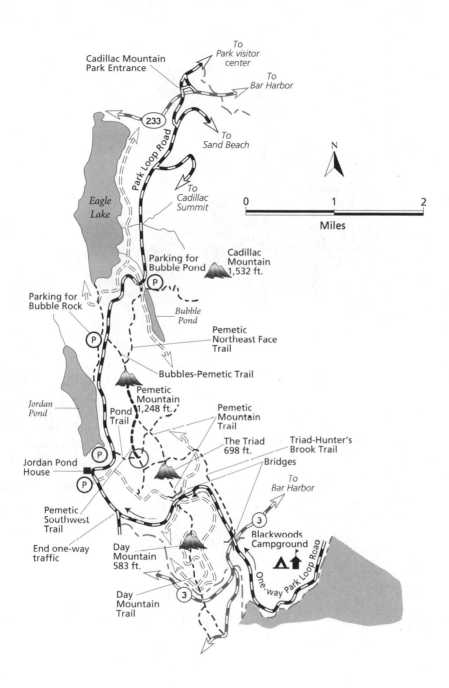

Cadillac Mountain
Park Entrance

To
Park visitor
center

To
Bar Harbor

233

Park Loop Road

To
Sand Beach

To
Cadillac
Summit

N

0   1   2

Miles

Eagle
Lake

Parking for
Bubble Pond

Cadillac
Mountain
1,532 ft.

Parking for
Bubble Rock

Bubble
Pond

Pemetic
Northeast Face
Trail

Bubbles-Pemetic Trail

Pemetic
Mountain
1,248 ft.

Jordan
Pond

Pond
Trail

Pemetic
Mountain
Trail

The Triad
698 ft.

Triad-Hunter's
Brook Trail

Bridges

Jordan Pond
House

To
Bar Harbor

Pemetic
Southwest
Trail

End one-way
traffic

Day
Mountain
583 ft.

3

Blackwoods
Campground

One-way Park Loop Road

Day
Mountain
Trail

3

Lichen on the ridge of Pemetic.

Turn right (west) at the carriage road and follow it for 1.5 miles to the Jordan Pond House. Take a short woods path that leads north from the Jordan Pond House to return to the Jordan Pond parking area. The loop is approximately 5 miles long.

31 Pemetic Northeast Face Trail

Highlights:	Hike up wooded northeast face of Pemetic Mountain to views at the summit.
Type of hike:	Day hike; out-and-back.
Total distance:	2.4 miles.
Difficulty:	Moderate.

Finding the trailhead: From the park visitor center, head south on the Park Loop Road for 5 miles, past the Cadillac Mountain entrance, to the Bubble Pond parking lot (not the Bubble Rock parking lot farther south). Walk toward Bubble Pond and bear right around the pond to the trailhead.

Parking and trailhead facilities: Park at the Bubble Pond parking lot, where there are a chemical toilet and a picnic table.

Key points:

   0.0   Pemetic Northeast Face Trailhead.
   0.1   Cross a carriage road.
   1.1   Junction with the Bubbles-Pemetic Trail.
   1.2   Pemetic Mountain summit.

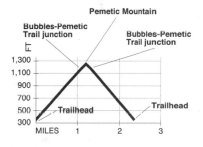

The hike: This is a longer but less steep way up to Pemetic than the nearby Bubbles-Pemetic Trail, and shorter than the Pemetic Mountain Trail along the largely open ridge to the south. Although some maps show this to be the northern spur of the Pemetic Mountain Trail, the trailhead at Bubble Pond calls this the Pemetic Northeast Face Trail.

Head right (southwest) on the trail away from Bubble Pond. At 0.1 mile, cross a carriage road. Watch out for bicyclists and horseback riders on this popular stretch of the carriage road. The trail immediately starts climbing Pemetic's wooded northeast face. Blue blazes, blue diamond-shaped metal markers nailed into trees, and cairns lead the way, but the trail can still be tricky to follow. The path is at times steep, rocky, and filled with roots.

At a particularly confusing spot at 0.6 mile with blowdowns at the base of a rock face, the trail bears left around the rock face. Cadillac Mountain comes into view to the left (east) through the trees. Cadillac is so close here, you can see cars going up the mountain's road.

The trail reaches a rocky, wooded ridge at 0.7 mile and bears right (west) down a rocky knob at 0.9 mile. The next stretch brings you up and down

Pemetic Northeast Face Trail

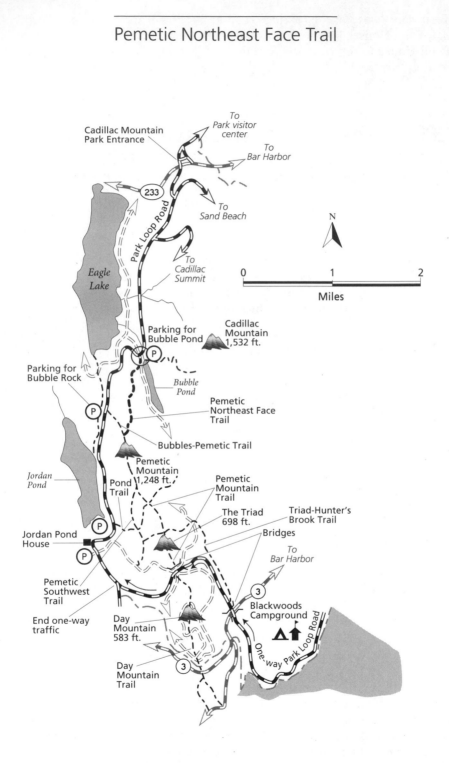

The Pemetic Northeast Face Trail begins to the right, off the shore of Bubble Pond.

knobs and into a bit of woods near the peak. Reach a junction at 1.1 miles with the Bubbles-Pemetic Trail. You get your first view of Penobscot Mountain on the right (west) here. Bear left to continue up the Pemetic Northeast Face Trail on an open ridge, reaching the 1,248-foot summit at 1.2 miles.

Views here include Cadillac Mountain to the northeast; the Triad, Day Mountain, and the Cranberry Isles to the south; Jordan Pond and Penobscot and Sargent mountains to the west; and the Bubbles to the northwest. Return the way you came.

32 Triad-Hunter's Brook Trail

> **Highlights:** Little-traveled woods walk along Hunter's Brook and up to the Triad, a 698-foot mountain with limited views.
> **Type of hike:** Day hike; out-and-back.
> **Total distance:** 4 miles.
> **Difficulty:** Moderate.

Finding the trailhead: From the Sieur de Monts entrance to the park, head south on the one-way Park Loop Road for 7 miles. The trailhead is on the right (east) side of the loop road just past the Maine Highway 3 overpass.

Parking and trailhead facilities: Park at the gravel pullout on the right (east) side of the loop road; there are no facilities.

Key points:
- 0.0   Triad-Hunter's Brook Trailhead.
- 1.4   Cross a carriage road.
- 1.9   Junction with the Pemetic Mountain Trail; turn left to the Triad.
- 2.0   Triad summit.

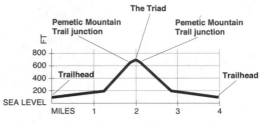

The hike: The reward of this trail is a little mountain called the Triad. Though the views are limited from the 698-foot summit, you can get a glimpse of the Cranberry Isles beyond Day Mountain to the south. From the Park Loop Road, the trail starts out relatively flat, along Hunter's Brook. After a couple of brook crossings—one in particular can be tricky in high water—the trail turns sharply left (east-southeast) just before crossing the carriage road at 1.4 miles.

The trail begins a sometimes steep climb toward the Triad, with sheer rock face and lots of limbs in some areas. Reach a four-way intersection with the Pemetic Mountain Trail at 1.9 miles. Turn left (south) here and reach the Triad summit at 2 miles. The spur to the Triad is technically part of the Pemetic Mountain Trail, whereas the Triad-Hunter's Brook Trail actually goes straight through the four-way intersection to a junction with the Pemetic Southwest Trail, then left (south) to the carriage road. But most hikers prefer to take in the views at the Triad and skip the rest of the Triad-Hunter's Brook Trail. Return the way you came.

Options: You can do a 4.2-mile loop by continuing south down the summit of the Triad. Reach the carriage road in 0.3 mile. Turn left and travel 0.5 mile on the carriage road, back to where the Triad-Hunter's Brook Trail first crossed the road. Turn right on the trail to head 1.4 miles back to the parking area on the loop road.

Triad-Hunter's Brook Trail

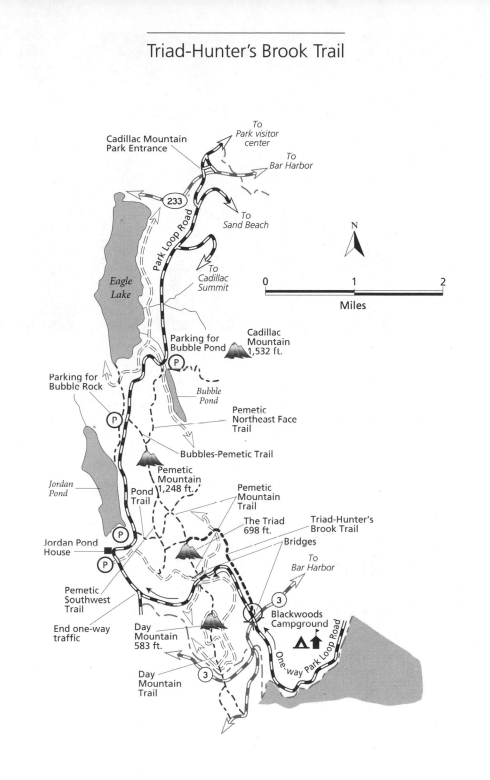

The skies in Acadia can be as dramatic as the mountains and sea, as this view from near the Triad summit shows.

It's also possible to add on Day Mountain by continuing south down the Triad to the carriage road, crossing the bridge there, and going up a trail on the other side. Day Mountain is reached in 0.8 mile from the Triad. Return the way you came, crossing over the carriage road bridge. But rather than going back up the trail to the Triad, turn right on the carriage road and travel 0.5 mile, back to where the Triad-Hunter's Brook Trail first crossed the road. Turn right on the trail to return the 1.4 miles back to the parking area. The loop is approximately 5.2 miles.

33 Day Mountain Trail

Highlights: Closest mountain views of the Cranberry Isles; hidden Champlain Monument.
Type of hike: Day hike; out-and-back.
Total distance: 2.6 miles.
Difficulty: Moderate.

Finding the trailhead: From the Sieur de Monts entrance to the park, head south on the one-way Park Loop Road for 8 miles, going under the Maine Highway 3 overpass to the next overpass, where the Day Mountain carriage road goes over the Park Loop Road on a stone bridge. Look for a wooden

Day Mountain Trail

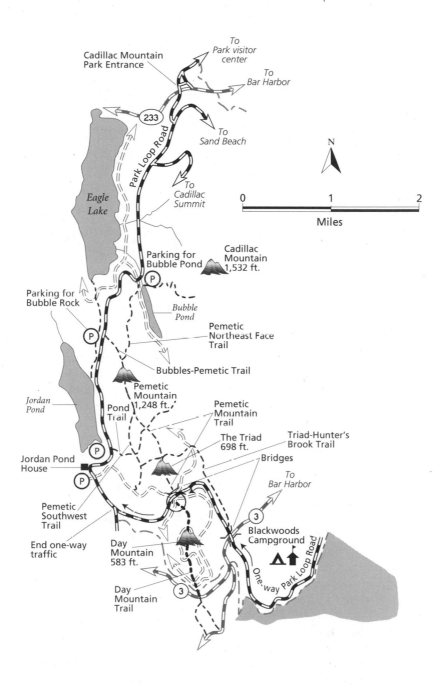

To
Park visitor
center

To
Bar Harbor

Cadillac Mountain
Park Entrance

233

Park Loop Road

To
Sand Beach

N

Eagle
Lake

To
Cadillac
Summit

0   1   2

Miles

Parking for
Bubble Pond

Cadillac
Mountain
1,532 ft.

Parking for
Bubble Rock

P

Bubble
Pond

Pemetic
Northeast Face
Trail

P

Bubbles-Pemetic Trail

Jordan
Pond

Pemetic
Mountain
1,248 ft.

Pond
Trail

Pemetic
Mountain
Trail

The Triad
698 ft.

Triad-Hunter's
Brook Trail

P

Bridges

To
Bar Harbor

Jordan Pond
House

P

3

Pemetic
Southwest
Trail

Blackwoods
Campground

End one-way
traffic

Day
Mountain
583 ft.

One-way Park Loop Road

Day
Mountain
Trail

3

sign that says "Path to Carriage Road," on the right side just before the carriage road overpass. Take the path up, turn left, and cross the Day Mountain carriage road bridge to the trailhead.

Parking and trailhead facilities: Park on a gravel pullout along Park Loop Road just before the Day Mountain carriage road overpass.

Key points:
- 0.0   Day Mountain Trailhead.
- 0.4   Cross a carriage road.
- 0.5   Day Mountain summit.
- 0.6   Cross a carriage road.
- 0.7   Bear left just before a carriage road, then cross over at a cairn.
- 1.0   Cross a carriage road.
- 1.1   Bear right on a carriage road to intersection No. 36 before crossing over.
- 1.3   ME 3; turn left to Champlain Monument.

The hike: Good things come in small packages, as this little hike proves. Day Mountain is only 583 feet and a mere half mile from the trailhead, but it provides close-up views of the Cranberry Isles to the south, and you can see spectacular sunsets to the west. The hike provides another lit-

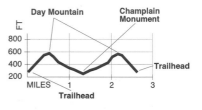

tle gem at trail's end—a hidden monument to the French explorer Samuel Champlain, who gave Mount Desert Island its name.

Heading south from the trailhead, the Day Mountain Trail rises swiftly through the woods, crosses a carriage road at 0.4 mile, and attains the summit with its views of the Cranberry Isles to the south and Gorham Mountain to the northeast at 0.5 mile. You can turn around here if you just came for the sunset, or you can continue south toward ME 3 and the Champlain Monument.

To continue, at 0.6 mile, cross a carriage road, the first of four road crossings you'll make on the way down, over the only carriage road that gradually winds up Day Mountain. You may see horse-drawn carriages from the nearby Wildwood Stables and bicyclists along this popular carriage road, so look both ways before crossing. At 0.7 mile, bear left and follow the cairns just before you come upon the carriage road again, and cross over at the final cairn. Some of the best views on the trail are visible along this part of the carriage road toward Otter Point to the east, the Cranberry Isles to the south, and Somes Sound to the west. The trail descends steeply at times.

At 1 mile, cross the carriage road again. Then at 1.1 miles, bear right on the carriage road to intersection No. 36 before crossing to the other side of the road for the fourth and final time. At 1.3 miles, bear left at the sign pointing to Champlain Monument, just before ME 3. The granite monument, hidden in the woods, says "In honor of Samuel de Champlain. Born in France 1567. Died at Quebec 1635. A soldier, sailor, explorer and administrator who gave this island its name." Return the way you came.

102

Options: To loop back on the carriage road rather than going back up Day Mountain again, turn right on the return from the Champlain Monument, at the first junction with the carriage road. Take the road 1.5 miles back to the stone carriage road bridge by the Day Mountain Trailhead and return to the parking area along Park Loop Road.

34 Pond Trail

Highlights:	Little-traveled trail from Jordan Pond to ridges of Pemetic and Cadillac mountains and a restful spot called the Featherbed.
Type of hike:	Day hike; out-and-back.
Total distance:	3.8 miles.
Difficulty:	Moderate to strenuous.

Finding the trailhead: From the park visitor center, head south on the Park Loop Road for 7.3 miles to a small pullout parking area on the right (west) side of the loop road, just before the Jordan Pond and Jordan Pond House parking lots. The trailhead is across the Park Loop Road from the small parking area.

Parking and trailhead facilities: Park at a small pullout parking area on the loop road just north of the Jordan Pond and Jordan Pond House parking lots. The restaurant, gift shop, and restrooms are open seasonally at the nearby Jordan Pond House.

Key points:
- 0.0   Pond Trailhead.
- 0.5   Junction with the Pemetic Southwest Trail.
- 0.8   Junction with the Pemetic Mountain Trail.
- 1.1   Cross a carriage road.
- 1.9   Featherbed and junction with the Cadillac Mountain South Ridge and Canon Brook trails.

The hike: Heading from the Jordan Pond area toward the ridges of Pemetic and Cadillac mountains, this trail provides important access to the peaks from the southwest. Along the way it passes near a low mountain called the Triad, up a steep stretch with iron rungs and

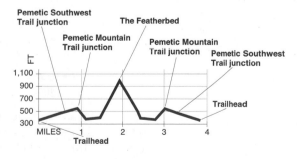

handrails for assistance, and ends at a surprising little pond on the Cadillac ridge, called the Featherbed.

Pond Trail

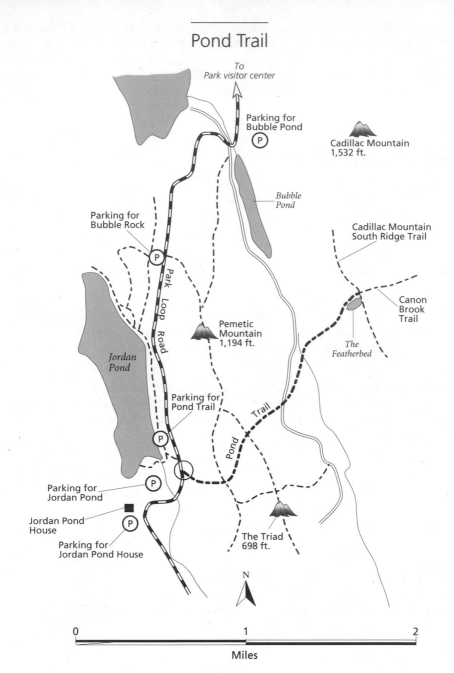

To
Park visitor center

Parking for
Bubble Pond

Cadillac Mountain
1,532 ft.

Bubble
Pond

Parking for
Bubble Rock

Cadillac Mountain
South Ridge Trail

Park Loop Road

Canon
Brook
Trail

Pemetic
Mountain
1,194 ft.

The
Featherbed

Jordan
Pond

Parking for
Pond Trail

Pond Trail

Parking for
Jordan Pond

Parking for
Jordan Pond

Jordan Pond
House

Parking for
Jordan Pond House

The Triad
698 ft.

N

| 0 | 1 | 2 |
Miles

Head east-southeast from the trailhead along a relatively flat section of
woods, then begin a moderate climb. At 0.5 mile, you'll come to an intersection with Pemetic Southwest Trail, which leads left to Pemetic Mountain.
A little farther up the Pond Trail, a spur leads right 0.6 mile to the Triad. At
0.8 mile, reach an intersection with the Pemetic Mountain Trail. To the left,
the Pemetic Mountain Trail leads to the Pemetic summit; to the right, it leads

to the Triad. The Pond Trail descends moderately off of the Pemetic ridge to a carriage road at 1.1 miles. Cross the road, bearing diagonally left. The trail parallels the carriage road north-northeast for a stretch, and then crosses a boggy area on log bridges as it cuts right to start the steep ascent up the Cadillac ridge.

Stone steps and iron rungs and handrails help you up rock faces and other tough terrain for part of the last half mile of the trail. When you first attain the ridge, you'll be rewarded with a view of pink granite cliffs. Then a short level stretch brings you to trail's end at 1.9 miles, at the Featherbed, a restful mountain pond with benches to sit on. Return the way you came.

Options: From trail's end, you can tag on 1.2 miles one way to ascend Cadillac via the Cadillac Mountain South Ridge Trail. Turn left at the four-way intersection at the Featherbed, heading north to Cadillac. Just before the summit road, bear right (northeast) to follow the trail as it parallels the road to the summit. Return the way you came.

For an approximately 4-mile loop up Pemetic, take the Pond Trail to either the Pemetic Southwest Trail at 0.5 mile, or the Pemetic Mountain Trail at 0.8 mile. Turn left (north) on either trail toward the summit. From the summit, continue heading north, descending to a junction with the Bubbles-Pemetic and Pemetic Northeast Face trails. Bear left (northwest) down the Bubbles-Pemetic Trail to the Bubble Rock parking area. Follow a path west from the parking area toward Bubble Rock, but turn left at the first intersection, to head south on the Jordan Pond Carry Trail toward the pond. At the shores of the pond, bear left (south) on the Jordan Pond Shore Trail, to the Jordan Pond parking lot. From the lot, head out to the Park Loop Road and turn left (north) back to the pullout parking area across from the Pond Trailhead.

35 Jordan Pond Nature Trail

Highlights: Self-guided nature trail through woods and along Jordan Pond.
Type of hike: Day hike; loop.
Total distance: 0.5 mile.
Difficulty: Easy.

Finding the trailhead: From the park visitor center, head south on the Park Loop Road for 7.6 miles and turn right into the Jordan Pond parking lot (not the Jordan Pond House parking lot). Park at the parking lot on the right. The trailhead is at the far end of the lot, at the top of a boat ramp road and on the right.

Parking and trailhead facilities: Park at the Jordan Pond parking lot; the only facility is a chemical toilet. The restaurant, gift shop, and restrooms are open seasonally at the nearby Jordan Pond House.

Jordan Pond Nature Trail

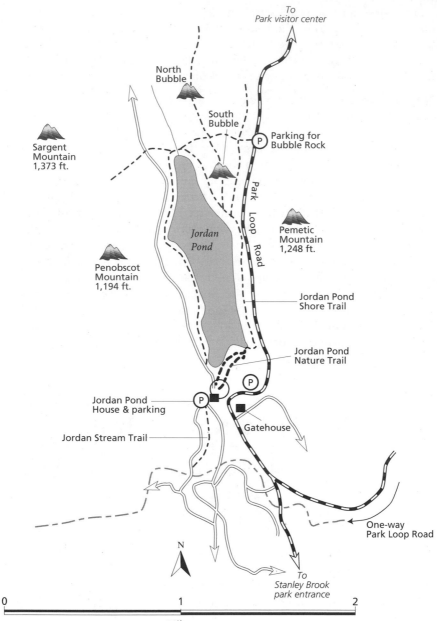

To
Park visitor center

North
Bubble

South
Bubble

Sargent
Mountain
1,373 ft.

Parking for
Bubble Rock

Park Loop Road

Jordan
Pond

Pemetic
Mountain
1,248 ft.

Penobscot
Mountain
1,194 ft.

Jordan Pond
Shore Trail

Jordan Pond
Nature Trail

Jordan Pond
House & parking

Gatehouse

Jordan Stream Trail

One-way
Park Loop Road

N

To
Stanley Brook
park entrance

0   1   2

Miles

Key points:

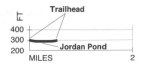

0.0   Jordan Pond Nature Trailhead.
0.2   Bear left (northwest) after trail post No. 3, at the shore of Jordan Pond and the junction with the Jordan Pond Shore Trail.
0.3   Cross the foot of a boat ramp after trail post No. 7.
0.4   Bear left twice, at the fork after post No. 8, and after post No. 9.
0.5   Jordan Pond Nature Trailhead.

The hike: A lot is packed into this short self-guided trail including panoramic views of Jordan Pond and the distinctive Bubbles on the far shore as well as lessons in history and nature. Be prepared for the trail to be crowded during the height of the season because it is so accessible. A descriptive brochure is available for purchase for 50 cents, or you can borrow one from the box provided and return it at trail's end.

The trail begins in the woods, heading right (northeast) at the top of the boat ramp road. The first two numbered trail posts take you through deep forests of balsam fir and red spruce, then under broad-leafed American beeches and towering northern white cedars.

At post No. 3, a short spur along a stone walk on the right leads you to the edge of a wetland. The main trail then brings you to the shores of Jordan Pond and a junction with the Jordan Pond Shore Trail. At post No. 5, you get a grand view of the distinctive twin mountains known as the Bubbles on the far shore. And at post No. 6, you get a lesson in the geology and history of Acadia, with the brochure describing the distinctive granite here and the dramatic scenery that has attracted artists since the 1840s. Cross

Jordan Pond with the Bubbles in the distance.

the foot of the boat ramp after post No. 7. At post No. 8, a plaque describes the power of glaciers in shaping Acadia. Then bear left at a fork back into the woods, to post No. 9. Here, the brochure describes how the Jordan Pond House tradition of afternoon tea and popovers came into being around 1900. Bear left at post No. 9 to circle back to the parking lot.

Options: If the walk has gotten you hungry for some of Jordan Pond House's famous popovers, bear right at post No. 9 for a short stroll to the restaurant.

36 Jordan Pond Shore Trail

Highlights:	Chance to glimpse a colorful merganser duck; expansive views of Jordan Pond, the Bubbles, and Jordan Cliffs.
Type of hike:	Day hike; loop.
Total distance:	3.3 miles.
Difficulty:	Easy to moderate.

Finding the trailhead: From the park visitor center, head south on the Park Loop Road for 7.6 miles and turn right into the Jordan Pond parking lot (not the Jordan Pond House parking lot). Park at the parking lot on the right. Follow the boat ramp road to the shore of the pond. The trailhead is on the right (east).

Parking and trailhead facilities: Park at the Jordan Pond parking lot. The restaurant, gift shop, and restrooms are open seasonally at the nearby Jordan Pond House.

Key points:

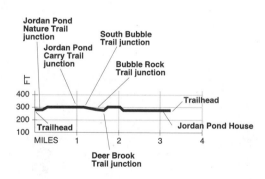

- 0.0   Jordan Pond Shore Trailhead.
- 0.1   Junction with the Jordan Pond Nature Trail.
- 1.0   Junction with the Jordan Pond Carry Trail.
- 1.1   Junction with the South Bubble Trail.
- 1.5   Junction with the Bubble Rock Trail.
- 1.6   Junction with the Deer Brook Trail.
- 3.2   Jordan Pond House.
- 3.3   Jordan Pond Shore Trailhead.

The hike: A vigorous walk around Jordan Pond, capped by afternoon tea and popovers on the lawn of the Jordan Pond House—one of those special Acadia experiences. The trail starts from the boat ramp at the Jordan Pond parking lot and immediately offers a spectacular view of the distinctive

Jordan Pond Shore Trail

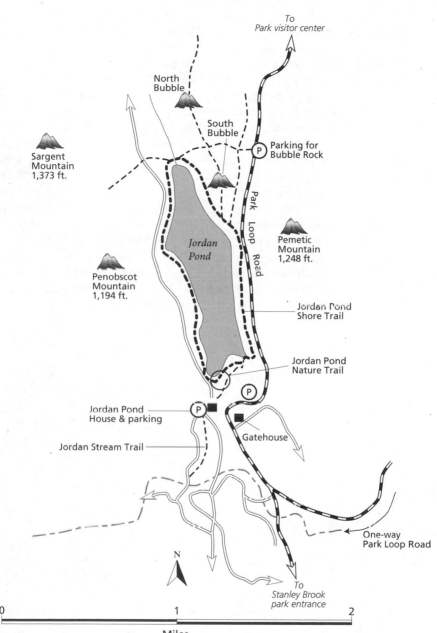

To
Park visitor center

North
Bubble

South
Bubble

Parking for
Bubble Rock

Sargent
Mountain
1,373 ft.

Jordan
Pond

Pemetic
Mountain
1,248 ft.

Penobscot
Mountain
1,194 ft.

Jordan Pond
Shore Trail

Jordan Pond
Nature Trail

Jordan Pond
House & parking

Jordan Stream Trail

Gatehouse

N

One-way
Park Loop Road

To
Stanley Brook
park entrance

Park Loop Road

0   1   2

Miles

rounded mountains known as the Bubbles, across the pond. Bear right (east), circling the pond counterclockwise.

The first half of the trail is along the easy eastern shore, but be prepared for the western shore's jagged rocks and exposed roots. Wear proper footwear. At 0.1 mile, you'll reach the first of several trails that diverge from Jordan Pond. Always bear left, paralleling the shore at each of the junctions. Soon, the trail rounds the bend and heads north. You'll soon see Jordan Cliffs to the west, across the pond.

There are plenty of boulders here along the shore to sit on and admire the crystal clear waters and the tremendous views. Jordan Pond serves as a public water supply, so no swimming is allowed. After passing over a series of wooden bridges, you'll soon come up under the towering pinkish granite of South Bubble. At a small coarse-sand beach, a log bench allows you to take in the long view back south across the pond, to the Jordan Pond House.

Cross another wooden bridge and at 1 mile, the Jordan Pond Carry Trail, which leads 1 mile to Eagle Lake, veers to the right. At 1.1 miles, the South Bubble Trail goes up 0.4 mile to the summit and the precariously perched Bubble Rock. The trail now gets more difficult, ascending a bit above the shoreline and crossing a boulder-strewn section. Birches and cedars dominate the woods here. At 1.5 miles, pass the junction with the Bubble Rock Trail, which heads up the gap between the North Bubble and South Bubble. Look back toward South Bubble, and you'll get a good view of Bubble Rock. You're now at the northernmost end of the pond and can get good views of the Jordan Pond House to the south and the Bubbles to the east.

A classic Acadia view from the Jordan Pond House.

Cross a series of intricate wooden bridges—one has an archway in the middle. At 1.6 miles, pass the junction with the Deer Brook Trail, which leads up toward Jordan Cliffs. Now begins the trail's traverse of the rough western shore of the pond, with its rocks, roots, and ups and downs. After a bit of hide-and-seek with the shore and a long stretch of rock hopping, you'll reach a series of wooden bridges and a long boardwalk that cross over creeks and fragile marshland. In addition to the dramatic views of the Bubbles here from the western shore, you may also catch a glimpse of a blue jay or a common merganser. It's hard to miss a merganser, especially the female with her distinctive rusty colored, crested head, and orange bill.

At 3.2 miles, pass near the Jordan Pond House, where you can stop for afternoon tea and popovers on the expansive lawn, with a grand view of the Bubbles as backdrop. At 3.3 miles, the trail ends back at the Jordan Pond parking lot.

Options: Walk just the easier eastern shore to the junction at 1 mile with the Jordan Pond Carry Trail. Return the way you came for a 2-mile hike. Or add on the short but steep trip up the South Bubble Trail, tagging on an extra 0.8 mile to the summit and back.

You can also loop around Jordan Pond yet skip the rocky western shore, by taking the Deer Brook Trail up to the carriage road. Turn left on the carriage road and walk 1.5 miles to the Jordan Pond House. From the Jordan Pond House, follow a woods path back to the Jordan Pond parking lot.

37 Jordan Stream Trail

Highlights:	Woods walk along stream; Cobblestone Bridge.
Type of hike:	Day hike; out-and-back or loop back on carriage road.
Total distance:	0.5 mile one way.
Difficulty:	Easy to moderate.

Finding the trailhead: From the park visitor center, head south on the Park Loop Road for 7.7 miles to the Jordan Pond House. Walk behind and to the left of the Jordan Pond House and follow a path marked "To Asticou, Jordan Cliff and Penobscot Mountain Trails" down to a carriage road. The trailhead is across the carriage road on the left.

Parking and trailhead facilities: Park at the Jordan Pond House or nearby Jordan Pond nature trail parking lot. The restaurant, gift shop, and restrooms are open seasonally.

Key points:
0.0 Jordan Stream Trailhead.
0.2 Junction with a carriage road; cross a wooden bridge to the trail on the other side.
0.5 Cobblestone Bridge.

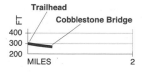

Jordan Stream Trail

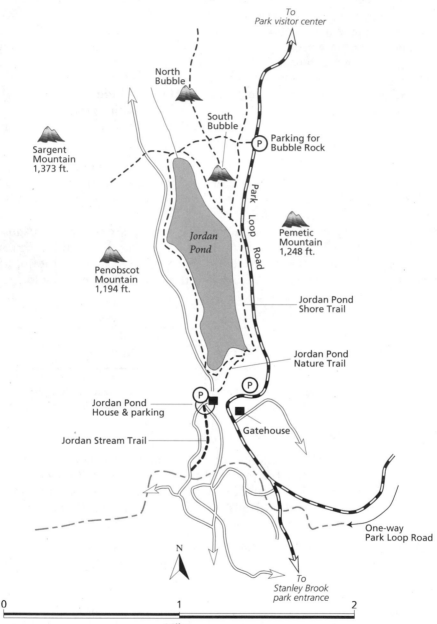

To
Park visitor center

North
Bubble

South
Bubble

Sargent
Mountain
1,373 ft.

Parking for
Bubble Rock

Jordan
Pond

Pemetic
Mountain
1,248 ft.

Penobscot
Mountain
1,194 ft.

Park Loop Road

Jordan Pond
Shore Trail

Jordan Pond
Nature Trail

Jordan Pond
House & parking

Jordan Stream Trail

Gatehouse

One-way
Park Loop Road

N

To
Stanley Brook
park entrance

0   1   2

Miles

The hike: Even in its short distance, the Jordan Stream Trail provides hikers with a historical flavor. About 100 years ago, the trail was laid out by the Seal Harbor Village Improvement Association as a scenic connector between the village and Jordan Pond. In the 1700s and earlier, it may have been part of a Native American canoe carry trail connecting Jordan Pond to the ocean. And it takes today's park visitors by some of the carriage roads and stone bridges built in the early 1900s by industrialist and Mount Desert Island summer resident John D. Rockefeller Jr.

From the Jordan Stream Trailhead at the carriage road behind Jordan Pond House, follow the narrow path through the woods, paralleling the stream as it tumbles south toward the ocean. Part of the trail features neatly laid stepping stones, making it seem like a garden path at times. At 0.2 mile, when you reach a junction with a carriage road, bear right (west) across an elegant, curved wooden bridge. Pick up the trail at the end of the bridge, heading left (south) down the other side of the stream. The trail descends and gets rougher here, with wet roots and rocks making the trail potentially slippery. A series of wooden footbridges take you across stream tributaries. Above you on your left you'll soon see an amazing stone wall made up of perfectly fitted granite blocks, bordering a carriage road.

At 0.5 mile, the trail brings you to the base of the Cobblestone Bridge, built in 1917. The park boundary ends here, although the trail continues toward Seal Harbor. You can return the way you came, or loop back on the

Cobblestone Bridge is among the elegant spans of hand-hewn granite bankrolled by Mount Desert Island summer resident John D. Rockefeller Jr. in the early 1900s.

carriage roads. To loop back, cross the stream on a wooden footbridge and climb the stone steps up to the Cobblestone Bridge and carriage road. You'll be at carriage road intersection No. 24. Take the road on the extreme left back toward Jordan Pond. Then at intersection No. 23, follow the road to the left back to the Jordan Pond House to complete the loop. Each carriage road intersection is well marked with carved wooden signs and rustic arrows.

38 Bubble Rock Trail

Highlights: 360-degree views from South Bubble; view of Bubble Rock.
Type of hike: Day hike; out-and-back.
Total distance: 1 mile.
Difficulty: Moderate.

Finding the trailhead: From the park visitor center, drive south on the Park Loop Road for 6 miles, past the Cadillac Mountain entrance and the Bubble Pond parking lot to the Bubble Rock parking lot. The trailhead leads from the Bubble Rock parking lot.

Parking and trailhead facilities: The Bubble Rock parking lot is on the right (west) side of the Park Loop Road; there are no facilities.

Key points:
- 0.0 Bubble Rock Trailhead.
- 0.1 Junction with the Jordan Pond Carry Trail.
- 0.3 Junction with the South Bubble and North Bubble trails; turn left (south).
- 0.5 South Bubble summit and Bubble Rock.

The hike: Going up the gap between South Bubble and North Bubble, this trail provides the shortest route up either of the distinctive rounded mountains overlooking Jordan Pond. It also takes you to Bubble Rock, precariously perched high above the Park Loop Road on the summit of South Bubble.

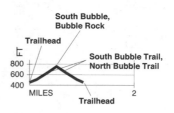

Heading west from the Bubble Rock parking lot, the trail crosses the Jordan Pond Carry Trail at 0.1 mile. Then at 0.3 mile, at the junction with the South Bubble and North Bubble Trails, turn left (south) to the South Bubble. Attain the 768-foot summit at 0.5 mile. A sign points to Bubble Rock nearby. Return the way you came.

Options: You can add on the North Bubble for another 0.8 mile round trip. On the way down from South Bubble, instead of turning right (east) through the gap to head back to the parking area, go straight, reaching the North Bubble in another 0.4 mile. Return the way you came.

Bubble Rock Trail

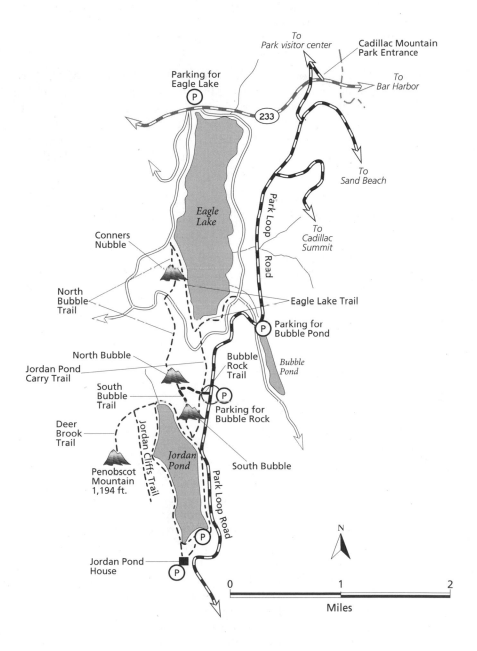

To
Park visitor center

Cadillac Mountain
Park Entrance

To
Bar Harbor

Parking for
Eagle Lake

233

To
Sand Beach

Eagle
Lake

Park Loop Road

To
Cadillac
Summit

Conners
Nubble

North
Bubble
Trail

Eagle Lake Trail

Parking for
Bubble Pond

Bubble
Pond

North Bubble

Bubble
Rock
Trail

Jordan Pond
Carry Trail

South
Bubble
Trail

Parking for
Bubble Rock

Deer
Brook
Trail

Jordan Cliffs Trail

Jordan
Pond

South Bubble

Penobscot
Mountain
1,194 ft.

Park Loop Road

Jordan Pond
House

N

0   1   2
Miles

39 South Bubble Trail

Highlights:	Climb to open summit of South Bubble; close-up view of Bubble Rock.
Type of hike:	Day hike; loop.
Total distance:	1.5 miles, including 0.6 mile to reach trailhead.
Difficulty:	Moderate to strenuous.

Finding the trailhead: From the park visitor center, drive south on the Park Loop Road for 6 miles, past the Cadillac Mountain entrance and the Bubble Pond parking lot, to the Bubble Rock parking lot. From the Bubble Rock parking lot, head straight on the Bubble Rock Trail to the first junction in 0.1 mile, then turn left on the Jordan Pond Carry Trail for 0.4 mile. Turn right on the Jordan Pond Shore Trail, and after 0.1 mile, South Bubble Trailhead is on the right.

Parking and trailhead facilities: The Bubble Rock parking lot is on the right (west) side of the Park Loop Road; there are no facilities.

Key points:
- 0.0   Bubble Rock parking lot.
- 0.6   South Bubble Trailhead, reached via the Bubble Rock Trail, Jordan Pond Carry Trail, and Jordan Pond Shore Trail.
- 1.0   South Bubble summit and Bubble Rock.
- 1.2   Junction with the Bubble Rock Trail and the North Bubble Trail; turn right (east).
- 1.4   Junction with Jordan Pond Carry Trail; go straight.
- 1.5   Bubble Rock parking lot.

The hike: Rising steeply from the shore of Jordan Pond, this trail takes you up the 768-foot South Bubble, providing a fresh perspective on one of the twin mountains that dominate the view in this part of Acadia. The trail also gives you a close-up view of another feature of the park—Bubble Rock, also known as Balanced Rock, precariously perched high above the Park Loop Road.

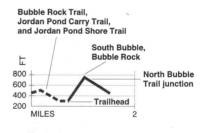

From the South Bubble Trailhead at 0.6 mile in from the Bubble Rock parking lot, the trail climbs steeply up from the pond along a rocky wash. Watch carefully for blue blazes. You soon confront the blocky face of South Bubble and must turn right, where you'll find a natural sitting spot to take in the gorgeous view of Jordan Pond to the south. In a couple of precarious spots, you need to hoist yourself through a narrow crevice or up a cliff face. At 1 mile, reach the summit of the South Bubble, where there are views all around. There's a big sign pointing to Bubble Rock near the peak. Be careful not to get too close to the edge. Descend along the blue-blazed trail, and reach the junction with the Bubble Rock Trail and North Bubble Trail at 1.2

South Bubble Trail

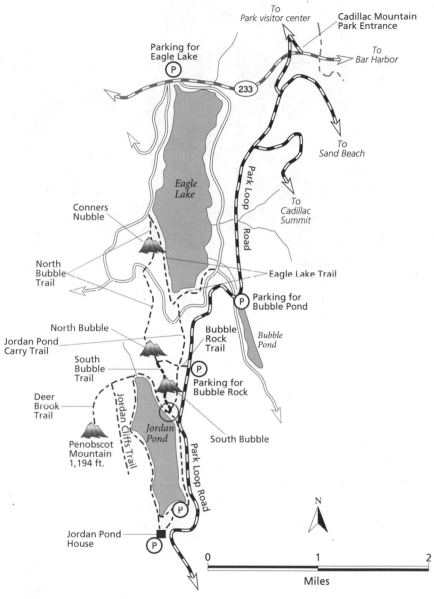

Bubble Rock sits precariously on the ridge.

miles. Turn right (east). Cross the Jordan Pond Carry Trail at 1.4 miles, and return to the Bubble Rock parking lot at 1.5 miles.

Options: To add another 0.8 mile round trip to the summit of the North Bubble, at the junction with the Bubble Rock Trail and North Bubble Trail, continue straight rather than turning right to the parking area. Reach the North Bubble summit in another 0.4 mile. Return to the junction and turn left (east) back to the Bubble Rock parking area.

40 North Bubble Trail

Highlights:	Open summits of North Bubble and Conners Nubble; views of Jordan Pond and Eagle Lake.
Type of hike:	Day hike; out-and-back.
Total distance:	3.4 miles, plus 0.2 mile to reach trailhead.
Difficulty:	Moderate.

Finding the trailhead: From the park visitor center, drive south on the Park Loop Road for 6 miles, past the Cadillac Mountain entrance and the Bubble Pond parking lot, to the Bubble Rock parking lot. Follow the Bubble Rock Trail west for 0.2 mile to the gap between the North Bubble and South Bubble. The North Bubble Trailhead is on the right, or north.

North Bubble Trail

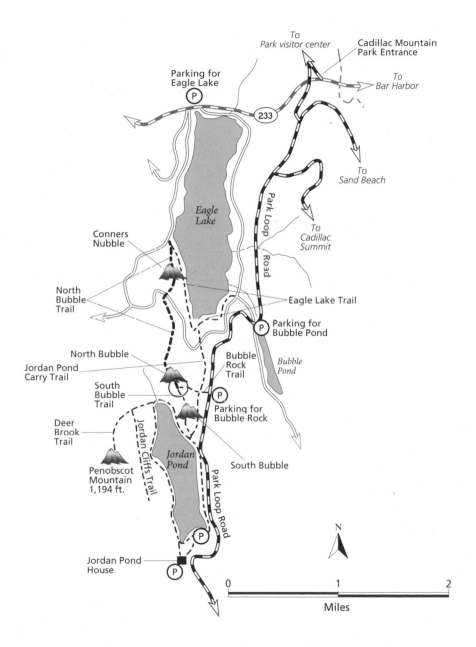

To
Park visitor center

Cadillac Mountain
Park Entrance

To
Bar Harbor

Parking for
Eagle Lake

P

233

To
Sand Beach

Eagle
Lake

To
Cadillac
Summit

Conners
Nubble

North
Bubble
Trail

Eagle Lake Trail

Parking for
Bubble Pond

P

Bubble
Pond

North Bubble

Jordan Pond
Carry Trail

Bubble
Rock
Trail

South
Bubble
Trail

P

Parking for
Bubble Rock

Deer
Brook
Trail

South Bubble

Penobscot
Mountain
1,194 ft.

Jordan Cliffs Trail

Jordan
Pond

Park Loop Road

P

Jordan Pond
House

P

N

0   1   2

Miles

Parking and trailhead facilities: The Bubble Rock parking lot is on the right (west) side of the Park Loop Road. There are no facilities.

Key points:
0.0   North Bubble Trailhead, reached after 0.2 mile on the Bubble Rock Trail.
0.3   North Bubble summit.
1.1   Cross a carriage road.
1.3   Conners Nubble summit.
1.7   Junction with the Eagle Lake Trail.
3.4   Return the same way you came.

The hike: This trail takes you over the higher of the two distinctive little mountains known as the Bubbles and a less traveled peak called Conners Nubble, providing views of Jordan Pond and Eagle Lake along the way. While both the North Bubble and South Bubble are easy to access

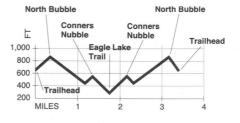

from the Bubble Rock parking area, more people head to the South Bubble for the chance to see the precariously perched Bubble Rock up close. That leaves the North Bubble Trail relatively less traveled, especially the most northerly stretches. The trail heads north from the Bubble Rock Trail and immediately takes you up pink granite steps tucked into an otherwise impassable sheer rock face. At 0.3 mile, after another ascent up pink granite steps, reach the summit of North Bubble, elevation 872 feet. Here you can see the lower South Bubble and Jordan Pond to the south. Most people turn around after getting the views from North Bubble. But if you want to climb the less-visited open summit of Conners Nubble, continue north along the trail, descending North Bubble into a blueberry-bush-filled sag. You'll soon get views of Conners Nubble, Eagle Lake, and Frenchman Bay. You can't miss the nubble, with its distinctive beehivelike appearance.

You'll also have views of Cadillac Mountain to the right, or northeast. Start descending from the ridge through a birch forest, and cross a carriage road at 1.1 miles. Then start ascending Conners Nubble via a switchback up a rocky ledge and a short clamber up a small cliff. Reach the nubble, elevation 588 feet, at 1.3 miles. From the open summit you can see north and northeast to Frenchman Bay and Porcupine Islands, east to Eagle Lake and Cadillac Mountain, west to Sargent and Penobscot Mountains, and south and southeast to the Bubbles and Pemetic Mountain. It's quite a spectacular 360-degree view. You can stop here or continue north, descending to the official trail's end at a junction with the Eagle Lake Trail, at 1.7 miles. Return the way you came.

Options: To do an approximately 3.5-mile loop, turn right on the Eagle Lake Trail and travel 1.1 miles to the Jordan Pond Carry Trail. Take a right on the carry trail and travel another 0.6 mile. At the intersection with the Bubble Rock Trail, turn left and return to the Bubble Rock parking lot in another 0.1 mile.

The views from the South Bubble include the faraway Cranberry Isles.

41 Eagle Lake Trail

Highlights: Hike along second largest lake in Acadia, providing access to little-traveled Conners Nubble, a low mountain north of the Bubbles.

Type of hike: Day hike; out-and-back.

Total distance: 3.6 miles, plus 0.2 mile to reach trailhead.

Difficulty: Easy to moderate.

Finding the trailhead: From the park visitor center, head south on the Park Loop Road for 5 miles, past the Cadillac Mountain entrance, to the Bubble Pond parking lot (not the Bubble Rock parking lot farther south). Cross to the other side of the Park Loop Road and walk on a carriage road for 0.2 mile, to carriage road intersection No. 7. Bear left. Eagle Lake Trailhead is on the right, along the southeast shore of Eagle Lake.

Parking and trailhead facilities: Park at the Bubble Pond parking lot where there are a chemical toilet and a picnic table.

Key points:
- 0.0 Eagle Lake Trailhead, reached after 0.2 mile on a carriage road.
- 0.6 Junction with the Jordan Pond Carry Trail.
- 1.7 Junction with the North Bubble Trail, with a 0.4-mile spur to Conners Nubble.
- 1.8 Carriage road.
- 3.6 Return the same way you came.

Eagle Lake Trail

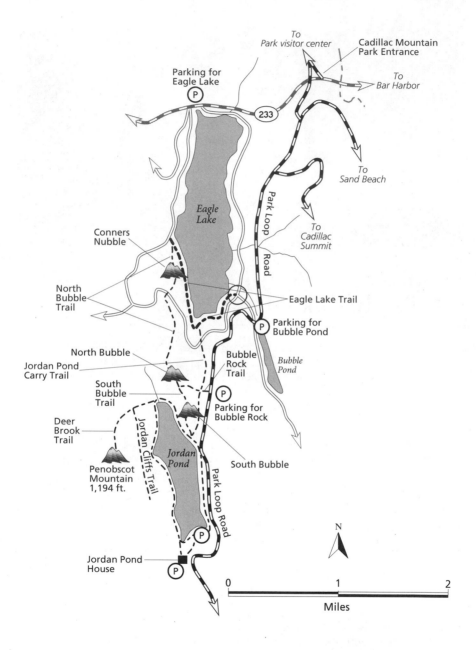

To
Park visitor center

Cadillac Mountain
Park Entrance

To
Bar Harbor

Parking for
Eagle Lake

233

To
Sand Beach

Eagle
Lake

Park Loop Road

To
Cadillac
Summit

Conners
Nubble

North
Bubble
Trail

Eagle Lake Trail

Parking for
Bubble Pond

North Bubble

Bubble
Rock
Trail

Bubble
Pond

Jordan Pond
Carry Trail

South
Bubble
Trail

Parking for
Bubble Rock

Deer
Brook
Trail

Jordan Cliffs Trail

Jordan
Pond

South Bubble

Penobscot
Mountain
1,194 ft.

Park Loop Road

N

Jordan Pond
House

0   1   2

Miles

The hike: Like other lake and pond hikes in Acadia, the Eagle Lake Trail can be walked just for its water views or for the access it provides to nearby mountains. What we've found particularly special about this trail is the access it provides to the lesser-

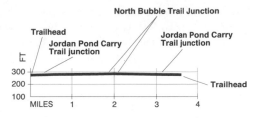

known Conners Nubble, just north of the highly popular Bubbles. And like other similar trails, the Eagle Lake Trail has its easy, flat sections and its rougher up-and-down sections.

The trail begins by following the easier east shore and heads west to the rougher side. Lots of cedars line the start of the trail. A long series of log bridges takes you over the wettest part of the path. At 0.6 mile, reach a junction with the Jordan Carry Trail, part of which had once been used by Native Americans to carry canoes from one body of water to another. This junction marks the start of the west shore of Eagle Lake.

The trail heads in and out of the woods and goes by a sandy beach: No swimming is allowed. At 0.8 mile, cross over a field of rocks straight ahead, rather than bearing left into the woods as so many others have mistakenly done, creating a worn-down, wrong-way path in the process. The path gets rockier, and more difficult here, as you skirt the western shore. You'll cross

From the North Bubble, the South Bubble is barely visible through the fog.

the base of a rock slide. After a final little uphill takes you inland into a birch grove, the trail levels off into a woods path once again. At 1.7 miles, reach a junction with the North Bubble Trail, which heads south to Conners Nubble and the North Bubble summit. The trail ends at 1.8 miles at a carriage road. Return the way you came.

Options: To add on the open summit of Conners Nubble, turn left (south) on the North Bubble Trail, for 0.4 mile. Return the way you came. To do a long loop up the Bubbles, turn left (south) on the North Bubble Trail, and take it up and over Conners Nubble, the North Bubble and the South Bubble. Descend to the shore of Jordan Pond, and turn left (southeast) along the Jordan Pond Shore Trail. Take your next left and head northwest on the Jordan Pond Carry Trail, looping back to Eagle Lake. Turn right (northeast) on the Eagle Lake Trail and return to the Bubble Pond parking area. The loop is approximately 5.4 miles.

42 Jordan Pond Carry Trail

Highlights:	Easy woods walk between Eagle Lake and Jordan Pond.
Type of hike:	Day hike; out-and-back.
Total distance:	2 miles, plus 0.6 mile to reach trailhead.
Difficulty:	Easy.

Finding the trailhead:. From the park visitor center, head south on the Park Loop Road for 5 miles, past the Cadillac Mountain entrance to the Bubble Pond parking lot (not the Bubble Rock parking lot farther south). Cross to the other side of the Park Loop Road and walk on a carriage road for 0.2 mile to carriage road intersection No. 7. Bear left and then take the Eagle Lake Trail for 0.6 mile. Jordan Pond Carry Trailhead is on the left.

Parking and trailhead facilities: Park at the Bubble Pond parking lot, where there are a chemical toilet and a picnic table.

Key points:
- 0.0 Jordan Pond Carry Trailhead, reached after 0.6 mile on the Eagle Lake Trail.
- 0.1 Cross a carriage road.
- 0.6 Junction with the Bubble Rock Trail; stay straight.
- 1.0 Jordan Pond, and a junction with the Jordan Pond Shore Trail.
- 2.0 Return the way you came.

The hike: Part of a pre–Revolutionary War carry trail, this easy woods path in the shadow of the Bubbles connects Eagle Lake to Jordan Pond. Head south from Eagle Lake, along log bridges through mossy bogs. At 0.1 mile,

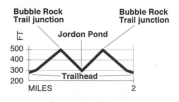

Jordan Pond Carry Trail

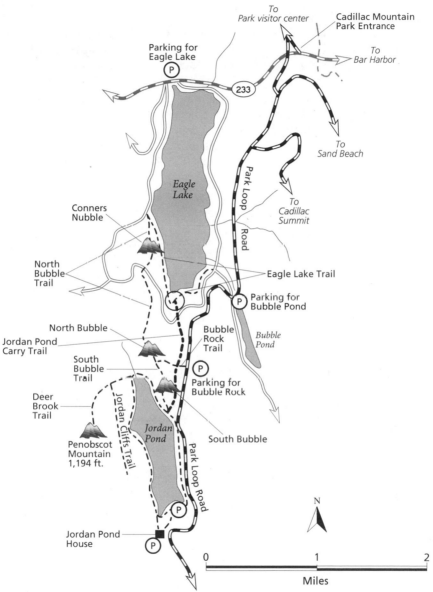

reach a carriage road; bear right and cross it. The trail soon begins ascending a bit. At 0.6 mile, reach a junction with the Bubble Rock Trail, which heads left (east) to the Bubble Rock parking area, and right (west) to the gap between the North Bubble and South Bubble. Stay straight. Reach the shore of Jordan Pond and a junction with the Jordan Pond Shore Trail at 1.0 mile. Return the way you came.

Options: For an approximately 5.7-mile loop up the Bubbles and back along the western shore of Eagle Lake, you can turn right (northwest) along the shore of Jordan Pond for 0.1 mile. Then take the South Bubble Trail for 0.6 mile, over the South Bubble and to the North Bubble Trail. Then take the North Bubble Trail for 1.7 miles, over the North Bubble and Conners Nubble, to the Eagle Lake Trail. Turn right along the lake and return to the carriage road near the Bubble Pond parking area in another 1.7 miles. The loop can be shortened by 0.7 mile if you turn right at the carriage road after descending from North Bubble. Follow the carriage road 1.5 miles, bearing right at carriage road intersection No. 7 back to the Bubble Pond parking area.

43 Asticou Trail

Highlights:	Less-traveled woods walk, providing access to some of the more remote trails up Penobscot and Sargent mountains.
Type of hike:	Day hike; out-and-back.
Total distance:	3.8 miles.
Difficulty:	Easy.

Finding the trailhead: From the park visitor center, head south on the Park Loop Road for 7.7 miles, to the Jordan Pond House parking lot, right after the Jordan Pond parking lot. Walk behind and to the left of Jordan Pond House, and follow path marked "To Asticou, Jordan Cliffs and Penobscot Mountain Trails," down to a carriage road. The trailhead is across the carriage road and wooden bridge, on the left.

Parking and trailhead facilities: Park at the Jordan Pond House or nearby Jordan Pond parking lot. The restaurant, gift shop, and restrooms are open seasonally.

Key points:
- 0.0   Asticou Trailhead.
- 1.0   Cross a carriage road.
- 1.1   Cross second carriage road. The Amphitheater Trail is 0.3 mile to the right on the road.
- 1.2   Junction with the Harbor Brook Trail over private land; stay straight.
- 1.6   Junction with the Asticou Ridge Trail over private land; bear right.
- 1.9   Junction with the Sargent Mountain South Ridge Trail.

Asticou Trail

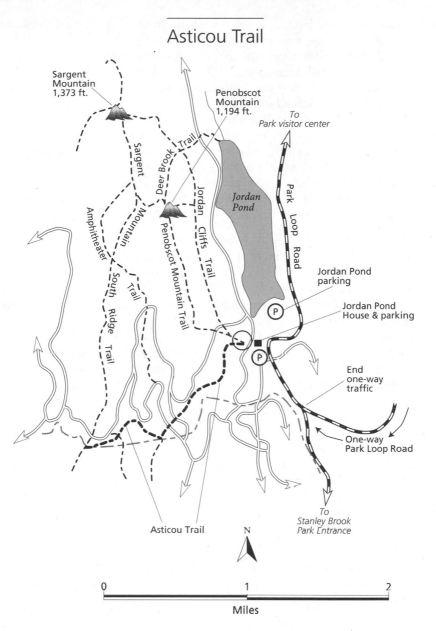

Sargent Mountain
1,373 ft.

Penobscot Mountain
1,194 ft.

To Park visitor center

Sargent Mountain Trail

Deer Brook Trail

Jordan Cliffs Trail

Jordan Pond

Amphitheater Trail

Sargent Mountain South Ridge Trail

Penobscot Mountain Trail

Park Loop Road

Jordan Pond parking

Jordan Pond House & parking

End one-way traffic

One-way Park Loop Road

Asticou Trail

N

To Stanley Brook Park Entrance

0   1   2
Miles

The hike: Easy enough by itself for novice hikers, yet challenging enough as part of a long loop up Penobscot for the most ambitious, this is a less-traveled gem of a trail. Leaving the crowd at the Jordan Pond House behind, the trail leads you quickly into woods of striped maple (also known as

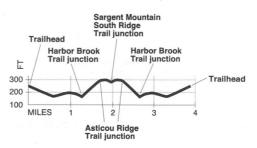

Sargent Mountain
South Ridge
Trail junction

Trailhead

Harbor Brook
Trail junction

Harbor Brook
Trail junction

Trailhead

FT

300
200
100

MILES   1   2   3   4

Asticou Ridge
Trail junction

moosewood because its shoots are a favorite food of moose) and towering cedars and pines. Pine needles carpet the forest floor.

At 1 mile, cross a carriage road; at 1.1 miles, cross a second carriage road. The even less traveled Amphitheater Trail is 0.3 mile to the right along this carriage road. At 1.2 miles, you'll cross over Harbor Brook on an elaborate wooden bridge with fancy handrails. The Harbor Brook Trail goes over private land to the left, paralleling the brook toward Maine Highway 3. Stay straight on the Asticou Trail. Several series of stone steps then take you over the biggest uphill on the trail, making the climb as easy as climbing a staircase. At the top of the rise at 1.6 miles, you'll reach a junction with the Asticou Ridge Trail that heads over private land to Eliot Mountain. Bear right to continue on the Asticou Trail. At 1.9 miles, the trail ends at the junction with the Sargent Mountain South Ridge Trail. Return the way you came.

Options: To loop up Penobscot or Sargent Mountain, turn right at trail's end and head north along the Sargent Mountain South Ridge Trail. Follow the trail signs for Sargent Mountain or Penobscot Mountain, 2.1 miles and 1.9 miles, respectively, from the end of the Asticou Trail. To close the loop up either mountain, follow the signs back to Jordan Pond, for a round trip of 5 to 6 miles.

Or you can loop up either Penobscot or Sargent Mountain along the little-traveled but steeper Amphitheater Trail. While this makes a 0.7-mile shorter loop, the trail is wooded and doesn't provide the panoramic views that the Sargent Mountain South Ridge Trail does. To do this loop, take a right at the second carriage road, at 1.1 miles on the Asticou Trail, and walk 0.3 mile on the road to the Amphitheater Trailhead, on the right (north). Take the Amphitheater Trail for 1.4 miles to a junction with the Sargent Mountain South Ridge Trail at Birch Spring. Take your first right on to the Sargent Mountain South Ridge Trail and follow the signs for Sargent Mountain or Penobscot Mountain. To close the loop up either mountain, follow the signs back to Jordan Pond.

44 Penobscot Mountain Trail

Highlights:	360-degree views atop 1,194-foot summit of Penobscot Mountain.
Type of hike:	Day hike; out and back.
Total distance:	3.2 miles.
Difficulty:	Moderate.

Finding the trailhead: From the park visitor center, head south on the Park Loop Road for 7.7 miles to the Jordan Pond House parking lot, right after the Jordan Pond parking lot. Walk behind and to the left of the Jordan Pond House and follow path marked "To Asticou, Jordan Cliffs and Penobscot Mountain Trails," down to a carriage road. The trailhead is across the carriage road on the right.

Penobscot Mountain Trail

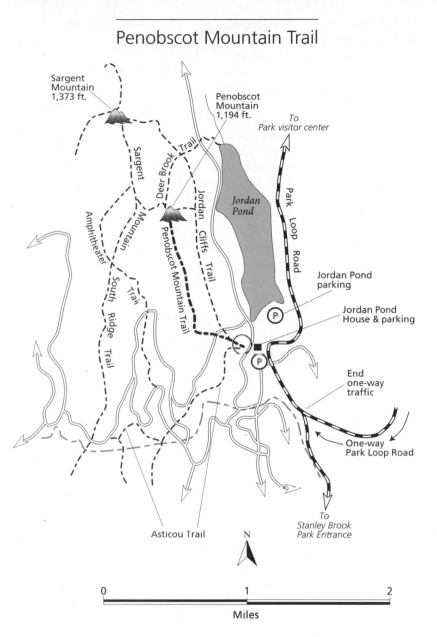

Parking and trailhead facilities: Park at Jordan Pond House or nearby Jordan Pond parking lot. A restaurant, gift shop, and restrooms are open seasonally.

Key points:

- 0.0   Penobscot Mountain Trailhead.
- 0.5   Cross a carriage road at the West Branch Bridge.
- 1.6   Penobscot Mountain summit; junction with a spur to the Jordan Cliffs Trail.

The hike: This is the most popular way up Penobscot because of the trail's ease of access from the Jordan Pond House and its open ridge views. It is also part of the most traveled route up Sargent Mountain. At 0.5 mile from the trailhead, cross a carriage road at the West Branch Bridge, one of the unique

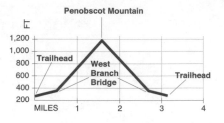

stone spans that dot the Acadia landscape. Turn left and begin the climb up Penobscot. Switchbacks take you along a wooden split rail fence. You may need to scramble up on your hands and knees at one tight spot. Look behind you to the south, and you'll see the Jordan Pond House.

You'll reach the open ridge with views south to the Cranberry Isles. It's easy to lose the trail on the ridge, so watch carefully for cairns and blue blazes. At 1.6 miles, reach the 1,194-foot summit of Penobscot, with its broad vistas. To the south are the Cranberry Isles, east are Pemetic and Cadillac mountains, north is Sargent, and west are Parkman Mountain and Bald Peak. Return the way you came.

Options: To add on the 1,373-foot-high Sargent Mountain, head north off Penobscot Mountain and bear left at the first junction, toward Sargent Pond, where there is a bench to rest on. Then turn right at the next junction, toward Sargent Mountain. The higher Sargent is 1 mile away from Penobscot.

45 Jordan Cliffs Trail

Highlights:	Climb along Jordan Cliffs to Penobscot Mountain, with views of Jordan Pond, Bubbles, and surrounding scenery; may be closed during peregrine falcon breeding season spring to late summer.
Type of hike:	Day hike; loop.
Total distance:	3.8 miles, including 0.5 mile to reach trailhead.
Difficulty:	Strenuous.

Finding the trailhead: From the park visitor center, head south on the Park Loop Road for 7.7 miles to the Jordan Pond House parking lot right after the Jordan Pond parking lot. Walk behind and to the left of Jordan Pond House and follow the path marked "To Asticou, Jordan Cliffs and Penobscot Mountain Trails" down to a carriage road. Cross the carriage road and take Penobscot Mountain Trail on the right for 0.5 mile. Jordan Cliffs Trailhead is on the right off the Penobscot Mountain Trail, just before next carriage road crossing.

Parking and trailhead facilities: Park at the Jordan Pond House or nearby Jordan Pond parking lot. The restaurant, gift shop, and restrooms are open seasonally.

Jordan Cliffs Trail

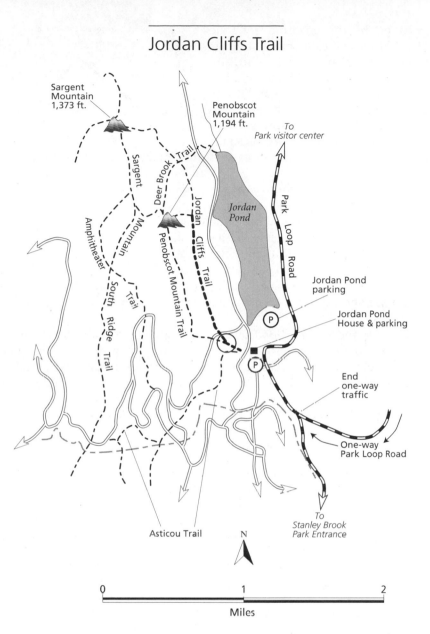

Key points:

- 0.0   Jordan Pond House.
- 0.5   Jordan Cliffs Trailhead, reached via the Penobscot Mountain Trail.
- 0.6   Cross a carriage road.
- 1.7   Junction; turn left up Penobscot Mountain.
- 2.2   Penobscot Mountain summit; turn left to descend via the Penobscot Mountain Trail.
- 3.2   Cross a carriage road.
- 3.8   Return to the Jordan Pond House.

The hike: This rugged climb along the Jordan Cliffs provides spectacular views down to Jordan Pond, across to the Bubbles and up to Penobscot Mountain. But like many of the cliff trails in Acadia, this one may be closed during peregrine falcon breeding season from spring to late summer, so check with park officials.

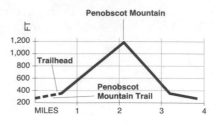

Also like other cliff trails, this one features iron rungs and precarious footing, so be prepared.

The trail starts by crossing a carriage road and ascending steeply, but soon levels off along the cliffs. To the south is an open view of the Cranberry Isles, and to the east is Jordan Pond. The Bubbles and Pemetic Mountain soon come into view to the northeast. A series of handrails helps you through some tricky spots along the cliff face. But the trickiest spot of all requires crossing a suspended one-log bridge nearly as narrow as a balance beam, with carved-out notches for footholds. After descending some log-and-stone steps and using a final iron handrail to get across a slippery spot, you'll come to a junction at 1.7 miles.

Technically, the Jordan Cliffs Trail continues straight, heading directly north-northwest to Sargent Mountain, but some of that section of trail has been closed because of unsafe conditions. Instead, turn left (west) at the junction and climb steeply up Jordan Cliffs to Penobscot Mountain. Reach the 1,194-foot summit at 2.2 miles. The only thing blocking the grand view here is the higher Sargent Mountain to the northwest. To loop back, descend south along the open ridge via the Penobscot Mountain Trail. Cross a carriage road at 3.2 miles and return to the Jordan Pond House at 3.8 miles.

Options: You can add on another 3 miles round trip up to Sargent Mountain. From the summit of Penobscot head north. At the next junction, bear left (west) toward Sargent Pond. Then at the next junction, turn right (north) and head straight to the 1,373-foot peak of Sargent. Return to Penobscot Mountain and follow the Penobscot Mountain Trail south back to the Jordan Pond House.

46 Deer Brook Trail

Highlights:	Steep climb up Penobscot Mountain along Deer Brook.
Type of hike:	Day hike; out-and-back.
Total distance:	3.2 miles, including 0.7 mile to reach trailhead.
Difficulty:	Strenuous.

Finding the trailhead: From the park visitor center, drive south on the Park Loop Road for 6 miles, past the Cadillac Mountain entrance and the Bubble

Deer Brook Trail

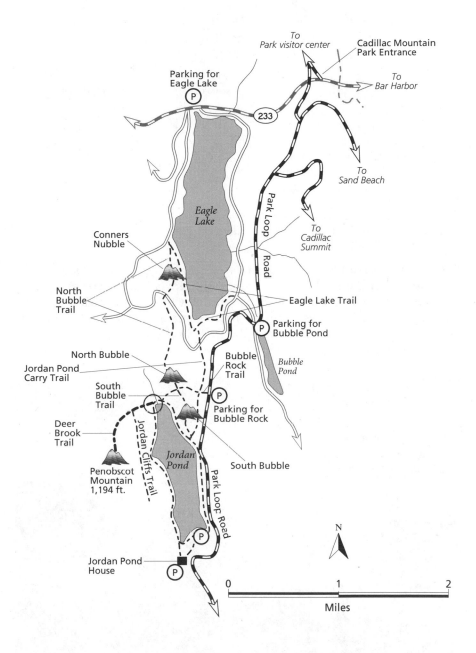

To Park visitor center

Cadillac Mountain Park Entrance

To Bar Harbor

Parking for Eagle Lake

233

To Sand Beach

Eagle Lake

Park Loop Road

To Cadillac Summit

Conners Nubble

Eagle Lake Trail

North Bubble Trail

Parking for Bubble Pond

Bubble Pond

North Bubble

Bubble Rock Trail

Jordan Pond Carry Trail

South Bubble Trail

Parking for Bubble Rock

Deer Brook Trail

Jordan Cliffs Trail

Jordan Pond

South Bubble

Penobscot Mountain 1,194 ft.

Park Loop Road

N

Jordan Pond House

0   1   2

Miles

Pond parking lot, to the Bubble Rock parking lot. From the Bubble Rock parking lot head straight on the Bubble Rock Trail for 0.6 mile to the shores of Jordan Pond. Turn right on the Jordan Pond Shore Trail for 0.1 mile. Deer Brook Trailhead is on the right.

Parking and trailhead facilities: The Bubble Rock parking lot is on the right (west) side of the Park Loop Road. There are no facilities.

Key points:

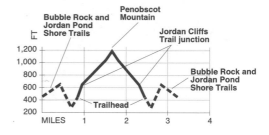

- 0.0   Bubble Rock parking lot.
- 0.7   Deer Brook Trailhead, reached via the Bubble Rock and Jordan Pond Shore trails.
- 0.8   Cross a carriage road.
- 0.9   Junction with the Jordan Cliffs Trail; stay straight.
- 1.5   Junction with a spur to Sargent Pond; stay straight.
- 1.6   Penobscot Mountain summit; junction with a spur to the Jordan Cliffs Trail.

The hike: This isn't the most scenic or easiest trail up Penobscot and, as a result, is one of the least-traveled routes. It follows Deer Brook steeply up through the woods and includes some difficult brook crossings, with rock hopping necessary at times. From the north shore of Jordan Pond at 0.7 mile from the Bubble Rock parking area, the trail climbs to a carriage road at 0.8 mile. Cross the road diagonally to the left.

Jordan Pond and the Bubbles as seen from the Jordan Cliffs Trail.

At 0.9 mile, reach a junction with the Jordan Cliffs Trail. Continue straight along Deer Brook, climbing steeply. At 1.5 miles, reach a junction with a spur to Sargent Pond. Stay straight (south) toward Penobscot. Reach the open 1,194-foot summit of Penobscot that provides views all around at 1.6 miles. A spur to the Jordan Cliffs Trail leads east from here. Return the way you came.

Options: To loop down via the Jordan Cliffs Trail, take the spur east off Penobscot. Reach the junction with the cliffs trail in another 0.5 mile and turn left. At the next junction in another 0.2 mile, turn right and follow the Deer Brook Trail back down another 0.2 mile to the north shore of Jordan Pond. Return to the Bubble Rock parking area in another 0.7 mile via the Jordan Pond Shore and Bubble Rock trails.

47 Sargent Mountain South Ridge Trail

Highlights:	Relatively less-traveled ridge walk to 1,373-foot summit of Sargent Mountain, with panoramic views toward the ocean and surrounding mountains.
Type of hike:	Day hike; out-and-back.
Total distance:	5.4 miles, including 0.7 mile to reach trailhead.
Difficulty:	Moderate.

Finding the trailhead: From Bar Harbor, head west on Maine Highway 233 for 4 miles, then left (south) on ME 198, for another 3.9 miles, past Upper Hadlock Pond on your left, to a carriage road parking lot on the left, just before the Brown Mountain Gatehouse. Bear left on the carriage road away from the gatehouse, which is now a private residence. Then bear right twice, at carriage road intersections No. 18 and No. 19, until you reach the trailhead on the left in about 0.7 mile.

Parking and trailhead facilities: Park at the carriage road and gatehouse parking area. The only facility is a chemical toilet.

Key points:

0.0	Brown Mountain Gatehouse.
0.7	Sargent Mountain South Ridge Trailhead, reached via a carriage road.
1.6	Junction with the Amphitheater Trail at Birch Spring.
2.0	Junction with the Sargent Pond Trail.

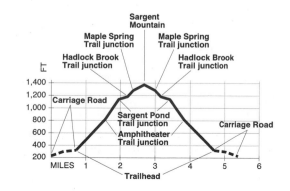

Sargent Mountain South Ridge Trail

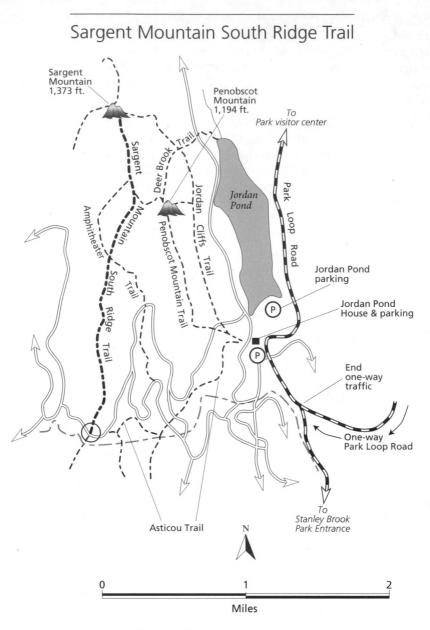

2.2   Junction with the Hadlock Brook Trail.
2.4   Junction with the Maple Spring Trail.
2.7   Sargent Mountain summit; return the way you came.

The hike: Most people who climb Sargent Mountain go up via the Penobscot Mountain Trail, making the Sargent Mountain South Ridge Trail a less-traveled route. As a result, you may see turkey vultures soaring on thermals, or a cluster of rare pink lady's slippers or showy yellow-and-pink columbines.

Even the pink granite cairns at the start of the trail are a treat, with the rocks stacked up like miniature architectural wonders.

From the trailhead that is 0.7 mile from the Brown Mountain Gatehouse, the trail heads north moderately up from the carriage road and soon hints at the dramatic views to come. It bears right and levels off, then ascends to an exposed pink granite ledge. The trail gently zigzags up the ridge of Sargent. Blueberry bushes line the path. In the spring, you can find columbine, with its delicate yellow-and-pink pipe-shaped flower; starflower, with its tiny six- or seven-pointed white flowers; and Canada dogwood, also known as bunchberry, with its four white petal-like bracts that look like a showy flower.

As the path takes you in and out of the woods and along exposed ledges, you get views of the Penobscot ridge to the right (east); the ocean behind you to the south; and Norumbega Mountain to the left (west). You reach the first full view of the Penobscot summit as the trail brings you along the edge of the natural amphitheater formed by the Sargent and Penobscot ridges. You can peer down through the trees and see a carriage road cutting along the side of the amphitheater. The trail makes one more turn to the east to a rocky outcropping with an expansive view of Penobscot, the amphitheater, the Gulf of Maine, and the Cranberry Isles. In the spring, purplish flowered rhodora and Canada dogwood bloom here.

Descend slightly to Birch Spring and the junction with the Amphitheater Trail at 1.6 miles. The trail continues up along woods and rocky ledges, then ascends steeply up open rock faces. Behind you lies the ridge you just climbed, snaking down toward the Gulf of Maine. You can also see the Cranberry Isles, Long Pond, and ME 3 to the south and Somes Sound and Norumbega to the west. At 2 miles, reach the junction with the Sargent Pond Trail, which heads east to Sargent Mountain Pond and 0.5 mile to the Penobscot summit. You're high enough on the open ridge of Sargent Mountain here to get views of Cadillac Mountain to the northeast and of Pemetic Mountain, which lies between Cadillac and Penobscot.

Reach a junction at 2.2 miles with the Hadlock Brook Trail, which heads southwest toward ME 198, and at 2.4 miles, a junction with the Maple Spring Trail, which also heads toward ME 198. At 2.7 miles, attain the 1,373-foot summit of Sargent to enjoy its 360-degree views. Return the way you came.

Options: You can add on the Penobscot summit on the descent by turning left (east) at the junction with the Sargent Pond Trail. Attain the 1,194-foot Penobscot summit in 0.5 mile. Return the way you came and head back down the Sargent Mountain South Ridge Trail. This adds an extra mile to the round trip. Or for a loop that brings you down the natural amphitheater on the return, turn left (southeast) at the junction with the Amphitheater Trail at Birch Spring, descending in another 0.6 mile to the Amphitheater Bridge. Climb up to the carriage road here, and turn right (west). Stay on the carriage road for 2 miles, bearing right at the first junction then left at the last two junctions, to return to the parking area. This makes for a 6.4-mile loop.

48 Sargent Mountain North Ridge Trail

Highlights:	Relatively less-traveled route up north ridge of Sargent Mountain, the second highest peak in Acadia.
Type of hike:	Day hike; out-and-back.
Total distance:	5 miles, including 1.2 miles to reach trailhead.
Difficulty:	Strenuous.

Finding the trailhead: From Bar Harbor, head west on Maine Highway 233 for 4 miles, then left (south) on ME 198 for a little more than a mile to Giant Slide Road on the left (east). Walk down Giant Slide Road, a private drive, to the Giant Slide Trailhead. Take the Giant Slide Trail for 1.2 miles to a four-way intersection. The Sargent Mountain North Ridge Trailhead is on the left.

Parking and trailhead facilities: Park along the east side of ME 198. There are no facilities.

Key points:
- 0.0 Giant Slide Trailhead.
- 1.2 Sargent Mountain North Ridge Trailhead, reached via the Giant Slide Trail.
- 1.8 Cross a carriage road.
- 2.5 Sargent Mountain summit; junction with the Grandgent Trail.

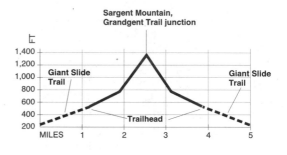

The hike: To reach the trailhead of this relatively short and less-traveled trail up Sargent Mountain, you must first hike 1.2 miles in on the rough and steep Giant Slide Trail to a four-way intersection. The Sargent Mountain North Ridge Trail heads left (east) from this intersection, immediately crossing what can be a wide rushing stream after heavy rains. Ascend steeply as the trail switchbacks through the forest.

At 1.8 miles from ME 198, cross a carriage road and climb stone steps to continue on the trail on the other side. As the trail continues climbing steeply, you'll get your first views to the left (west) of Eagle Lake. If you hike this trail in late spring, you'll also have views of an explosion of purple flowers known as rhodora. The trail dips then ascends along an open ridge with views all around. The trail here is marked only by cairns and becomes tricky to follow. There's a sharp right up to Sargent's peak that's easy to miss, so if you find yourself descending rather than heading up to the peak, you'll need to backtrack.

Sargent's 1,373-foot summit, reached at 2.5 miles from ME 198, is marked by a giant cairn and a series of trail signs. The second highest mountain in

Sargent Mountain North Ridge Trail

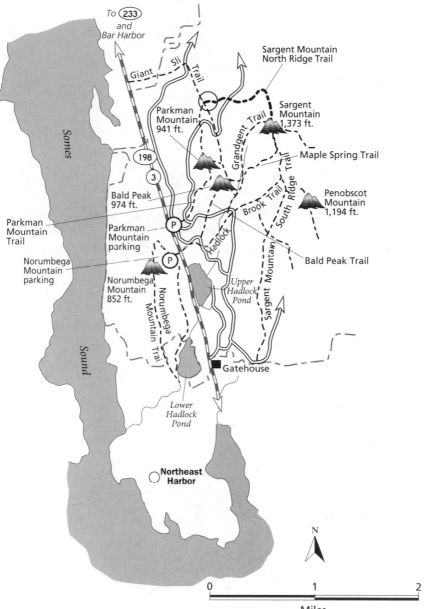

To (233)
and
Bar Harbor

Giant Sli Trail

Sargent Mountain
North Ridge Trail

Parkman
Mountain
941 ft.

Grandgent Trail

Sargent
Mountain
1,373 ft.

Maple Spring Trail

Bald Peak
974 ft.

Brook Trail

South Ridge Trail

Penobscot
Mountain
1,194 ft.

Parkman
Mountain
Trail

Parkman
Mountain
parking

Hadlock

Sargent Mountain

Bald Peak Trail

Norumbega
Mountain
parking

Norumbega
Mountain
852 ft.

Norumbega Mountain Trail

Upper
Hadlock
Pond

Somes

Sound

Gatehouse

Lower
Hadlock
Pond

Northeast
Harbor

N

0   1   2
Miles

The open ridge of Sargent Mountain provides expansive views of the Cranberry Isles and the Gulf of Maine to the south.

Acadia, behind only Cadillac, provides spectacular 360-degree views of Somes Sound and Western Mountain to the right (west); the Cranberry Isles and the Gulf of Maine to the south; Pemetic and Cadillac Mountains to the east; and Porcupine Islands and Frenchman Bay to the northeast. Return the way you came.

Options: To loop back to the Giant Slide via the Maple Spring Trail, head south down Sargent Mountain for 0.3 mile to a junction. Turn right to descend the steep Maple Spring Trail, reaching the Giant Slide Trail in 0.8 mile. Turn right (north) to follow the Giant Slide Trail another 2.2 miles back to ME 198. The loop is 5.8 miles long.

49 Amphitheater Trail

Highlights:	Less-traveled trail to natural amphitheater and Amphitheater Bridge between ridges of Penobscot and Sargent mountains, with access to either peak possible.
Type of hike:	Day hike; out-and-back, or long loop over Penobscot Mountain.
Total distance:	4.4 miles, including 1.4 miles to reach trailhead.
Difficulty:	Moderate to strenuous.

Amphitheater Trail

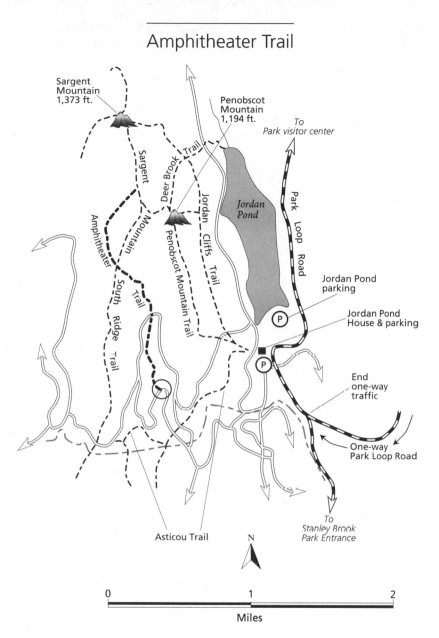

Finding the trailhead: From the park visitor center, head south on the Park Loop Road for 7.7 miles to the Jordan Pond House parking lot right after the Jordan Pond parking lot. Walk behind and to the left of the Jordan Pond House and follow the path marked "To Asticou, Jordan Cliffs and Penobscot Mountain Trails," down to a carriage road. Asticou Trailhead is across the carriage road and wooden bridge on the left. Take the Asticou Trail for 1.1 miles to the second carriage road. Turn right (northwest) on the carriage road, reaching the Amphitheater Trailhead on the right in another 0.3 mile.

Parking and trailhead facilities: Park at the Jordan Pond House or nearby Jordan Pond parking lot. The restaurant, gift shop, and restrooms are open seasonally.

Key points:
  0.0 Asticou Trailhead.
  1.4 Amphitheater Trailhead, reached via the Asticou Trail and a carriage road.
  2.2 Amphitheater Bridge; return the way you came.

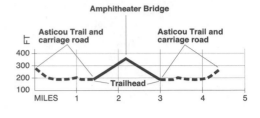

The hike: On this less-traveled trail, it's possible to see plenty of wildlife as well as the Little Harbor Brook Bridge and the long span of the Amphitheater Bridge. The trail is named after the natural amphitheater between the ridges of Sargent and Penobscot mountains.

From the trailhead, reached after a 1.4-mile walk along the Asticou Trail and carriage road, the Amphitheater Trail parallels the carriage road on the right, going by the Little Harbor Brook Bridge and the brook itself. Cairns mark this section of the trail, which can be hard to follow. Soon, distinctive blue blazes mark a change in the trail direction to the right (north) away from the carriage road and toward the amphitheater. The trail crosses from one side of the brook to the other.

At 2.2 miles, reach the grand Amphitheater Bridge towering above the trail and spanning the long, rocky rim of the natural amphitheater. You have to admire the engineering that went into constructing the bridge as well as the natural forces that created the amphitheater. Return the way you came.

Options: Although the Amphitheater Bridge is a natural turnaround point, the trail does officially continue for another 0.9 mile, passing a junction with the Sargent Mountain South Ridge Trail at Birch Spring and ending at a junction in the woods with the Hadlock Brook Trail. The continuation of the trail beyond the bridge to Sargent Mountain South Ridge Trail provides access to Penobscot or Sargent Mountain.

To loop over Penobscot Mountain, follow the trail beyond the Amphitheater Bridge, paralleling the brook for a bit, then steeply ascending to open ledges. You get views behind you (south) of the Cranberry Isles. In another 0.6 mile from the bridge, reach a four-way intersection with the Sargent Mountain South Ridge Trail. Take your first right and ascend north 0.4 mile along the ridge. Turn right (east) at the junction with the Sargent Pond Trail and head 0.5 mile to the summit of Penobscot Mountain. Follow the 1.6-mile-long Penobscot Mountain Trail back down to Jordan Pond's south shore. The loop is approximately 5.3 miles.

If you want to continue on to Sargent Mountain before heading down over Penobscot, follow the Sargent Mountain South Ridge Trail 1.1 miles from Birch Spring all the way up to that higher peak, passing the junctions with the Sargent Pond, Hadlock Brook, and Maple Spring Trails along the way. Then to loop down over Penobscot, descend the Sargent summit back to the junction with the Sargent Pond Trail and turn left (east) for 0.5 mile, passing Sargent Pond and climbing Penobscot Mountain. Finally, at the Penobscot summit, turn right (south) and follow the 1.6-mile Penobscot Mountain Trail back down to the south shore of Jordan Pond. The loop is 6.7 miles long.

50 Giant Slide Trail

Highlights: Less-traveled trail along rock slide, providing access to Sargent Mountain from northwest.
Type of hike: Day hike; out-and-back.
Total distance: 4.4 miles.
Difficulty: Moderate to strenuous.

Finding the trailhead: From Bar Harbor, head west on Maine Highway 233 for 4 miles, then left (south) on ME 198, for a little more than a mile, to Giant Slide Road, on the left, or east. The trailhead is down Giant Slide Road, a private drive. (The trailhead may be moved in the future. Check with the park before your hike.)

Parking and trailhead facilities: Park along the east side of ME 198. There are no facilities.

Key points:

0.0 Giant Slide Trailhead.

0.7 Cross a carriage road.

1.2 Junction with the Parkman Mountain and Sargent Mountain North Ridge trails.

1.5 Cross a carriage road.

1.8 Junction is with a spur trail to Parkman Mountain and with the Grandgent trail.

2.2 Junction with the Maple Spring Trail; return the way you came.

The hike: Huge boulders and slabs of granite, evidence of a long-ago massive slide, make this trail particularly challenging. At one point, the opening between the granite is so narrow, you have to turn sideways to get through. At another point, you walk under a 15- to 20-foot rock overhang.

The first part of the trail, much of it along private land, is relatively flat. But once you cross the first carriage road at 0.7 mile, inside the Acadia boundary, the trail turns right (south) and starts a steep, steady ascent. If you hike after heavy rains, Sargent Brook's cascades and waterfalls make for a wet and wonderful show along here.

Giant Slide Trail

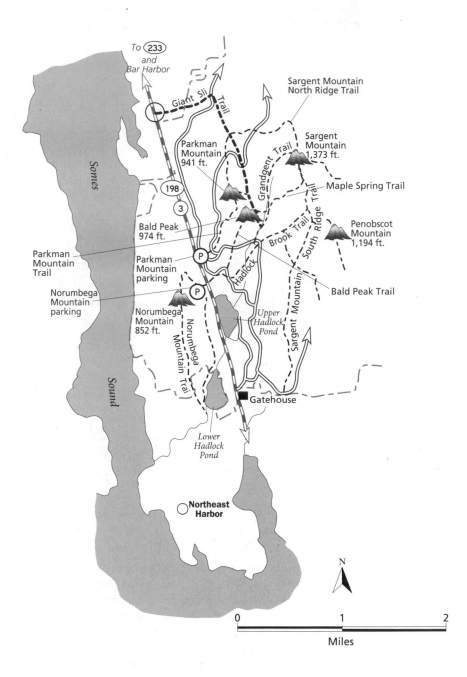

To (233) and Bar Harbor

Giant Sli__ Trail

Sargent Mountain North Ridge Trail

Parkman Mountain 941 ft.

Grandgent Trail

Sargent Mountain 1,373 ft.

Maple Spring Trail

198

3

Bald Peak 974 ft.

Penobscot Mountain 1,194 ft.

Parkman Mountain Trail

Parkman Mountain parking

Brook Trail

South Ridge Trail

Norumbega Mountain parking

Bald Peak Trail

Norumbega Mountain 852 ft.

Hadlock

Upper Hadlock Pond

Sargent Mountain

Norumbega Mountain Trail

Gatehouse

Lower Hadlock Pond

○ Northeast Harbor

Somes

Sound

N

0   1   2
Miles

At 1.2 miles, reach the junction with the Parkman Mountain Trail and the Sargent Mountain North Ridge Trail. Go straight on the Giant Slide Trail, squeezing sideways through the tumbled-down slabs of granite and clambering over boulders. The trail next follows Sargent Brook, crossing from one side of the brook to the other. At one point, a sheer rock wall towers over the trail on the left (east). Watch your step on the moss-covered rocks.

Climb to the next gravel road at 1.5 miles and cross it diagonally to the right. The trail levels off a bit and at 1.8 miles reaches a junction with a spur trail to the right (west) up Parkman Mountain and the Grandgent Trail to the left (east) up Gilmore Peak and Sargent Mountain. The trail then descends to end at 2.2 miles, at a junction with the Maple Spring Trail. Return the way you came.

Options: To hike a loop that includes Sargent Mountain, take the Giant Slide Trail to the first junction and turn left (east) up the 1.3-mile Sargent Mountain North Ridge Trail. From the summit, descend right (west) along the steep 0.8-mile Grandgent Trail, going over Gilmore Peak and then down to the Giant Slide Trail. Turn right (north) on the Giant Slide Trail to return in another 1.8 miles back to the parking area. The loop is approximately 5.1 miles long.

Another possible loop can be done up Parkman Mountain. Take the Giant Slide Trail to the first junction and turn right (west) up the Parkman Mountain Trail, reaching the open summit in another 0.7 mile. Then turn left (east) off the summit down a 0.3-mile spur trail to loop down to the Giant Slide Trail. Turn left (north) on the Giant Slide Trail to return to the parking area in another 1.8 miles. The loop is approximately 4 miles.

51 Grandgent Trail

Highlights:	Difficult trail up west face of Sargent via Gilmore Peak.
Type of hike:	Day hike; out-and-back or part of loop.
Total distance:	4.6 miles, including 1.5 miles to reach trailhead.
Difficulty:	Strenuous.

Finding the trailhead: From Bar Harbor, head west on Maine Highway 233 for 4 miles, then left (south) on ME 198 for another 2.5 miles to the Parkman Mountain parking area on the left (east) side of the road. Bear right on a carriage road, then left at carriage road intersection No. 13 to reach Parkman Mountain Trailhead on the left (north) side of the road in 0.1 mile. Take the Parkman Mountain Trail for 1.2 miles to the summit of Parkman Mountain and a junction with a spur to the Giant Slide Trail. Turn right (east) on the spur and head 0.3 mile to the Giant Slide Trail. The Grandgent Trailhead is straight ahead.

Parking and trailhead facilities: Parking is available at the Parkman Mountain parking area; there is a chemical toilet here.

Grandgent Trail

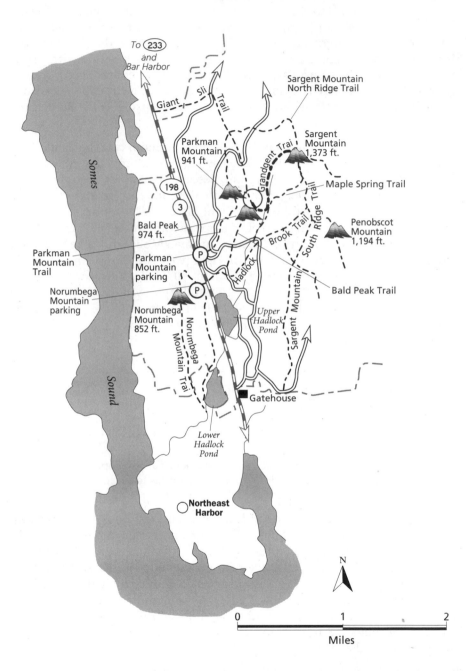

To (233) and Bar Harbor

Sargent Mountain North Ridge Trail

Giant Sli Trail

Parkman Mountain 941 ft.

Grandgent Trail

Sargent Mountain 1,373 ft.

Maple Spring Trail

Somes

198

3

Bald Peak 974 ft.

Brook Trail

South Ridge Trail

Penobscot Mountain 1,194 ft.

Parkman Mountain Trail

Parkman Mountain parking

P

Hadlock

Norumbega Mountain parking

P

Bald Peak Trail

Norumbega Mountain 852 ft.

Sargent Mountain

Upper Hadlock Pond

Norumbega Mountain Trail

Sound

Gatehouse

Lower Hadlock Pond

Northeast Harbor

N

0   1   2

Miles

Key points:

0.0 Parkman Mountain parking area.
1.5 Grandgent Trailhead via the Parkman Mountain Trail and a spur to the Giant Slide Trail.
1.8 Gilmore Peak.
2.3 Sargent Mountain summit; return the way you came.

The hike: This hard-to-reach and strenu-ous trail is primarily used as a connector for loops up and down the steep west face of Sargent Mountain. It also takes you over the less-traveled Gilmore Peak with views from its 1,036-foot summit.

From the trailhead at the junction with the Giant Slide Trail, 1.5 miles in from ME 198, ascend steeply east up Gilmore Peak along loose rock. At 1.8 miles from ME 198,

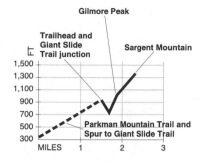

reach the summit of Gilmore, with views west to Somes Sound, Echo Lake, and Long Pond, and east to Sargent Mountain. Descend Gilmore, turning sharply left (north) off the peak. The trail continues along open ledges, then drops into the woods, where there's a creek crossing. Climb out of the sag and reach Sargent and 360-degree views at 2.3 miles. Return the way you came or loop back.

Options: You can make a loop with either the Maple Spring or Hadlock Brook Trails by heading south off Sargent on the Sargent Mountain South Ridge Trail. To go down the Maple Spring Trail, turn right at the first junction off the Sargent Mountain South Ridge Trail. Pass a junction with the Giant Slide Trail in another 0.8 mile, the Deer Brook Bridge in another 0.1 mile, and then turn right in another 0.3 mile on to the Hadlock Brook Trail. At a carriage road, turn right and travel another 0.4 mile, bearing left at carriage road intersection No. 13, back to the Parkman Mountain parking area.

To go down the Hadlock Brook Trail, turn right at the second junction off the Sargent Mountain South Ridge Trail. Head down 1.4 miles to the second carriage road crossing. Turn right on the carriage road and travel another 0.4 mile, bearing left at carriage road intersection No. 13 back to the Park-man Mountain parking area.

52 Hadlock Brook Trail

Highlights: Steep, less-traveled trail up to Sargent Mountain.
Type of hike: Day hike; out-and-back or as part of loop.
Total distance: 4.2 miles.
Difficulty: Strenuous.

Hadlock Brook Trail

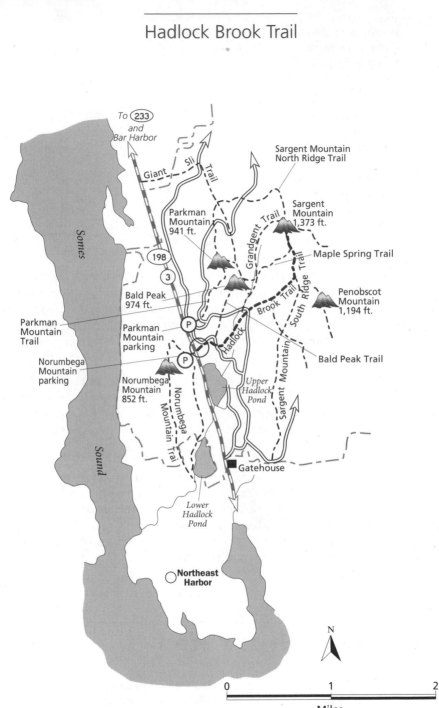

To (233) and Bar Harbor

Sargent Mountain North Ridge Trail

Giant Sli Trail

Parkman Mountain 941 ft.

Grandgent Trail

Sargent Mountain 1,373 ft.

Maple Spring Trail

(198)

(3)

Bald Peak 974 ft.

Brook Trail

South Ridge Trail

Penobscot Mountain 1,194 ft.

Parkman Mountain Trail

Parkman Mountain parking

P

Hadlock

Bald Peak Trail

Norumbega Mountain parking

P

Norumbega Mountain 852 ft.

Norumbega Mountain Trail

Upper Hadlock Pond

Sargent Mountain

Somes

Gatehouse

Lower Hadlock Pond

Sound

Northeast Harbor

N

0   1   2

Miles

Finding the trailhead: From Bar Harbor, head west on Maine Highway 233 for 4 miles, then left (south) on ME 198 for nearly 3 miles past the Parkman Mountain parking area to the Norumbega Mountain parking area. The Hadlock Brook Trailhead is on the left (east) side of ME 198, across from the Norumbega Mountain parking area.

Parking and trailhead facilities: Park at the Norumbega Mountain parking area. There are no facilities.

Key points:
- 0.0 Hadlock Brook Trailhead.
- 0.1 Junction with the Parkman Mountain Trail.
- 0.2 Junction with the Bald Peak Trail; cross a carriage road.
- 0.4 Junction with the Maple Spring Trail.
- 0.7 Cross a carriage road.
- 1.1 Junction with the Amphitheater Trail.
- 1.6 Junction with the Sargent Mountain South Ridge Trail; bear left to the summit.
- 2.1 Sargent Mountain summit; return the way you came.

The hike: This rough trail provides access to Sargent Mountain from the west and can be done as a loop with the equally steep Maple Spring Trail. Mosquitoes can be fierce near the beginning of the trail where it skirts a marshland north of Upper Hadlock Pond. Bring repellent.

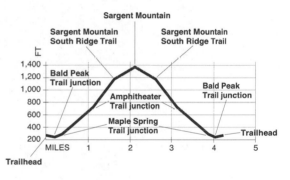

At 0.1 mile, the Parkman Mountain Trail heads left. At 0.2 mile, the Bald Peak Trail heads left and you cross the first of two carriage roads. And at 0.4 mile, the Maple Spring Trail goes left. Ascend to the second carriage road at 0.7 mile by the pink granite Waterfall Bridge.

On the other side of the road, the trail begins its rough, steep climb, repeatedly crossing Hadlock Brook. Reach a junction with the Amphitheater Trail at 1.1 miles. The footing is particularly tricky here, with roots snaking across the trail. Climb steeply through the woods and up the pink granite face. You know you're nearing the end of the steepest climb when you see a trail sign high up on the ridge ahead above treeline.

At 1.6 miles, reach the junction with the Sargent Mountain South Ridge Trail. Although the Hadlock Brook Trail officially ends here, turn left and head north on the ridge to reach the spectacular Sargent Mountain summit at 2.1 miles. Return the way you came.

The Grandgent Trail ends at the top of Sargent Mountain.

Options: You can loop back down from Sargent Mountain via the equally steep Maple Spring Trail. Heading south from the summit for 0.3 mile to the first trail junction, descend sharply right (southwest) off the ridge on the Maple Spring Trail. After another 0.9 mile, cross a carriage road. At the next trail junction in another 0.3 mile, bear right on to the Hadlock Brook Trail, looping back to the trailhead in another 0.4 mile. The loop is approximately 4 miles long.

53 Maple Spring Trail

Highlights: Steep, less-traveled trail up to Sargent Mountain.
Type of hike: Day hike; out-and-back.
Total distance: 3.8 miles, including 0.4 mile to reach trailhead.
Difficulty: Strenuous.

Finding the trailhead: From Bar Harbor, head west on Maine Highway 233 for 4 miles, then left (south) on ME 198 for nearly 3 miles past the Parkman Mountain parking area to the Norumbega Mountain parking area. The Hadlock Brook Trailhead is on the left (east) side of ME 198, across from the Norumbega Mountain parking area. Follow the Hadlock Brook Trail for 0.4 mile to reach the Maple Spring Trailhead on the left.

Parking and trailhead facilities: Park at the Norumbega Mountain parking area. There are no facilities.

Key points:

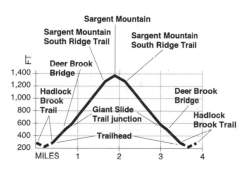

0.0   Norumbega Mountain parking area.
0.4   Maple Spring Trailhead via the Hadlock Brook Trail.
0.7   Deer Brook Bridge.
0.8   Junction with the Giant Slide Trail.
1.6   Junction with the Sargent Mountain South Ridge Trail; bear left to the Sargent Mountain summit.
1.9   Sargent Mountain summit; return the way you came.

The hike: There's not much difference between this and the Hadlock Brook Trail. They're both steep, rocky routes up to the Sargent Mountain ridge, with lots of brook crossings. But the Maple Spring Trail does end a bit closer to the summit of Sargent than the Hadlock Brook Trail and goes by the double-arched Deer Brook Bridge on the carriage road rather than by the Waterfall Bridge.

Hike 0.4 mile on the Hadlock Brook Trail to reach the Maple Spring Trailhead; then head left (north-northeast). At 0.7 mile, go under the carriage road's

Maple Spring Trail

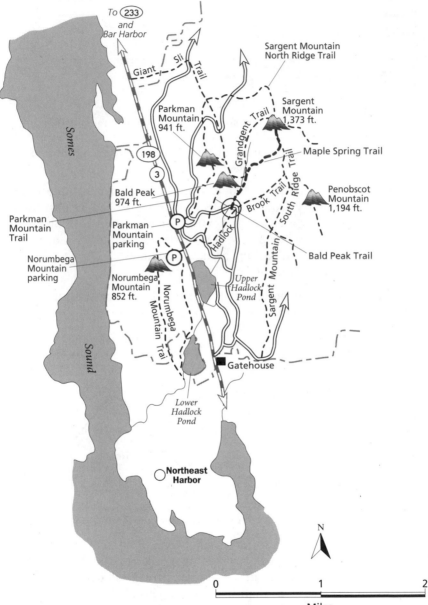

To 233 and Bar Harbor

Giant Sli Trail

Parkman Mountain 941 ft.

Sargent Mountain North Ridge Trail

Sargent Mountain 1,373 ft.

Grandgent Trail

Maple Spring Trail

Somes

198

3

Bald Peak 974 ft.

Penobscot Mountain 1,194 ft.

Brook Trail

South Ridge Trail

Parkman Mountain Trail

Parkman Mountain parking

P

Hadlock

Bald Peak Trail

Norumbega Mountain parking

P

Norumbega Mountain 852 ft.

Upper Hadlock Pond

Norumbega Mountain Trail

Sargent Mountain

Sound

Gatehouse

Lower Hadlock Pond

Northeast Harbor

N

0   1   2

Miles

Deer Brook Bridge. The Giant Slide Trail bears left (north) at 0.8 mile. Ascend steeply until you reach the junction with the Sargent Mountain South Ridge Trail at 1.6 miles. The trail officially ends here, but turn left (north) and reach Sargent Mountain summit at 1.9 miles. Return the way you came.

54 Parkman Mountain Trail

Highlights: 360-degree views from 941-foot summit of Parkman Mountain.
Type of hike: Day hike; out-and-back.
Total distance: 2.4 miles, plus 0.1 mile to reach trailhead.
Difficulty: Moderate to strenuous.

Finding the trailhead: From Bar Harbor, head west on Maine Highway 233 for 4 miles, then left (south) on ME 198 for another 2.5 miles to the Parkman Mountain parking area on the left (east) side of the road. Bear right on a carriage road, then left at carriage road intersection No. 13 to reach the trailhead on the left (north) side of the carriage road, in about 0.1 mile.

Parking and trailhead facilities: Park at the Parkman Mountain parking area or Norumbega Mountain parking area farther south on ME 198. The only facility is a chemical toilet at the Parkman Mountain parking area.

Key points:
    0.0   Parkman Mountain Trailhead, reached after 0.1 mile on a carriage road.
    0.1   Cross a carriage road.
    1.1   Junction with the Bald Peak Trail.
    1.2   Parkman Mountain summit; junction with a spur to the Giant Slide Trail.

The hike: The great views from Parkman Mountain make this a popular little trail. The trail heads north from the carriage road off the parking area, crossing another carriage road at 0.1 mile. Parallel the carriage road for a bit, then take a right at a huge rock.

The trail soon takes a sharp left. Just about halfway up, at treeline, a lone iron rung helps you up a rock face. Next, in a series of switchbacks, the trail ascends the open ridge, with views west to Somes Sound and south to the Gulf of Maine. Watch for loose gravel on the path. As the trail takes you higher, you get glimpses of Upper and Lower Hadlock Ponds to the south. The trail levels off a bit and enters a short stretch of woods with huge birch trees, then begins a steep climb up dramatic pink granite ledges.

At 1.1 miles, the Bald Peak Trail heads to the right (east). Reach Parkman Mountain summit at 1.2 miles, where a spur trail leads right (east) to the

Parkman Mountain Trail

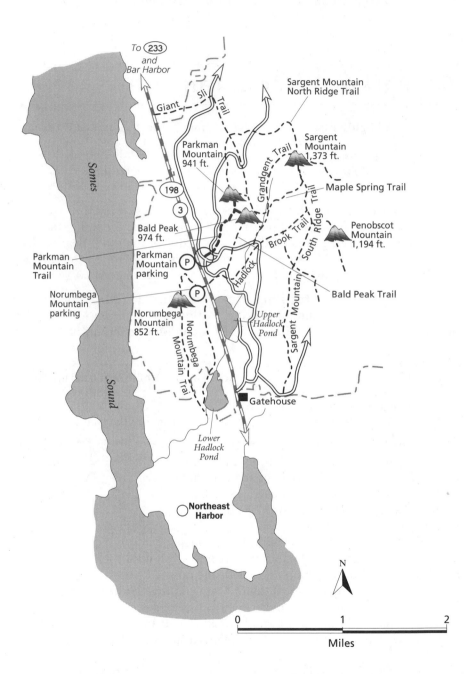

To (233)
and
Bar Harbor

Giant Sli Trail

Sargent Mountain
North Ridge Trail

Parkman
Mountain
941 ft.

Grandgent Trail

Sargent
Mountain
1,373 ft.

Maple Spring Trail

198

3

Bald Peak
974 ft.

Brook Trail

South Ridge Trail

Penobscot
Mountain
1,194 ft.

Parkman
Mountain
Trail

Parkman
Mountain
parking

P

Hadlock

Bald Peak Trail

Norumbega
Mountain
parking

P

Somes

Norumbega
Mountain
852 ft.

Norumbega Mountain Trail

Upper
Hadlock
Pond

Sargent Mountain

Sound

Gatehouse

Lower
Hadlock
Pond

Northeast
Harbor

N

0   1   2

Miles

Giant Slide Trail. From the open summit, you can see Bald Peak to the southeast; Sargent Mountain to the east; Somes Sound, Western Mountain, and Norumbega Mountain to the west; and the Gulf of Maine to the south. While Parkman summit is a natural ending point for the hike, the trail does continue north down the ridge on the other side for another 0.7 mile, crossing a carriage road and ending at a junction with the Giant Slide and Sargent Mountain North Ridge Trails. Return the way you came.

Options: You can loop back via Bald Peak. On the return from the summit of Parkman Mountain, bear left (east) over Bald Peak. Head down the Bald Peak Trail and turn right (west) on the first carriage road. At the fork in the road, bear left to get back to the Parkman Mountain parking area.

For an especially ambitious 5.1-mile loop up Sargent Mountain, take the Parkman Mountain trail north beyond Parkman summit across a carriage road to the junction with the Giant Slide and Sargent Mountain North Ridge trails. Head up the 1.3-mile-long Sargent Mountain North Ridge Trail, passing a junction with the Grandgent Trail, to the Sargent summit. Head down on the Sargent Mountain South Ridge Trail for 0.3 mile, and turn right (southwest) to descend 0.9 mile on the steep Maple Spring Trail. At the first carriage road, turn right (west) and walk 0.5 mile. Bear left at the fork in the carriage road to get back to the Parkman Mountain parking area in another 0.2 mile.

55 Bald Peak Trail

Highlights:	360-degree views from 974-foot summit of Bald Peak.
Type of hike:	Day hike; out-and-back, or part of loop up Parkman Mountain.
Total distance:	1.8 miles, including 0.2 mile to reach trailhead, or 2.7-mile loop up Parkman Mountain.
Difficulty:	Moderate.

Finding the trailhead: From Bar Harbor, head west on Maine Highway 233 for 4 miles then left (south) on ME 198 for nearly 3 miles past the Parkman Mountain parking area to the Norumbega Mountain parking area. The Hadlock Brook Trailhead is on the left (east) side of ME 198 across from the Norumbega Mountain parking area. Follow the Hadlock Brook Trail 0.2 mile to reach the Bald Peak Trailhead on the left.

Parking and trailhead facilities: Park at Norumbega Mountain parking area. There are no facilities.

Key points:
- 0.0 Norumbega Mountain parking area.
- 0.2 Bald Peak Trailhead, reached via Hadlock Brook Trail.
- 0.9 Bald Peak summit.

Bald Peak Trail

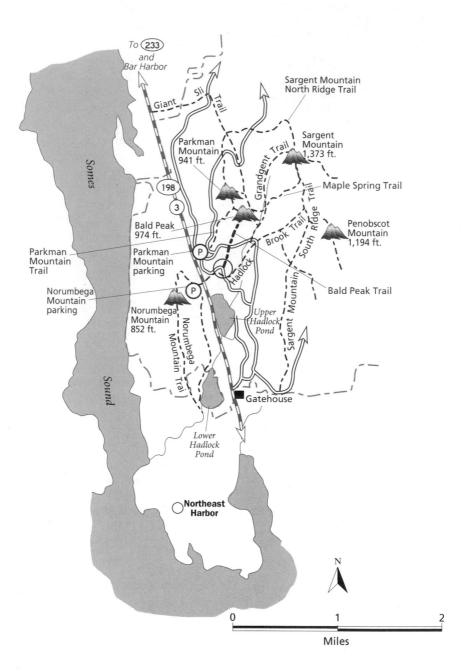

To (233) and Bar Harbor

Giant Sli Trail

Sargent Mountain North Ridge Trail

Parkman Mountain 941 ft.

Grandgent Trail

Sargent Mountain 1,373 ft.

Maple Spring Trail

198

3

Somes

Bald Peak 974 ft.

Brook Trail

South Ridge Trail

Penobscot Mountain 1,194 ft.

Parkman Mountain Trail

Parkman Mountain parking

P

Hadlock

Sargent Mountain

Bald Peak Trail

Norumbega Mountain parking

P

Norumbega Mountain 852 ft.

Upper Hadlock Pond

Sound

Norumbega Mountain Trail

Gatehouse

Lower Hadlock Pond

Northeast Harbor

N

0   1   2

Miles

The hike: Bald Peak offers great views with little effort, as does the nearby Parkman Mountain. But the proximity of ME 198 to the trail means you can sometimes hear the traffic on the way up, and you'll most likely have company at the top. You will also need to bring insect repellent, especially after a rain. Luckily, it doesn't take long to reach more open terrain, where the wind can keep the mosquitoes at bay.

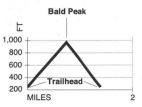

The Bald Peak Trail, which leads left (north) off the Hadlock Brook Trail, immediately crosses a carriage road then ascends fairly steeply up rocky ledges. The trail dips down a bit, circling around the back of some of the ledges you just climbed up. A final clamber up a rock face brings you to Bald Peak at 0.9 mile, with 360-degrees views of Sargent Mountain and Gilmore Peak to the right (east), Parkman Mountain to the north, Norumbega Mountain to the west, and the Cranberry Isles to the south. Chances are you can also see hikers on the nearby Gilmore Peak and Parkman Mountain. Return the way you came.

Options: To do a loop up Parkman Mountain, bear left (west) off Bald Peak, into a dip in the trail. In another 0.2 mile, reach a junction with the Parkman Mountain Trail. Turn right (north) and reach that summit in another 0.1 mile. Descend the summit the same way, back to the trail junction between Parkman Mountain and Bald Peak. Turn right (west) to loop back down on the Parkman Mountain Trail, rather than left to get back onto the Bald Peak Trail. Head 1.4 miles southwest toward ME 198. Cross three carriage roads and turn right on the Hadlock Brook Trail to return to the Norumbega Mountain parking area. The loop is approximately 2.7 miles.

56 Norumbega Mountain Trail (Goat Trail)

Highlights:	Views atop Norumbega of Somes Sound and Western Mountain.
Type of hike:	Day hike; out-and-back.
Total distance:	3.8 miles.
Difficulty:	Strenuous.

Finding the trailhead: From Bar Harbor, head west on Maine Highway 233 for 4 miles, then left (south) on ME 198 for nearly 3 miles, past the Parkman Mountain parking area, to the Norumbega Mountain parking area on the right (west) side of the road. The trailhead is at the northern end of the lot.

Parking and trailhead facilities: Park at the Norumbega Mountain parking area. There are no facilities.

Norumbega Mountain Trail (Goat Trail)

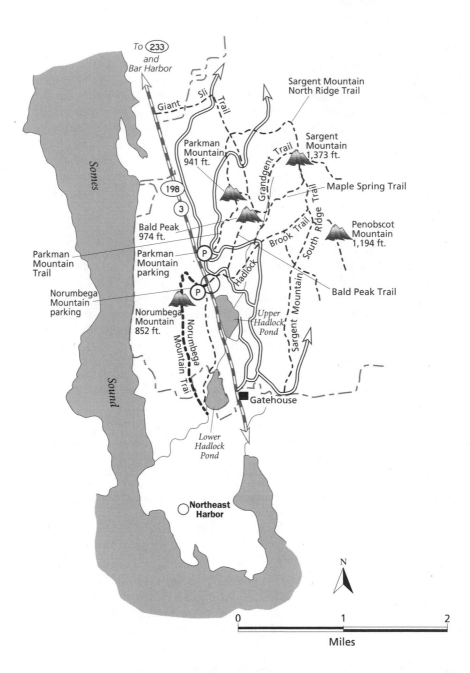

To (233)
and
Bar Harbor

Sargent Mountain
North Ridge Trail

Giant Sli Trail

Parkman
Mountain
941 ft.

Grandgent Trail

Sargent
Mountain
1,373 ft.

Maple Spring Trail

198

3

Somes

Bald Peak
974 ft.

Brook Trail

South Ridge Trail

Penobscot
Mountain
1,194 ft.

Parkman
Mountain
Trail

Parkman
Mountain
parking

P

Hadlock

Bald Peak Trail

Norumbega
Mountain
parking

P

Norumbega
Mountain
852 ft.

Norumbega Mountain Trail

Upper
Hadlock
Pond

Sargent Mountain

Sound

Gatehouse

Lower
Hadlock
Pond

Northeast
Harbor

N

0   1   2

Miles

Key points:
- 0.0   Norumbega Mountain Trailhead.
- 0.5   Norumbega Mountain summit.
- 1.2   Junction with a spur to the golf course; bear left.
- 1.9   Lower Hadlock Pond.
- 3.8   Return the way you came.

The hike: Norumbega Mountain parallels the eastern edge of Somes Sound, providing fine views of the fjord and mountains to the west. The toughest part of this hike is at the beginning, with a short, steep climb to the mountaintop along open ledges. This part of the trail is sometimes referred to as the Goat Trail.

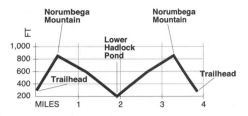

Reach the 852-foot summit at 0.5 mile, soon after the trail turns sharply south. A weather-beaten sign marks the summit, as well as a stone with this inscription: "M.C.M. 1943-1982." The fine views here include Parkman Mountain to the east, Somes Sound to the west, and the Cranberry Isles to the south. We've seen rare pink and yellow lady's slippers off this trail. Many people turn around here for a 1-mile round trip. The trail next descends the long south ridge with more views along the way, west to Western Mountain and east to Sargent Mountain. At 1.2 miles, after a sharp climb down, reach a junction with a spur to a golf club. Bear left toward Lower Hadlock Pond. Reach the shore of Lower Hadlock Pond at 1.9 miles, where there is a nice view to the northeast of Bald Peak. Return the way you came.

Options: It's possible to do a loop by turning left at Lower Hadlock Pond and walking along the northwest shore toward Upper Hadlock Pond. At the north end of Lower Hadlock, cross a log bridge and walk by beautiful cascades and waterfalls. Cross another wooden bridge, then turn left and continue back to the Norumbega Mountain parking area.

From Bald Peak, you can see Parkman Mountain ahead.

159

MOUNT DESERT ISLAND, WEST OF SOMES SOUND

This is the quieter side of the island. The major Acadia National Park trails here go up and around such landmarks as Acadia, St. Sauveur, and Flying mountains; Beech Mountain; Beech Cliff; Long Pond; Echo Lake; and Bernard and Mansell mountains, known collectively as Western Mountain. The most popular trails in this section of Mount Desert Island are Acadia and Flying mountains, with their close-up views of Somes Sound; Beech Mountain with its fire tower; and Beech Cliff with its views down to Echo Lake. The highest peak in this part of the park is Bernard Mountain, at 1,071 feet. The summits of both Bernard and Mansell are wooded and therefore relatively less climbed, but there are views from nearby observation points and along some of the trails' rocky ledges. The most popular starting point for trails up these mountains is at the Long Pond pumping station. Less-traveled trails up Bernard or Mansell begin off either the gravel Western Mountain Road or Long Pond Fire Road.

Mount Desert Island, West of Somes Sound

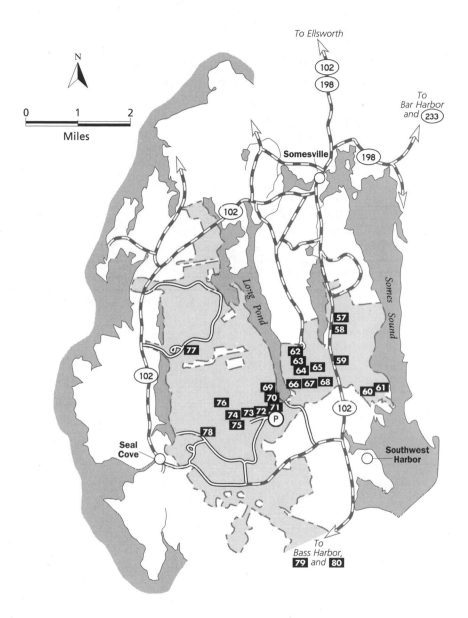

57 Acadia Mountain Trail

Highlights: Views of Somes Sound, Echo Lake, Gulf of Maine, Cranberry Isles, and surrounding mountains.
Type of hike: Day hike; loop.
Total distance: 2.8 miles.
Difficulty: Strenuous.

Finding the trailhead: From Somesville, head south on Maine Highway 102 for 3 miles, past Ikes Point, to the Acadia Mountain parking lot. The trailhead is on the left (east) side of ME 102.

Parking and trailhead facilities: The Acadia Mountain parking lot is on the right (west) side of ME 102. The only facility is a chemical toilet.

Key points:
- 0.0 Acadia Mountain Trailhead.
- 0.1 Junction with the St. Sauveur Mountain Trail; bear left.
- 0.2 Cross the gravel Man O' War Truck Road.
- 0.8 Acadia Mountain summit.
- 1.1 Robinson Mountain.
- 1.7 Junction with the spur to Man O' War Truck Road and the spur to Man O' War Brook; turn left to the brook.
- 1.8 Man O' War Brook.
- 1.9 Return to the junction with the spur to Man O' War Truck Road; head straight on the road.
- 2.6 Junction; turn left into the woods.
- 2.7 Bear right at a junction.
- 2.8 Return to ME 102 and the parking lot.

The hike: One of Acadia's more popular trails west of Somes Sound, the Acadia Mountain Trail is a tough scramble up to spectacular views of Somes Sound, the ocean, and surrounding mountains. But as strenuous as it is, you may see families with small children making the trek.

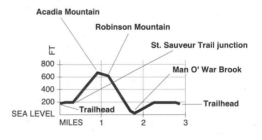

At the junction with the St. Sauveur Mountain Trail at 0.1 mile, bear left toward Acadia Mountain. At 0.2 mile, cross the gravel Man O' War Truck Road and continue on the Acadia Mountain Trail. Now the rough climb begins. At times you need to pull yourself up 20-foot-long rock crevices. Although the trail here is largely well marked with cairns, there is a sharp left that is easy to miss. The trail continues to climb steadily through forest, then takes you up a rocky section with switchbacks. You may hear the sound of boats on Somes Sound, and you'll soon get good views of the fjord. Resume the steep ascent up the rock face via switchbacks.

Acadia Mountain Trail

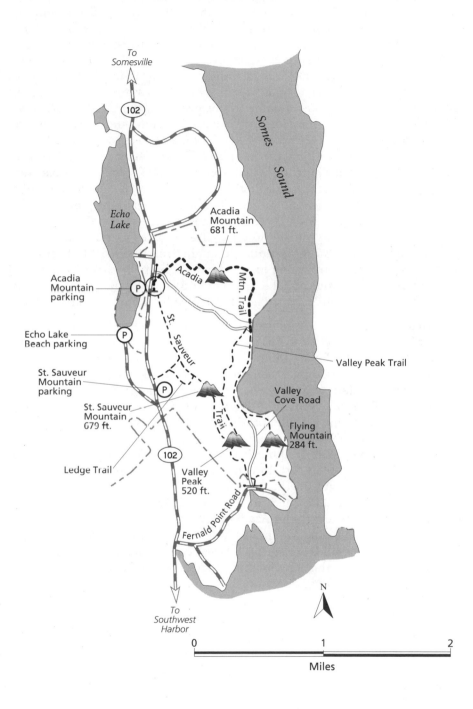

To
Somesville

102

Somes Sound

Echo
Lake

Acadia
Mountain
681 ft.

Acadia Mtn. Trail

Acadia
Mountain
parking

P

Echo Lake
Beach parking

P

St. Sauveur Trail

Valley Peak Trail

St. Sauveur
Mountain
parking

P

Valley
Cove Road

St. Sauveur
Mountain
679 ft.

Flying
Mountain
284 ft.

Ledge Trail

102

Valley
Peak
520 ft.

Fernald Point Road

To
Southwest
Harbor

N

0   1   2

Miles

You'll see Echo Lake for the first time behind you, to the west. The trail levels off a bit now as you reach the 681-foot Acadia Mountain summit at 0.8 mile. Here, from a rock promontory, you get expansive views of Somes Sound, as well as of Somesville to the north and the Gulf of Maine and the Cranberry Isles to the south. There's also a hidden trail that leads to the right, providing great views of Northeast Harbor and Southwest Harbor.

You may choose to turn around here, even though better and closer views of the sound await you farther on. The trail next takes you steeply down jagged rock. At 1.1 miles you come to a gorgeous view atop a broad open summit. There is no sign here giving a name to this peak, but the USGS map shows this as Robinson Mountain. Here you can see Beech Mountain with its fire tower to the west; Valley Cove, and the Gulf of Maine to the south; and Somes Sound and Norumbega Mountain to the east. The trail next descends steeply.

At 1.7 miles, reach a junction with a spur to Man O' War Truck Road and a spur to Man O' War Brook. Turn left (southeast) to get a view of the brook cascading down into Somes Sound, at 1.8 miles. Return to the junction with the spur to the Man O' War Truck Road, following the gravel road northwest back to where the Acadia Mountain Trail crosses it at 2.6 miles. Turn left into the woods onto the Acadia Mountain Trail, then right at the next junction at 2.7 miles, returning to the Acadia Mountain parking lot at 2.8 miles. Alternatively, you can take the Man O' War Truck Road until it ends at ME 102, then left on ME 102 back to the Acadia Mountain parking lot.

Options: For a rigorous 5.5-mile loop, rather than heading back on the Man O' War Truck Road, follow the sign at another junction that's closer to Man O' War Brook toward Flying Mountain. The 1.6-mile long Flying Mountain Trail takes you south along the rocky shore of Somes Sound and Valley Cove, over Flying Mountain with its great views of the narrows at the mouth of the sound and Fernald Point, and down to a parking area. Cross the parking area, turn right for 0.1 mile on the gravel Valley Cove Road, and then left onto the Valley Peak Trail.

Follow the Valley Peak Trail northwest 0.4 mile to Valley Peak. Continue northwest, taking the left fork toward the wooded summit of St. Sauveur Mountain. Stay straight on the 1.6-mile-long St. Sauveur Trail along the mountain ridge, until it descends to the junction with the Acadia Mountain Trail. Turn left to return to the Acadia Mountain parking area. The Valley Cove section of the Flying Mountain Trail may be closed during peregrine falcon breeding season from spring to late summer, as it was for the first time in 2000, making this long loop impossible to do. Check with the park officials before attempting this route.

58 St. Sauveur Trail

> **Highlights:** Wooded St. Sauveur Mountain; views from Valley Peak.
> **Type of hike:** Day hike; out-and-back.
> **Total distance:** 3.2 miles.
> **Difficulty:** Moderate.

Finding the trailhead: From Somesville, head south on Maine Highway 102 for about 3 miles, past Ikes Point to the Acadia Mountain parking lot. The trailhead is on the left (east) side of ME 102.

Parking and trailhead facilities: The Acadia Mountain parking lot is on the right (west) side of ME 102. The only facility is a chemical toilet.

Key points:
- 0.0 St. Sauveur Trailhead.
- 0.1 Junction with the Acadia Mountain Trail; bear right (south).
- 0.7 Junction with the north end of the Ledge Trail.
- 1.0 Junction with the south end of the Ledge Trail.
- 1.2 St. Sauveur Mountain summit.
- 1.6 Valley Peak summit.

The hike: This is not the shortest or most scenic route to the peaks on the west shore of Somes Sound. But the St. Sauveur Trail provides relatively easy ridge walking and serves as an important link for ambitious hikers wanting to do a long multiple-peak loop. First

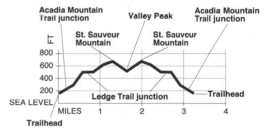

described in the late 1800s and early 1900s as the Dog Mountain Trail, after the former name of St. Sauveur Mountain, the trail begins across ME 102 from what can be a crowded Acadia Mountain parking area during the height of the season. Most hikers head to Acadia Mountain from here, so the St. Sauveur is the trail less traveled.

At 0.1 mile from the trailhead, at a junction with the Acadia Mountain Trail, turn right (south) and head toward St. Sauveur Mountain. You'll get views toward Echo Lake to the northwest and Long Pond to the west as you reach some open ledges. The trees here are predominantly gnarled pitch pines and cedars. Once you attain the ridge at 0.4 mile, the trail stays fairly level but zigzags a bit, so follow it carefully. At one particularly tricky spot, where the trail zigs left, some hikers have mistakenly gone straight—if a short, well-worn path that dead-ends is an indication. Someone laid a log across the path to discourage others from making the same mistake.

At 0.7 mile, you'll reach a junction with the north end of the Ledge Trail, which comes in from the right. Continue straight (southeast) on the St.

St. Sauveur Trail

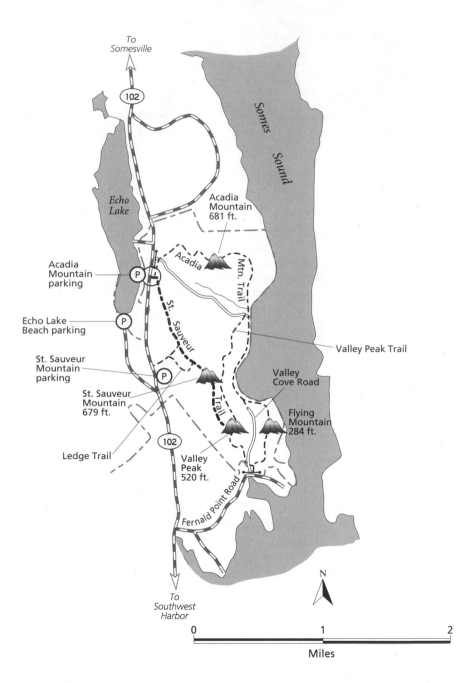

To
Somesville

102

Somes

Sound

Echo
Lake

Acadia
Mountain
681 ft.

Acadia
Mountain
parking

Acadia

Mtn. Trail

Echo Lake
Beach parking

St. Sauveur

Valley Peak Trail

St. Sauveur
Mountain
parking

Valley
Cove Road

St. Sauveur
Mountain
679 ft.

Flying
Mountain
284 ft.

Ledge Trail

Trail

102

Valley
Peak
520 ft.

Fernald Point Road

To
Southwest
Harbor

N

0   1   2

Miles

Sauveur Trail, passing a junction with the southern end of the Ledge Trail at 1 mile. Reach the wooded summit of 679-foot St. Sauveur Mountain at 1.2 miles. A trail sign near the summit indicates two routes to Valley Peak. Head straight on the St. Sauveur Trail (south) for the less confusing route.

Reach Valley Peak on the shoulder of St. Sauveur Mountain at 1.6 miles. Although only 520 feet in elevation, Valley Peak offers grand vistas of the nearby Greening Island, the more distant Cranberry Isles, Northeast Harbor, Fernald Cove, and the narrows at the mouth of Somes Sound, the only fjord on the east coast of the United States. The St. Sauveur Trail officially ends here. Return the way you came for a 3.2-mile round trip.

Options: For a 3.7-mile loop that takes you along open ledges with views of Somes Sound, and then steeply down, turn left (northeast) at Valley Peak. Follow the Valley Peak Trail and reach a junction near the gravel Man O' War Truck Road in another 1.1 miles. Turn left (northwest) on to the gravel road, and travel another 0.8 mile to a junction with the Acadia Mountain Trail. From here, head left (southwest) for 0.1 mile, then turn right (northwest) onto the St. Sauveur Trail, returning to your car in another 0.1 mile.

For a lengthy 4.9-mile loop incorporating the open summit of Flying Mountain and a rugged shoreline walk along Somes Sound, turn right (southwest) at Valley Peak and descend the Valley Peak Trail for 0.4 mile to the gravel Valley Cove Road. Turn right and travel 0.2 mile on the gravel road to a parking area and the Flying Mountain Trailhead. Take the 1.7-mile-long Flying Mountain Trail northeast, over Flying Mountain and along the rocky shore of Somes Sound, until it reaches a junction near the gravel Man O' War Truck Road. Turn left (northwest) onto the gravel road, and travel another 0.8 mile to a junction with the Acadia Mountain Trail. From here, head left (southwest) for 0.1 mile, then turn right (northwest) on to the St. Sauveur Trail, returning to your car in another 0.1 mile.

59 Ledge Trail

Highlights:	Shortest route to wooded summit of St. Sauveur Mountain; views from Valley Peak.
Type of hike:	Day hike; loop.
Total distance:	2.6 miles.
Difficulty:	Moderate.

Finding the trailhead: From Somesville, head south on Maine Highway 102 for 3.5 miles to a sign for St. Sauveur Mountain. The trailhead is on the east side of ME 102.

Parking and trailhead facilities: The St. Sauveur Mountain parking lot is on the left (east) side of ME 102. There are no facilities.

Key points:
0.0 Ledge Trailhead.
0.2 Junction; bear right (southeast) toward St. Sauveur Mountain.

Ledge Trail

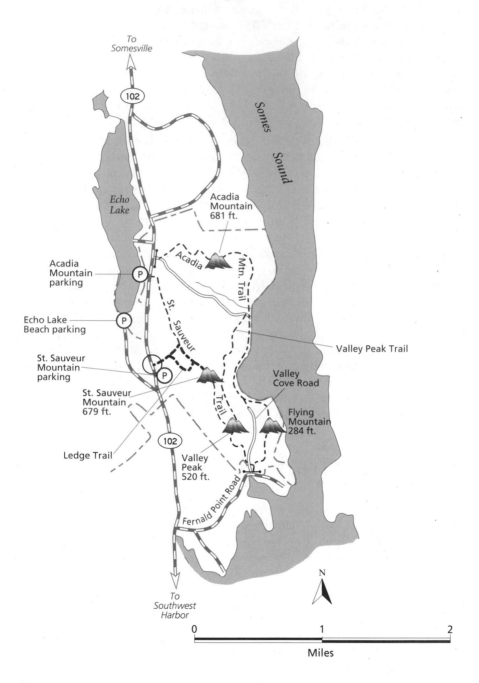

To
Somesville

102

Somes Sound

Echo
Lake

Acadia
Mountain
681 ft.

Acadia

Mtn. Trail

Acadia
Mountain
parking

P

St. Sauveur

Echo Lake
Beach parking

P

Valley Peak Trail

St. Sauveur
Mountain
parking

P

Valley
Cove Road

St. Sauveur
Mountain
679 ft.

Trail

Flying
Mountain
284 ft.

102

Ledge Trail

Valley
Peak
520 ft.

Fernald Point Road

To
Southwest
Harbor

N

0   1   2

Miles

0.6　Junction with the St. Sauveur Trail; bear right (southeast).

0.8　St. Sauveur Mountain summit.

1.2　Valley Peak summit.

1.8　Retrace your steps northwest along the St. Sauveur Trail; skip the first junction with the Ledge Trail.

2.1　Turn left (southwest) at the second junction with the Ledge Trail.

2.4　Bear right at a junction.

2.6　Ledge Trailhead.

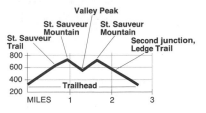

The hike: Built in the early 1900s, the Ledge Trail is a loop that connects to the St. Sauveur Trail and provides the shortest way up the 679-foot wooded summit of St. Sauveur Mountain. It also provides a less strenuous approach to the views of Valley Peak than the shorter but steeper Valley Peak Trail.

From the Ledge Trailhead, go left over a wooden bridge and take a sharp left along a rock face. Climb gradually up stone steps to a junction at 0.2 mile. Head right (southeast) toward St. Sauveur Mountain. The trail climbs fairly steeply up a wooded mountainside here with rocks and roots along the way. Follow the blue blazes along the rocky ledges that the trail is named

after. When the trail begins to curve left (north), views of the fire tower on Beech Mountain are visible through the trees to the west. At 0.6 mile, reach a junction with the St. Sauveur Trail. Bear right (southeast).

Reach the wooded summit of St. Sauveur Mountain at 0.8 mile and continue straight to Valley Peak at 1.2 miles for the views. Retrace your steps north on the St. Sauveur Trail, turning left not at the first junction with the Ledge Trail at 1.8 miles, but at the second one at 2.1 miles. Bear right at the junction at 2.4 miles, closing the Ledge Trail loop, and return to your car at 2.6 miles.

Man O' War Brook tumbles into Somes Sound at the base of Acadia Mountain.

60 Valley Peak Trail

Highlights:	Great views of the Cranberry Isles, Somes Sound, Norumbega, Sargent, and Penobscot mountains.
Type of hike:	Day hike; out-and-back or part of loop with Flying Mountain Trail.
Total distance:	3 miles.
Difficulty:	Moderate to strenuous.

Finding the trailhead: From Somesville, head south on Maine Highway 102 for 4.5 miles, past the St. Sauveur Mountain parking lot. Turn left (east) onto Fernald Point Road, and travel 1 mile to the foot of gravel Valley Cove Road. The trailhead is down Valley Cove Road 0.2 mile on the left (west) side of the gravel road.

Parking and trailhead facilities: There is a small parking area on Fernald Point Road at the foot of gravel Valley Cove Road, but no facilities.

Key points:
- 0.0   Valley Peak Trailhead.
- 0.4   Valley Peak; junction with the south end of the St. Sauveur Trail; bear right.
- 0.7   Junction with a spur to St. Sauveur Mountain; bear right.
- 1.5   Man O' War truck road.

The hike: The Valley Peak Trail provides some of the most spectacular views of the Cranberry Isles and of Somes Sound, the only fjord on the east coast of the United States. A short but steep climb from the trailhead brings you to the 520-foot Valley Peak at 0.4 mile. The view to

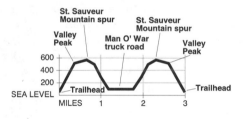

the southeast includes the nearby Greening Island, the more distant Cranberry Isles, Northeast Harbor, Fernald Cove, and the narrows at the mouth of Somes Sound.

Bear right (northeast) to continue along the Valley Peak Trail. Somes Sound soon appears below you as the trail continues north on the ridge that parallels the fjord. Although the vistas are as grand as anything you might get from a much higher elevation, the sound of motor boats and people talking, especially during the summer, reminds you of how low the trail really is. Next, the trail crosses rocky ledges, going in and out of the woods and up and down the ridge, with frequent views of the sound and the Cranberry Isles. East, across the sound, rise Sargent, Penobscot, Parkman, Bald, and Norumbega mountains.

At 0.7 mile, reach a junction with a short spur to the wooded summit of St. Sauveur Mountain. Eagle Cliff is below you here, facing the sound. Bear right (north) along the main trail, which has now leveled off. Low blueberry bushes border the trail. Then the steep descent to Man O' War truck road

Valley Peak Trail

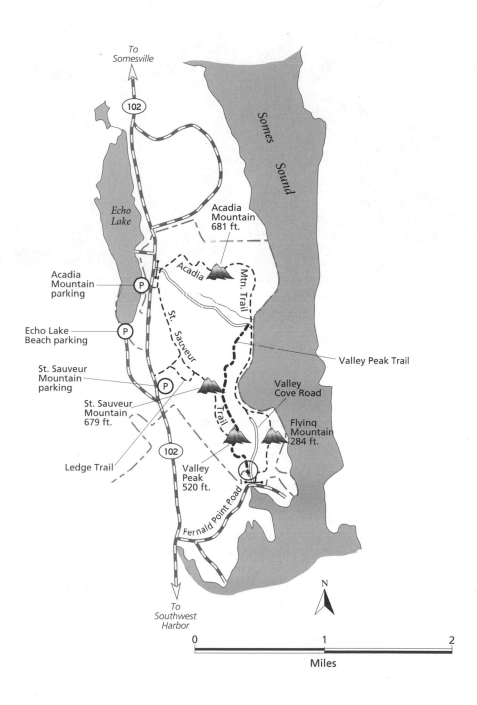

To Somesville

102

Somes Sound

Echo Lake

Acadia Mountain 681 ft.

Acadia Mountain parking

Echo Lake Beach parking

St. Sauveur Mountain parking

St. Sauveur Mountain 679 ft.

Ledge Trail

102

Acadia Mtn. Trail

St. Sauveur Trail

Valley Peak Trail

Valley Cove Road

Flying Mountain 284 ft.

Valley Peak 520 ft.

Fernald Point Road

To Southwest Harbor

N

0   1   2

Miles

From the Valley Peak Trail, some super scenes of Somes Sound, the only fjord on the eastern seaboard.

begins, with switchbacks and slick rock faces to navigate. More blueberry bushes and low-lying juniper line the trail.

As the trail goes farther below treeline, you'll see giant moosewood with its distinctive striped bark and large maple leaf. The trail levels off and crosses a log bridge over a creek and a series of stone steps. Turn right and you'll soon reach a junction marked by a trail sign at 1.4 miles. The gravel Man O' War truck road is to the left at 1.5 miles.

Return the way you came, if you don't mind the steep climb back up, or do a less-strenuous 3.2-mile loop by returning along the rocky shores of Somes Sound and over Flying Mountain. But be aware that the section of the Flying Mountain Trail near Valley Cove may be closed from spring to late summer, if peregrine falcon chicks have hatched here, as they did for the first time in decades in 2000. If it's possible to do the loop, turn right at the junction near Man O' War truck road and turn right again to follow the 1.7-mile-long Flying Mountain Trail back to your car.

Options: For a longer 4.5-mile loop, turn left at the end of the Valley Peak Trail onto the gravel Man O' War truck road. Travel 0.8 mile on the gravel road, and turn left (southwest) at the junction with the Acadia Mountain Trail. Stay straight as the trail joins the St. Sauveur Trail, leading over St. Sauveur Mountain and on to Valley Peak in another 1.6 miles. Bear right at Valley Peak back on to the Valley Peak Trail, and descend 0.4 mile southwest to

Valley Peak affords sweeping views of Greening Island and the Cranberry Isles.

the gravel Valley Cove Road. Turn right on the gravel road, returning to the parking area in another 0.2 mile.

For a shorter 1.8-mile loop, getting most of the views and avoiding the steep descent to Man O' War truck road, turn left (west) at the ridge overlooking Somes Sound onto the spur to St. Sauveur Mountain at 0.7 mile. Reach the wooded summit in another 0.1 mile, then turn left to head south on the St. Sauveur Trail, looping back to Valley Peak in another 0.4 mile. Bear right at Valley Peak back onto the Valley Peak Trail, and descend 0.4 mile southwest to the gravel Valley Cove Road. Turn right onto the gravel road, returning to the parking area in another 0.2 mile.

61 Flying Mountain Trail

Highlights:	Views of Somes Sound, Fernald Cove, and the Cranberry Isles.
Type of hike:	Day hike; out-and-back or loop.
Total distance:	3.2 miles.
Difficulty:	Moderate.

Finding the trailhead: From Somesville, head south on Maine Highway 102 for 4.5 miles, past the St. Sauveur Mountain parking lot. Turn left (east) onto Fernald Point Road, and travel 1 mile to the parking area at the foot of gravel Valley Cove Road. The trailhead is on the right (east) side of the parking area.

Parking and trailhead facilities: There is a small parking area on Fernald Point Road at the foot of gravel Valley Cove Road, but no facilities.

Key points:

0.0   Flying Mountain Trailhead.
0.3   Flying Mountain.
0.7   Junction with gravel Valley Cove Road.
0.9   Valley Cove.
1.6   Junction with trails to Acadia and St. Sauveur mountains, Valley Peak, and Man O' War Truck Road.

The hike: Flying Mountain is one of the lowest peaks in Acadia, yet it offers some of the best views. It can be climbed as part of a short out-and-back scramble of as little as a 0.6-mile round trip, or a longer loop of up to 4.6 miles. In 2000, for the first time in decades, peregrine falcon chicks hatched near the Valley

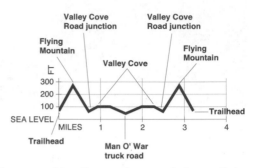

Cove section of the trail. While the most heavily used part of the trail (to Flying Mountain) remained open, the more northerly section by Valley Cove was closed as a result. Falcons are known to return to the same area to breed year after year, so the Valley Cove section of the trail may be closed in future years from spring to late summer.

The trail ascends swiftly from the parking area, first through deep woods and then up rocky ledges. At one point, the ledges serve as stone steps. Once you're above treeline and at the top of the rock face, you'll get views to the southeast of Greening Island and the Cranberry Isles. To the northwest are the rocky cliffs of Valley Peak, along the shoulder of St. Sauveur Mountain.

Dominating the view at the 284-foot Flying Mountain summit at 0.3 mile is the sandy peninsula known as Fernald Point. Across the narrows at the mouth of Somes Sound is the town of Northeast Harbor, and in the distance are Greening Island and the Cranberry Isles. From here, you can see kayakers rounding Fernald Point and boaters entering and leaving Somes Sound.

Some hikers turn around here, content with the views on Flying Mountain. But those who go on will be rewarded with scenes of Somes Sound and views of Norumbega, Penobscot, Sargent, and

Stone steps carry hikers over the rocky face of the Flying Mountain Trail.

174

Flying Mountain Trail

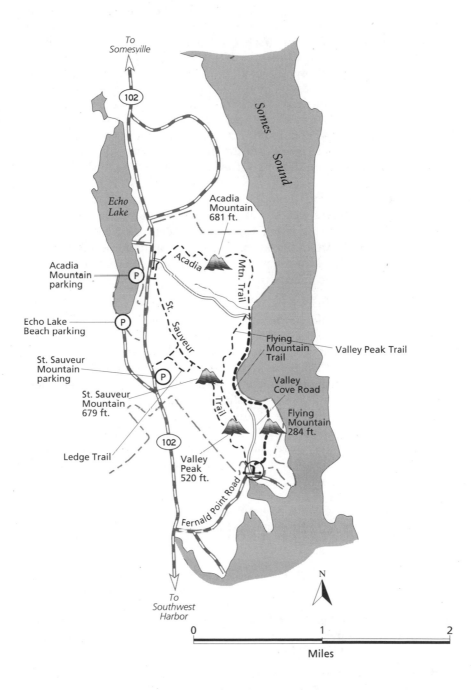

To
Somesville

102

Somes
Sound

Echo
Lake

Acadia
Mountain
681 ft.

Acadia
Mountain
parking

P

Acadia

Mtn. Trail

St. Sauveur

Echo Lake
Beach parking

P

Flying
Mountain
Trail

Valley Peak Trail

St. Sauveur
Mountain
parking

P

Valley
Cove Road

St. Sauveur
Mountain
679 ft.

Trail

Flying
Mountain
284 ft.

Ledge Trail

102

Valley
Peak
520 ft.

Fernald Point Road

N

To
Southwest
Harbor

0   1   2

Miles

other mountains of Acadia. They will also be challenged by the up-and-down nature of the trail along the rough, rocky shores of Valley Cove.

Just beyond the summit of Flying Mountain at 0.4 mile, you'll get the first glimpse of the northern reaches of Somes Sound, as well as of Acadia Mountain to the north and Norumbega Mountain on the other side of the sound to the northeast. The trail descends steeply toward Valley Cove and turns left (northwest) along the shore. At 0.7 mile, after crossing a creek that leads to the sound, you'll reach a junction with the gravel Valley Cove Road.

Continuing along the cove's rocky shore, the Flying Mountain Trail soon crosses huge boulders and rock faces. Pink granite steps take you over some of the biggest slabs. At one particularly treacherous spot when wet, you need to carefully make your way over a rock face to reach the top of a series of stone steps. The steps are held against the side of a cliff only with iron rods. Beyond Valley Cove, one more series of stone steps takes you up and over rocky cliffs. The trail then flattens out. A long series of log bridges takes you across a boggy area.

You'll soon cross a cool creek meandering into Somes Sound and climb a rocky ledge that offers views of St. Sauveur Mountain and a last glimpse of the sound. At 1.6 miles, reach a major intersection where trails diverge to Acadia Mountain, Valley Peak, St. Sauveur Mountain, and Man O' War truck road. The Flying Mountain Trail officially ends here. Return the way you came for a 3.2-mile round trip.

Options: For a 1.5-mile loop that skips the rocky shore of Valley Cove, turn left (southeast) at 0.7 mile at the junction with the gravel Valley Cove Road. Follow the road back to the parking area in another 0.8 mile. For an ambitious 4.7-mile loop that circles back on the St. Sauveur Trail over both St. Sauveur Mountain and Valley Peak, turn left at 1.7 miles onto the gravel Man O' War truck road. In another 0.8 mile, turn left (southwest) at the junction with the Acadia Mountain Trail. Stay straight as the trail joins the St. Sauveur Trail, leading over St. Sauveur Mountain and onto Valley Peak in another 1.6 miles. Bear right at Valley Peak, onto the Valley Peak Trail, and descend 0.4 mile southwest to the gravel Valley Cove Road. Turn right onto the gravel road, returning to the parking area in another 0.2 mile.

62 Beech Cliff Trail

Highlights:	Cliff-top views of Echo Lake and beyond; may be closed during peregrine falcon breeding season from spring to late summer.
Type of hike:	Day hike; loop.
Total distance:	0.8 mile.
Difficulty:	Moderate.

Finding the trailhead: Head south of Somesville on Maine Highway 102, turn right at the flashing yellow light toward Pretty Marsh. Take the second

Beech Cliff Trail

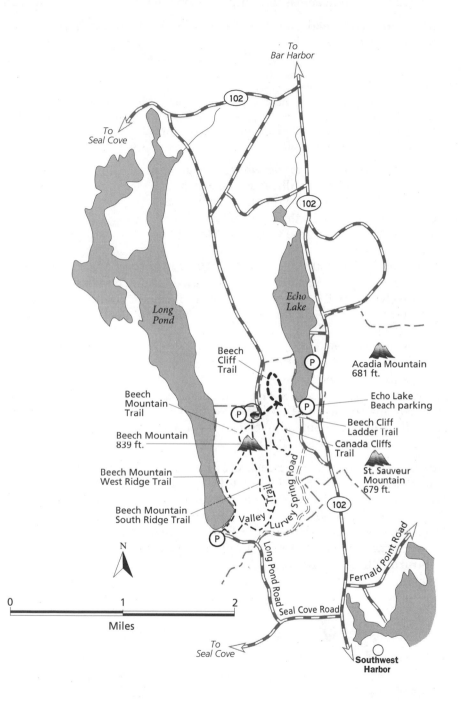

To
Bar Harbor

102

To
Seal Cove

102

Echo
Lake

Long
Pond

Beech
Cliff
Trail

P

Acadia Mountain
681 ft.

Beech
Mountain
Trail

P

P

Echo Lake
Beach parking

Beech Cliff
Ladder Trail

Beech Mountain
839 ft.

Canada Cliffs
Trail

St. Sauveur
Mountain
679 ft.

Beech Mountain
West Ridge Trail

Lurvey Spring Road

Beech Mountain
South Ridge Trail

Valley
Trail

P

Long Pond Road

Fernald Point Road

N

102

Seal Cove Road

0   1   2

Miles

To
Seal Cove

Southwest
Harbor

left onto Beech Hill Road, at a sign pointing to Beech Mountain and Beech Cliff. Follow Beech Hill Road 3.2 miles to the parking lot at the end. The trailhead leaves from across the parking lot on the left (east) side of the road.

Parking and trailhead facilities: Park at the Beech Mountain parking lot; there are no facilities.

Key points:
- 0.0   Beech Cliff Trailhead.
- 0.2   Junction with the Canada Cliffs Trail; bear left to the Beech Cliff loop.
- 0.3   Beech Cliff.
- 0.6   Close loop; bear right back to the parking area.
- 0.8   Beech Cliff Trailhead.

The hike: This is the easier of two ways to access Beech Cliff because the trailhead is basically at the same elevation as the cliff. From the parking area, the trail rises gradually through the woods and reaches a junction with the Canada Cliffs Trail at 0.2 mile.

Bear left (northeast) to head to the Beech Cliff loop, where you have a choice of taking the inland or the cliff-side half of the loop first. Either way is relatively flat, with some granite steps to make the footing easier. To get the views first, bear right on the cliff-side half of the loop, reaching Beech Cliff at 0.3 mile.

From here you can look down onto Echo Lake Beach and the AMC Camp, but don't get too close to the edge. Farther east is Acadia and St. Sauveur mountains. To the south are Somes Sound, the Gulf of Maine, and the Cranberry Isles, and to the southwest is Beech Mountain and its fire tower. You may hear the traffic on ME 102, across the lake. The trail continues along the cliff, then circles inland, closing the loop at 0.6 mile. Bear right to return to the parking area at 0.8 mile.

Options: After closing the Beech Cliff loop, turn left on the Canada Cliffs Trail to add another 1-mile loop that leads you back to the parking area in a different way. You'll come to two trail junctions on the Canada Cliffs ridge. The first one leads left down to Echo Lake, but stay straight on the ridge. The second one leads right off the ridge, but bear left. The trail finally circles west and down off the ridge. Continue straight at the next junction, and then turn right at the final junction to return to the Beech Mountain parking area.

63 Beech Cliff Ladder Trail

Highlights: Nearly vertical climb up Beech Cliff along several long iron ladders; trail may be closed during peregrine falcon breeding season from spring to late summer.

Type of hike: Day hike; loop.

Total distance: 1.2 miles.

Difficulty: Strenuous

Finding the trailhead: From the flashing yellow light just south of Somesville, head south on Maine Highway 102 for 3.5 miles. Turn right at the Echo Lake Beach entrance and follow the road to the parking lot. Go to the far end of the parking lot, walk down the stairs, and turn left along a paved walkway to the trailhead.

Parking and trailhead facilities: You can park at the Echo Lake Beach parking lot, where there are seasonally open changing rooms, water fountain, and flush toilets.

Key points:

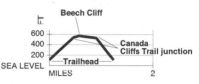

0.0   Beech Cliff Ladder Trailhead.

0.4   Junction with the Canada Cliffs Trail; turn right, then bear right again at the Beech Cliff loop.

0.5   Beech Cliff.

0.8   Close Beech Cliff loop; bear left on the Canada Cliffs Trail, then left again back down to Echo Lake.

1.2   Beech Cliff Ladder Trailhead.

The hike: This tough little trail climbs from Echo Lake straight up Beech Cliff and is as challenging as the better-known Precipice Trail on Champlain Mountain. And like the Precipice, this trail may be closed from spring to late summer during peregrine falcon breeding season.

At the start, a sign gives fair warning: "Caution: Trail Steep with Exposed Cliffs and Fixed Iron Rungs." The first stretch of the trail is fairly level. But at a sign warning hikers to stay on the path to prevent erosion, the trail makes a left and begins to climb via switchbacks. Cross a rock slide at the base of Beech Cliff, then watch for an overlook on the right, with views of Acadia

and St. Sauveur mountains east and Echo Lake below. Continue climbing via switchbacks and stone stairs with a wooden handrail for protection. At one point, you'll walk under a huge birch tree growing sideways out of the

The Beech Cliff Ladder Trail isn't for people afraid of heights.

Beech Cliff Ladder Trail

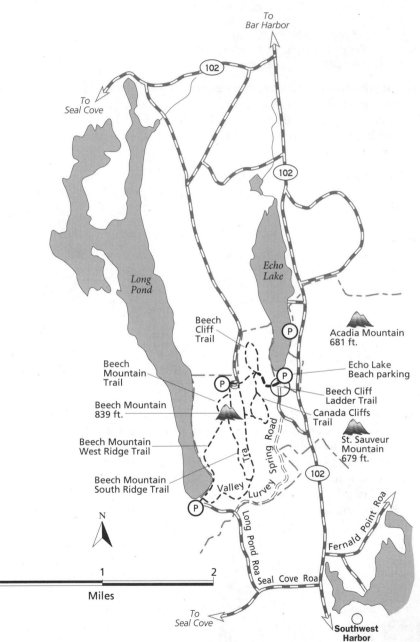

To
Bar Harbor

102

To
Seal Cove

102

Long
Pond

Echo
Lake

P

Beech
Cliff
Trail

Acadia Mountain
681 ft.

Beech
Mountain
Trail

P

P

Echo Lake
Beach parking

Beech Cliff
Ladder Trail

Beech Mountain
839 ft.

Canada Cliffs
Trail

Beech Mountain
West Ridge Trail

St. Sauveur
Mountain
679 ft.

Beech Mountain
South Ridge Trail

Valley Trail

Lurvey Spring Road

102

P

Fernald Point Roa

N

Long Pond Roa

Seal Cove Roa

0   1   2
Miles

To
Seal Cove

Southwest
Harbor

The Cranberry Isles and the ocean in the distance, as seen from Beech Cliff.

cliffside. Go up one more set of stone stairs with a wooden handrail.

Now begins the part of the trail that is so steep you need to climb up several iron ladders bolted into the rock face. The first ladder has 10 rungs, and the second has 18 rungs and handholds made of steel poles and cable. Two more 15-rung ladders follow. After a final set of stone steps, you attain the ridge and the junction with the Canada Cliffs Trail at 0.4 mile. Turn right toward the Beech Cliff loop, then bear right on the half of the loop that brings you close to the edge of the cliff. Reach Beech Cliff and its dramatic clifftop views at 0.5 mile. Circle inland and close the Beech Cliff loop at 0.8 mile. Bear left on the Canada Cliffs Trail, then left again back down the Ladder Trail to Echo Lake. Return to the Echo Lake Beach parking lot at 1.2 miles.

64 Canada Cliffs Trail

Highlights: Views of Acadia and St. Sauveur mountains, Somes Sound, and Beech Mountain.
Type of hike: Day hike; loop.
Total distance: 1.2 miles.
Difficulty: Moderate.

Finding the trailhead: Head south of Somesville on Maine Highway 102, and turn right at the flashing yellow light toward Pretty Marsh. Take the second left onto Beech Hill Road, at a sign pointing to Beech Mountain and Beech Cliff. Follow Beech Hill Road 3.2 miles to the parking lot at the end. Take the Beech Cliff Trail, across from the parking lot, for 0.2 mile to a junction. The Canada Cliffs Trailhead is on the right.

Canada Cliffs Trail

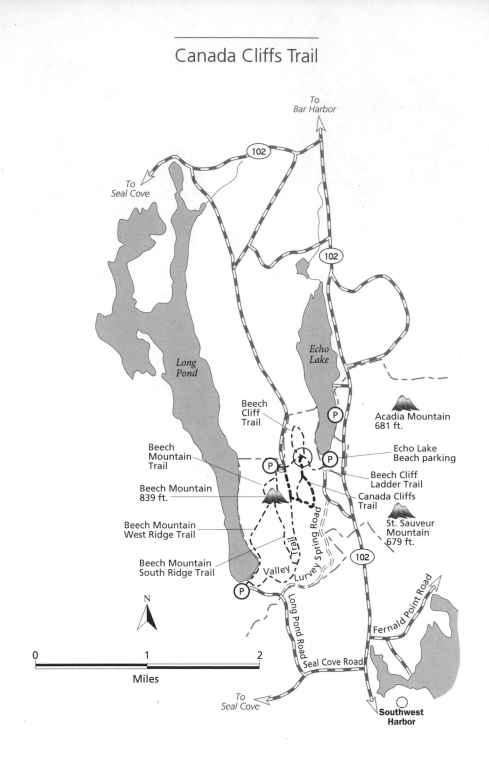

To
Bar Harbor

102

To
Seal Cove

102

Long
Pond

Echo
Lake

Beech
Cliff
Trail

Acadia Mountain
681 ft.

Beech
Mountain
Trail

Echo Lake
Beech parking

Beech Cliff
Ladder Trail

Beech Mountain
839 ft.

Canada Cliffs
Trail

Beech Mountain
West Ridge Trail

St. Sauveur
Mountain
679 ft.

Beech Mountain
South Ridge Trail

Valley
Trail

Lurvey Spring Road

102

Long Pond Road

Fernald Point Road

N

Seal Cove Road

0   1   2

Miles

To
Seal Cove

Southwest
Harbor

Parking and trailhead facilities: Park at the Beech Mountain parking lot; there are no facilities.

Key points:
- 0.0   Beech Mountain parking lot.
- 0.2   Canada Cliffs Trailhead, reached via Beech Cliff Trail.
- 0.3   Junction with the Beech Cliff Ladder Trail; stay straight.
- 0.4   Junction with a spur to the right off-ridge; bear left.
- 0.9   Junction with a spur to the right up-ridge; stay straight.
- 1.0   Junction with the Valley Trail; turn right.
- 1.2   Return to the Beech Mountain parking lot.

The hike: The Canada Cliffs Trail doesn't provide the same dramatic views down to Echo Lake as the neighboring Beech Cliff Trail, but it does give you similar vistas of Acadia and St. Sauveur mountains to the east, Somes Sound, Gulf of Maine, and the Cranberry Isles to the

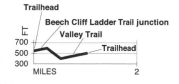

south, and Beech Mountain with its fire tower to the west.

At 0.1 mile from the trailhead (and 0.3 mile from the parking lot), the Beech Cliff Ladder Trail comes in on the left. Stay straight. In another 0.1 mile, bear left at a fork to continue on the Canada Cliffs ridge to the views. Although the trail doesn't get as close to the cliff's edge as the Beech Cliff Trail does, there are still fine views of surrounding mountains and ocean. Follow the trail southeast along the ridge, descending steeply at first along open rock ledges, then more gradually through the woods as the path circles northwest. At the next junction where a spur comes in on the right, stay straight. At 1 mile, at a junction with the Valley Trail, turn right and return to the Beech Mountain parking area at 1.2 miles.

Options: Before getting on the Canada Cliffs Trail, you can do the 0.4-mile-long Beech Cliff loop first. Pass the Canada Cliffs Trailhead and continue on the Beech Cliff Trail to the Beech Cliff loop. Bear right at the fork to get the cliff-top views first, then circle around inland, closing the short loop. Backtrack to the Canada Cliffs Trail and do that 1-mile loop back to the Beech Mountain parking lot.

65 Beech Mountain Trail

Highlights:	Views of Long Pond, Somes Sound, and surrounding scenery from 839-foot Beech Mountain, topped by a fire tower.
Type of hike:	Day hike; loop.
Total distance:	1.1 miles.
Difficulty:	Moderate.

Finding the trailhead: Head south of Somesville on Maine Highway 102, and turn right at the flashing yellow light toward Pretty Marsh. Take the second left onto Beech Hill Road at a sign pointing to Beech Mountain and Beech Cliff. Follow Beech Hill Road 3.2 miles to the parking lot at the end. The trailhead leaves from the northwest end of the parking lot.

Parking and trailhead facilities: Park at the Beech Mountain parking lot; there are no facilities.

Key points:
- 0.0   Beech Mountain Trailhead.
- 0.1   Bear right at a fork, going around the loop counterclockwise.
- 0.6   Junction with the Beech Mountain West Ridge Trail; bear left.
- 0.7   Beech Mountain summit; junction with the Beech Mountain South Ridge Trail; bear left.
- 1.1   Return to the Beech Mountain parking lot.

The hike: Beech Mountain rises from a thin peninsula-like ridge of land sandwiched between Long Pond and Echo Lake, providing views all around. The 839-foot peak is also distinctive for its fire tower—the only mountain in Acadia to have one—and is a good place to watch hawks migrate. In fact, we saw four kestrels dive and soar above us when we hiked here one fall.

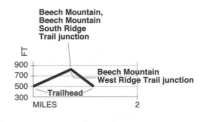

At 0.1 mile at the fork in the Beech Mountain Trail, bear right to head the easier way around the loop up to the summit. You'll soon begin getting spectacular views of Long Pond to the right (west) of the wide-open trail. At 0.6 mile, reach the junction with the Beech Mountain West Ridge Trail. Bear left. You'll next hit a series of log steps leading to the summit.

At 0.7 mile, reach the steel fire tower atop Beech Mountain and the junction with the Beech Mountain South Ridge Trail. Access to the deck of the U.S. government–owned fire tower is blocked, although you can climb a dozen steps to the first platform and its almost 360-degree views of the ocean and surrounding mountains. Echo Lake, Acadia Mountain, and St. Sauveur Mountain are to the east; Southwest Harbor, Northeast Harbor, and the Cranberry Isles are to the southeast; and Long Pond is to the west. The loop trail next heads down quickly along the rough mountain face to the northeast. Descend along switchbacks, open cliff face, and through boulder fields. Pass what must be an erratic—an out-of-place boulder plopped there by retreating glaciers. Go down a series of stone steps, then log steps. Bear right at the fork and return to the parking area at 1.1 miles.

Beech Mountain Trail

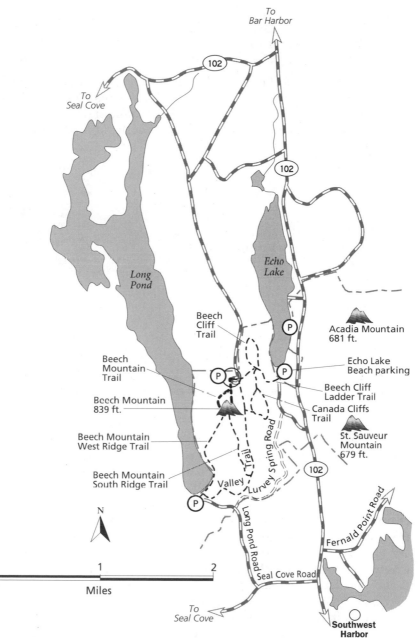

To
Bar Harbor

102

To
Seal Cove

Long
Pond

Echo
Lake

Beech
Cliff
Trail

P

Acadia Mountain
681 ft.

Beech
Mountain
Trail

P

P

Echo Lake
Beach parking

Beech Mountain
839 ft.

Beech Cliff
Ladder Trail

Canada Cliffs
Trail

Beech Mountain
West Ridge Trail

St. Sauveur
Mountain
679 ft.

Beech Mountain
South Ridge Trail

Valley

Trail

Lurvey Spring Road

102

P

N

Long Pond Road

Fernald Point Road

0   1   2

Miles

Seal Cove Road

To
Seal Cove

Southwest
Harbor

66 Beech Mountain West Ridge Trail

> **Highlights:** Climb up Beech Mountain from Long Pond; stunning views.
> **Type of hike:** Day hike; out-and-back.
> **Total distance:** 1.8 miles.
> **Difficulty:** Moderate to strenuous.

Finding the trailhead: From Southwest Harbor, head north 0.5 mile on Maine Highway 102. Turn left (west) at Seal Cove Road and travel for 0.5 mile. Then go right (north) on Long Pond Road to the end to a pumping station on the shore of the pond. The trailhead is at the far end of the parking area to the east.

Parking and trailhead facilities: Park at the Long Pond pumping station; there are no facilities.

Key points:

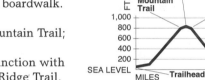

0.0   Beech Mountain West Ridge Trailhead.
0.2   Head right (east) away from Long Pond, and right again away from a boardwalk. Cross a gravel road.
0.8   Junction with the Beech Mountain Trail; bear right.
0.9   Beech Mountain summit; junction with the Beech Mountain South Ridge Trail.

The hike: The roughest of three hikes up Beech Mountain, the Beech Mountain West Ridge Trail rises steeply from Long Pond and climbs the mountain's open face. But the beginning of the trail gives no hint of the ruggedness to come. Like an easy woods walk paralleling Long Pond at the start, the only challenge here is to walk across a dozen wood bridges through wet areas.

At 0.2 mile, the trail heads right away from the pond and then right again away from a wooden boardwalk that leads to private property. Cross a gravel road. Soon the trail begins its steep ascent over a smooth rock face that can be extremely slick when wet. There are no carefully laid stone steps as found on other Acadia trails to make the going more civilized. As the trail goes up the steep open west face, you get views down to Long Pond and farther west to Mansell Mountain.

At 0.8 mile, the Beech Mountain Trail comes in from the left. Bear right, reaching 839-foot-high Beech Mountain and the summit fire tower at 0.9 mile. Access to the deck of the U.S. government–owned fire tower is blocked, although you can climb a dozen steps to the first platform and its almost 360-degree views of the ocean and surrounding mountains. Echo Lake, Acadia Mountain, and St. Sauveur Mountain are to the east; Southwest Harbor, Northeast Harbor, and the Cranberry Isles are to the southeast; and Long Pond is to the west. Return the way you came.

Beech Mountain West Ridge Trail

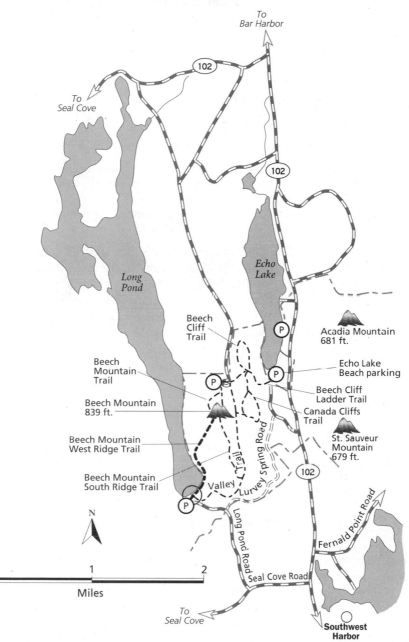

To
Bar Harbor

102

To
Seal Cove

102

Long
Pond

Echo
Lake

Beech
Cliff
Trail

Acadia Mountain
681 ft.

Beech
Mountain
Trail

P

Echo Lake
Beach parking

P

Beech Cliff
Ladder Trail

Beech Mountain
839 ft.

Canada Cliffs
Trail

Beech Mountain
West Ridge Trail

St. Sauveur
Mountain
679 ft.

Beech Mountain
South Ridge Trail

Valley Trail

Lurvey Spring Road

102

P

N

Long Pond Road

Fernald Point Road

0   1   2

Miles

Seal Cove Road

To
Seal Cove

Southwest
Harbor

Options: For an approximately 2.4-mile loop, head southeast from the summit down the 0.8-mile-long Beech Mountain South Ridge Trail, with its long stretches of stone steps and switchbacks. Turn right at the junction with the Valley Trail and head another 0.7 mile back to the Long Pond pumping station parking area.

67 Beech Mountain South Ridge Trail

Highlights:	Climb up switchbacks and stone steps to Beech Mountain and its fire tower and views.
Type of hike:	Day hike; out-and-back.
Total distance:	3 miles, including 0.7 mile to reach trailhead.
Difficulty:	Moderate to strenuous.

Finding the trailhead: From Southwest Harbor, head north 0.5 mile on Maine Highway 102. Turn left (west) at Seal Cove Road and travel for 0.5 mile. Then head right (north) on Long Pond Road to the end to a pumping station on the shore of the pond. Take the Valley Trail, which leads across from the pumping station on the south end of the parking area, for 0.7 mile. The Beech Mountain South Ridge Trailhead is on the left.

Parking and trailhead facilities: Park at the Long Pond pumping station; there are no facilities.

Key points:

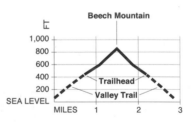

0.0	Parking area.
0.7	Beech Mountain South Ridge Trailhead, reached via the Valley Trail.
1.1	Reach an open rock ridge at the top of a switchback made up of stone steps; turn right. At a T intersection, go right up a rock ledge.
1.5	Junction with the Beech Mountain Trail; bear right to the Beech Mountain summit.

The hike: Of the three ways up to Beech Mountain, this is the longest if you count the Valley Trail on which you must first hike. It is also the most architecturally fascinating, with its carefully laid stone steps. At 0.7 mile from the Long Pond pumping station, the Beech Mountain South Ridge Trail heads left (north) off the Valley Trail and starts with long stretches of stone steps that take you up switchbacks. The steps make what would be an extremely difficult trail a more manageable one.

At 1.1 miles from Long Pond, reach an open rock ridge. The trail appears to lead left, but go right to continue on the ridge. At a T intersection, go right once again, up a rock ledge. For the rest of the way, the trail takes you up

Beech Mountain South Ridge Trail

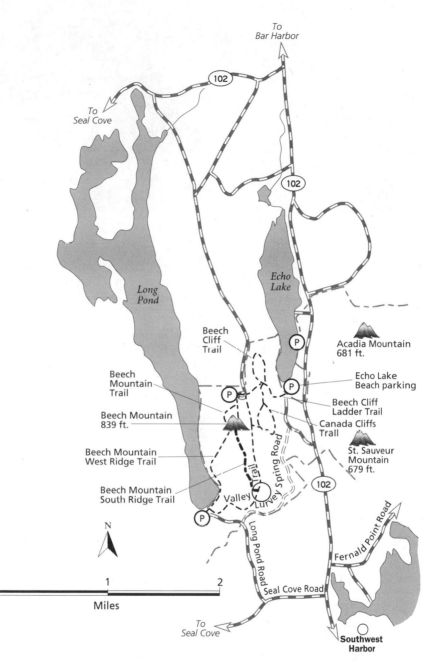

To
Bar Harbor

102

To
Seal Cove

102

Echo
Lake

Long
Pond

Beech
Cliff
Trail

P

Acadia Mountain
681 ft.

Beech
Mountain
Trail

P

P

Echo Lake
Beach parking

Beech Cliff
Ladder Trail

Beech Mountain
839 ft.

Canada Cliffs
Trail

St. Sauveur
Mountain
679 ft.

Beech Mountain
West Ridge Trail

Lurvey Spring Road

Beech Mountain
South Ridge Trail

Valley Trail

102

P

N

Long Pond Road

Fernald Point Road

0   1   2

Miles

To
Seal Cove

Seal Cove Road

Southwest
Harbor

The fire tower atop Beech Mountain can be seen from miles away.

the open ridge and through wooded knobs, providing views south, east, and west. At 1.5 miles from Long Pond, bear right at a junction with the Beech Mountain Trail and attain 839-foot-high Beech Mountain and its fire tower.

Access to the deck of the U.S. government–owned fire tower is blocked, although you can climb a dozen steps to the first platform and its almost 360-degree views of the ocean and surrounding mountains. Echo Lake, Acadia Mountain, and St. Sauveur Mountain are to the east; Southwest Harbor, Northeast Harbor, and the Cranberry Isles are to the southeast; and Long Pond is to the west. Return the way you came.

Options: To loop back to the Long Pond pumping station parking area, you can descend Beech Mountain via the 1-mile-long Beech Mountain West Ridge Trail. Head down the summit as if you were going back down the Beech Mountain South Ridge Trail, but bear right at the junction with the Beech Mountain Trail to the next junction with the West Ridge Trail. Bear left to head southwest down the West Ridge Trail, toward the Long Pond pumping station parking area.

68 Valley Trail

Highlights:	Less-traveled walk through lush valley between Beech Mountain and Canada Cliffs.
Type of hike:	Day hike; out-and-back.
Total distance:	3 miles.
Difficulty:	Easy to moderate.

Finding the trailhead: From Southwest Harbor, head north 0.5 mile on Maine Highway 102. Turn left (west) at Seal Cove Road and travel for 0.5 mile. Then head right (north) on Long Pond Road to the end to a pumping station on the shore of the pond. The trailhead is across from the pumping station on the south end of the parking area.

Parking and trailhead facilities: Park at the Long Pond pumping station. There are no facilities.

Key points:
   0.0   Valley Trailhead.
   0.3   Cross the foot of a private drive; bear left on a gravel road.
   0.7   Junction with the Beech Mountain South Ridge Trail; bear right.
   1.3   Junction with the Canada Cliffs Trail; keep straight.
   1.5   Beech Mountain parking area.

The hike: Although there are no dramatic cliff-top or ocean views on this trail, you can view lush valley scenery and get a different perspective on Acadia National Park. As if in a hanging garden, ferns drape over the top of huge slabs of granite that sheared off Beech Mountain. And chances

are you'll be able to get away from the crowds here, although you may hear ME 102 traffic in the distance.

At the start, the trail goes up a few granite steps and ascends a bit, before leveling off into a well-graded path. At 0.3 mile, cross the foot of a private drive and bear left on a gravel road, watching for the sign pointing out the trail's continuation through the woods. The trail gets rougher here. Roots and rocks make the footing more difficult, and the uphill climb here takes you over stone steps and a long switchback.

At 0.7 mile, the Beech Mountain South Ridge Trail heads steeply left up the mountain. Bear right to continue on the Valley Trail. The path flattens out a bit here as it goes through the lush forested valley sandwiched between Beech Mountain and Canada Cliffs. It winds gradually up the valley, taking you among house-sized granite slabs with ferns growing on top. The only sign of civilization you may find here is the distant sound of traffic on ME 102.

At 1.3 miles, the Canada Cliffs Trail comes in on the right. Stay straight and reach the trail's end at the Beech Mountain parking area at 1.5 miles. Return the way you came.

Options: You can tag on the 0.8-mile-long Beech Cliff Trail for some spectacular cliff-top views down to Echo Lake. At the end of the Valley Trail at the Beech Mountain parking area, head straight to the Beech Cliff Trailhead on the right (northeast). Follow the signs to Beech Cliff, then loop back to the Beech Mountain parking area. Follow the Valley Trail back to the Long Pond pumping station parking area.

Valley Trail

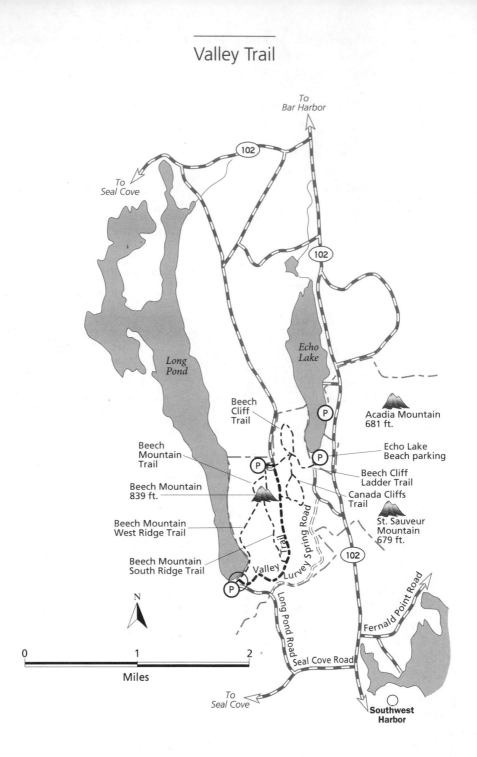

To
Bar Harbor

To
Seal Cove

102

102

Long
Pond

Echo
Lake

Beech
Cliff
Trail

P

Acadia Mountain
681 ft.

Beech
Mountain
Trail

P

P

Echo Lake
Beach parking

Beech Mountain
839 ft.

Beech Cliff
Ladder Trail

Canada Cliffs
Trail

St. Sauveur
Mountain
679 ft.

Beech Mountain
West Ridge Trail

102

Beech Mountain
South Ridge Trail

Valley Trail

Lurvey Spring Road

Fernald Point Road

P

N

Long Pond Road

Seal Cove Road

0   1   2

Miles

To
Seal Cove

Southwest
Harbor

For an approximately 2.7-mile-long loop up Beech Mountain and back down the Beech Mountain South Ridge Trail, take the Valley Trail to the Beech Mountain parking area. Cross the parking area to the Beech Mountain Trailhead on the left (northwest) end of the lot. At a fork, bear left to ascend to Beech Mountain. At the next fork, bear left again down the 0.8-mile-long South Ridge Trail. Then turn right on the Valley Trail, returning to the Long Pond pumping station parking area in another 0.7 mile.

69 Great Pond Trail

      Highlights: Mostly flat walk along southwest shore of Long (Great) Pond, the largest body of fresh water on Mount Desert Island.
      Type of hike: Day hike; out-and-back, or part of loop up Western Mountain.
      Total distance: 5.8 miles, or 4.7-mile loop.
      Difficulty: Easy to moderate.

Finding the trailhead: From Southwest Harbor, head north 0.5 mile on Maine Highway 102. Turn left (west) at Seal Cove Road and travel for 0.5 mile. Then head right (north) on Long Pond Road to the end to a pumping station on the pond's shore. The trailhead is to the left of the pumping station.

Parking and trailhead facilities: Park at the Long Pond pumping station; there are no facilities.

Key points:
    0.0   Great Pond Trailhead; junction with the Cold Brook Trail.
    0.2   Junction with the Perpen-dicular Trail.
    2.9   Junction with the Western Trail.

The hike: The Great Pond Trail is a pleasant walk offering the possibility of sunning on big, flat rocks or seeing dozens of herring gulls soar on the wind above what is

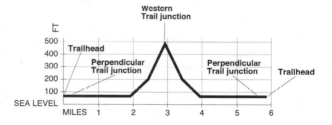

also known as Long Pond. The trail can also serve as a jumping-off point for some of the challenging hikes up Western Mountain.

The trail heads left (west) from the pumping station. Cold Brook Trail goes inland, and the Great Pond Trail stays along the shore. At 0.2 mile, the Perpendicular Trail heads steeply up toward the twin wooded summits—Mansell and Bernard—that make up Western Mountain. Continue straight on the Great Pond Trail.

Great Pond Trail

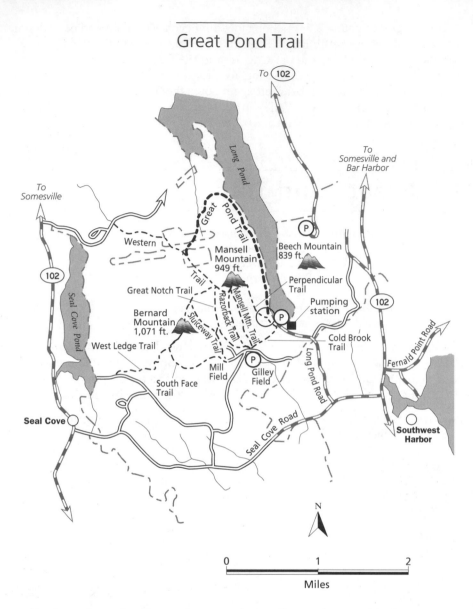

Farther along the shore, there are large, flat rocks suitable for sunning. Although the beginning of the trail is well graded, roots and rocks make the footing a bit more difficult farther in. As the trail hits its northernmost point, it heads inland and up the northern shoulder of Western Mountain. At one point you cross a creek on a long log bridge. At 2.9 miles, the trail ends at the junction with the Western Trail. Return the way you came.

Options: For a 4.7-mile loop back via 949-foot Mansell Mountain, continue another 0.4 mile beyond the junction with the Western Trail farther up the northern shoulder of Western Mountain to the Great Notch. Turn left

The trail takes you along Long Pond, also known as Great Pond, with views of Beech Mountain.

(east) 0.3 mile over the wooded summit of Mansell Mountain, and then hike down the 0.9-mile Perpendicular Trail. Turn right at the shore of the pond to return to the pumping station parking area in another 0.2 mile.

70 Perpendicular Trail

Highlights: Steep ascent up rock steps to 949-foot Mansell Mountain.
Type of hike: Day hike; out-and-back.
Total distance: 2.2 miles.
Difficulty: Strenuous.

Finding the trailhead: From Southwest Harbor, head north 0.5 mile on Maine Highway 102. Turn left (west) at Seal Cove Road and travel for 0.5 mile. Then head right (north) on Long Pond Road to the end to a pumping station on the shore of the pond. Take the Great Pond Trail to the left of the pumping station for 0.2 mile to reach the Perpendicular Trailhead.

Parking and trailhead facilities: Park at the Long Pond pumping station; there are no facilities.

Key points:
- 0.0 Parking area.
- 0.2 Perpendicular Trailhead, via Great Pond Trail.
- 1.0 View down to Long Pond.
- 1.1 Wooded Mansell Mountain summit.
- 2.2 Return the same way you came.

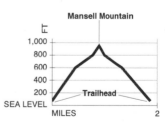

The hike: The name of this trail is no exaggeration. Although it's easier to go down rather than up the Perpendicular Trail, some ambitious hikers have been known to scale this because it's there. From the trailhead, begin ascending steeply. You'll climb an iron ladder and rungs, then switchback across some of the steepest stuff and clamber up a finely crafted, winding stone staircase. The trail has hundreds of stone steps. You'll get views down to Long Pond and northeast to Beech Mountain.

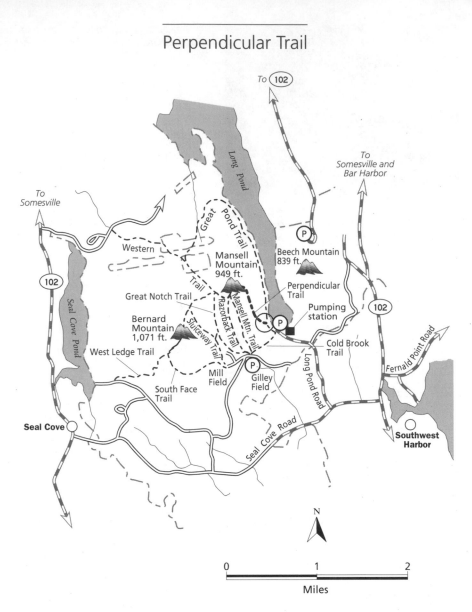

At 1.0 mile, reach a rocky ledge with the best views on the trail of Long Pond below and Beech Mountain and its fire tower to the northeast. You can also see the Cranberry Isles and the mouth of Somes Sound to the south. At 1.1 mile, the trail ends at the wooded summit of Mansell Mountain where there are no views. The only markers here are a wooden post and cairn and a flat gray stone with the words "Arlie: Her last mountain" etched on it. Return the way you came.

Options: To avoid ascending the Perpendicular Trail while still coming down it, you can loop up via the 0.9-mile Mansell Mountain Trail to the summit and then down. From the pumping station parking area, head left (southwest) away from the pond on the 0.4-mile Cold Brook Trail to Gilley Field. Then turn right (northwest) up the Mansell Mountain Trail. Turn right (northeast) over the summit and then head down the Perpendicular Trail.

71 Cold Brook Trail

Highlights: Short connector to Western Mountain trails from Long Pond pumping station.
Type of hike: Day hike; out-and-back, or part of loop up Western Mountain.
Total distance: 0.8 mile.
Difficulty: Easy.

Finding the trailhead: From Southwest Harbor, head north 0.5 mile on Maine Highway 102. Turn left (west) at Seal Cove Road and travel for 0.5 mile. Then head right (north) on Long Pond Road to the end to a pumping station on the shore of the pond. Head left of the pumping station onto the Great Pond Trail. The Cold Brook Trailhead is an immediate left, going inland from the Great Pond Trailhead.

Parking and trailhead facilities: Park at the Long Pond pumping station; there are no facilities.

Key points:
0.0 Cold Brook Trailhead.
0.4 Gilley Field; junction with the Mansell Mountain Trail.
0.8 Return the same way you came.

The hike: This short, easy trail provides important access to trails up the twin wooded summits—Mansell and Bernard—of Western Mountain. From the Long Pond pumping station, head left onto the Great Pond Trail, then make another immediate left onto the

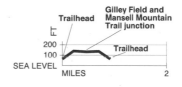

Cold Brook Trail. At 0.4 mile, the woods walk takes you out to the Gilley Field parking area, where a series of trails up Western Mountain start. Return the way you came.

Options: For a loop up 949-foot Mansell Mountain, from Gilley Field take the 0.9-mile Mansell Mountain Trail, the first trail heading up the mountain. From the wooded summit, descend east-southeast along the 0.9-mile Perpendicular Trail. Turn right at the pond's shore to return in another 0.2 mile to the pumping station parking area. The loop is approximately 2.4 miles. You can also hike other, longer loops up Mansell and the higher but equally wooded Bernard summit by using the Cold Brook Trail to access the other paths that lead from Gilley Field: the strenuous Razorback, the Great Notch Trail, the Sluiceway, or the South Face Trail.

Cold Brook Trail

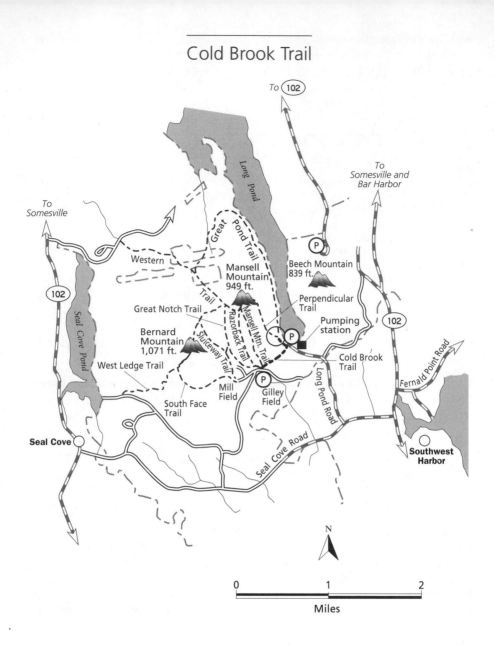

To (102)

To
Somesville and
Bar Harbor

Long Pond

To
Somesville

Great Pond Trail

Western

Mansell
Mountain
949 ft.

Beech Mountain
839 ft.

(P)

(102)

Seal Cove Pond

Great Notch Trail

Razorback Trail

Mansell Mtn. Trail

Perpendicular
Trail

Pumping
station

(P)

(102)

Bernard
Mountain
1,071 ft.

Sluiceway Trail

Cold Brook
Trail

Fernald Point Road

West Ledge Trail

Mill
Field

(P)

Gilley Field

Long Pond Road

South Face
Trail

Seal Cove

Seal Cove Road

Southwest
Harbor

N

0   1   2
Miles

The Cold Brook Trail heads inland from Long Pond, toward Western Mountain trails.

72 Mansell Mountain Trail

> **Highlights:** Climb up wooded summit of 949-foot Mansell Mountain, with nearby overlook of Long Pond.
> **Type of hike:** Day hike; out-and-back.
> **Total distance:** 2.2 miles.
> **Difficulty:** Moderate to strenuous.

Finding the trailhead: From Southwest Harbor, head north 0.5 mile on Maine Highway 102. Turn left (west) at Seal Cove Road and follow the road for 2.9 miles as it turns from pavement to gravel. Then turn right at a gravel road, where a sign points to Seal Cove Pond and Western Mountain Road. At the next two junctions, bear right toward Gilley Field. The trailhead leads northwest from Gilley Field.

Parking and trailhead facilities: Park at Gilley Field; there are no facilities.

Key points:

- 0.0 Mansell Mountain Trailhead.
- 0.8 Overlook.
- 0.9 Junction at the top of the ridge; bear right.
- 1.0 Mansell Mountain summit; junction with the Perpendicular Trail.
- 1.1 Overlook down to Long Pond, at the top of the Perpendicular Trail.

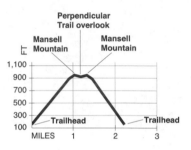

The hike: Although this is a relatively short trail, and less steep than the neighboring Perpendicular Trail, the Mansell Mountain Trail should not be underestimated. First described as part of a pre–Revolutionary War road, the Mansell Mountain Trail starts off by going up a wide but steep path through the woods. Switchbacks and blue blazes mark the way. By the time you reach the mountain's exposed granite, the pitch is very steep.

The trail jogs to the left around the first rock face. Soon you get your first views of Southwest Harbor, Bass Harbor, and the Cranberry Isles to the south and southeast, and Blue Hill Bay to the west. Amazingly, you can hear traffic on ME 102 from here. At 0.8 mile near the top of the ridge, finally above the din below, a sign points to an overlook. The path to the overlook was hidden by a blowdown when we hiked the trail, so you may need to look carefully for it.

At 0.9 mile, reach the ridge. Turn right at the junction and at 1 mile attain the wooded Mansell Mountain, elevation 949 feet. There are no views here. The only markers are a wooden post and cairn and a flat gray stone with the words "Arlie: Her last mountain" etched on it. This is also where the Perpendicular Trail ends. To cap the climb with some views, head east along the Perpendicular Trail. At 1.1 miles, reach a rocky ledge with good views of Long Pond below, and Beech Mountain and its fire tower, to the

Mansell Mountain Trail

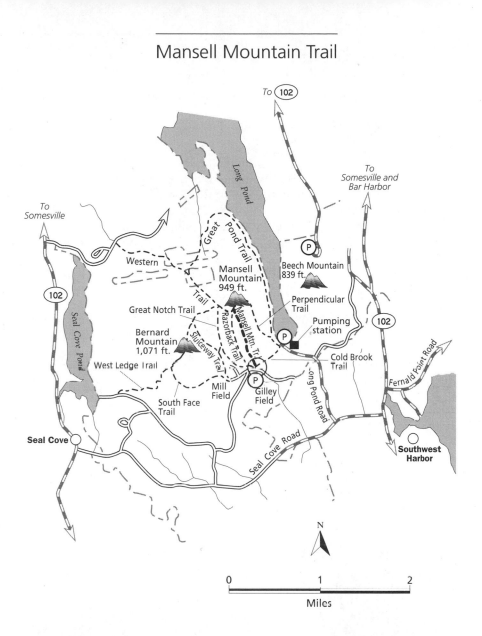

northeast. You can also see the Cranberry Isles and Somes Sound to the south. Return the way you came.

Options: If you're not afraid of exposed heights, you can loop down via the steep Perpendicular Trail on the return. Descend 0.8 mile from the rocky ledge with good views down to Long Pond. At the pond's shore, turn right for 0.2 mile. Just before the Long Pond pumping station parking area, turn right on the Cold Brook Trail and follow it 0.4 mile back to Gilley Field. The loop is approximately 2.5 miles long.

73 Razorback Trail

Highlights:	Climb up rocky spine to Mansell Mountain; good views.
Type of hike:	Day hike; out-and-back.
Total distance:	3 miles.
Difficulty:	Moderate.

Finding the trailhead: From Southwest Harbor, head north 0.5 mile on Maine Highway 102. Turn left (west) at Seal Cove Road and follow the road for 2.9 miles as it turns from pavement to gravel. Then turn right at a gravel road where a sign points to Seal Cove Pond and Western Mountain Road. At the next two junctions, bear right toward Gilley Field. Follow the Great Notch Trail that leads straight west from Gilley Field for 0.2 mile. The Razorback Trailhead is the second right off the trail, after the Mansell Mountain Trail, and may not be marked by a trailhead sign.

Parking and trailhead facilities: Park at Gilley Field; there are no facilities.

Key points:

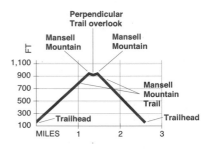

- 0.0   Gilley Field.
- 0.2   Razorback Trailhead reached via the Great Notch Trail.
- 1.2   Junction; bear right to Mansell Mountain.
- 1.3   Junction with the Mansell Mountain Trail; bear left.
- 1.4   Mansell Mountain summit; junction with the Perpendicular Trail.
- 1.5   Overlook down to Long Pond.

Snaking up a rocky spine of Mansell Mountain, the Razorback Trail provides great views.

202

Razorback Trail

To (102)

To
Somesville and
Bar Harbor

To
Somesville

Long Pond

Great Pond Trail

Western

Mansell
Mountain
949 ft.

Beech Mountain
839 ft.

102

Great Notch Trail

Perpendicular
Trail

Pumping
station

Bernard
Mountain
1,071 ft.

Seal Cove Pond

Mansell Mtn. Tr.

Razorback Trail

Sluiceway Trail

Cold Brook
Trail

West Lodge Trail

102

Mill
Field

Gilley
Field

South Face
Trail

Long Pond Road

Fernald Point Road

Seal Cove

Seal Cove Road

Southwest
Harbor

N

0   1   2

Miles

The hike: Going up a nearly razor-thin spine of Mansell Mountain, the Razorback Trail provides some spectacular views south to the Gulf of Maine and the Cranberry Isles. The trailhead, not marked when we hiked this, is 0.2 mile west of Gilley Field and heads right (north) off the Great Notch Trail. Follow the cairns and blue blazes steeply up what begins as a wide-open path carpeted with pine needles. Then climb a series of stone steps.

The trail next takes you along the narrow spine up Mansell Mountain, bringing you along cliffs and providing some wonderful open-ridge views. To the left (west) you can see the wooded hulk of Knight's Nubble and Bernard

Mountain, and to the south the Gulf of Maine and the Cranberry Isles. If you hike soon after a rain, you may find water cascading down the smooth rock face that you're hiking along. At 1.2 miles, reach a junction at the top of the ridge. You can turn around here because Mansell Mountain is wooded and a nearby overlook offers no better views than what you already get on the Razorback. If you choose to continue, bear right at the top of the ridge. At 1.3 miles, pass the Mansell Mountain Trail coming in on the right. Reach the wooded Mansell Mountain summit, elevation 949 feet, and the junction with the Perpendicular Trail at 1.4 miles. Continue on the Perpendicular Trail and reach an overlook at 1.5 miles that gives views down to Long Pond, northeast to Beech Mountain and its fire tower, and south to the Gulf of Maine. Return the way you came.

Options: To loop down via the Mansell Mountain Trail, backtrack to where that trail comes in from the south. Turn left and head 0.9 mile down the Mansell Mountain Trail back to the Gilley Field parking area.

74 Great Notch Trail

Highlights: Most gradual climb up Western Mountain's rugged south face.
Type of hike: Day hike; out-and-back.
Total distance: 3.2 miles.
Difficulty: Moderate.

Finding the trailhead: From Southwest Harbor, head north 0.5 mile on Maine Highway 102. Turn left (west) at Seal Cove Road and follow the road for 2.9 miles as it turns from pavement to gravel. Then turn right at a gravel road, where a sign points to Seal Cove Pond and Western Mountain Road. At the next two junctions, bear right toward Gilley Field. The Great Notch Trailhead is to the west of the field.

Parking and trailhead facilities: Park at Gilley Field; there are no facilities.

Key points:
- 0.0 Great Notch Trailhead; junction with the Mansell Mountain Trailhead, stay straight.
- 0.2 Junction with the Razorback Trailhead; stay straight.
- 0.6 Junction with a spur to the Sluiceway; stay straight.
- 1.2 Great Notch; junction with the Western Trail; turn right to Mansell Mountain.

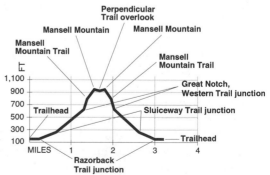

Great Notch Trail

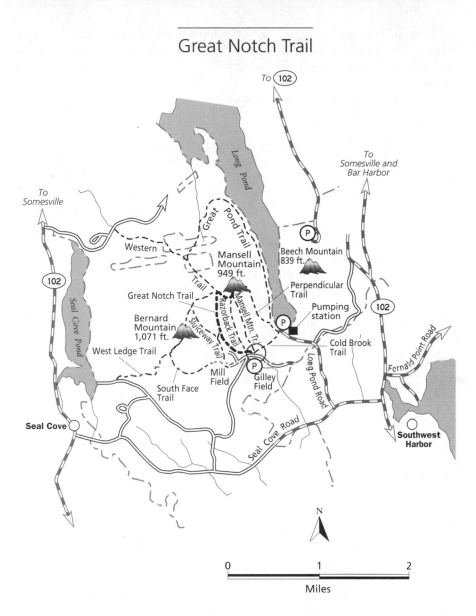

1.3   Junction with the top of the Razorback Trail; bear left.

1.4   Junction with the Mansell Mountain Trail, bear left.

1.5   Mansell Mountain summit; junction with the Perpendicular Trail.

1.6   Overlook down to Long Pond, at the top of the Perpendicular Trail.

The hike: Of the half-dozen trails up the rugged southern face of Western Mountain, the Great Notch Trail is the most gradual. Also known as the Gilley Trail, it climbs from Gilley Field to the Great Notch, separating Mansell Mountain and Bernard Mountain. Whereas the trail provides access to either one of the peaks, Mansell Mountain is closer and that route is described here.

Head west from Gilley Field, passing the Mansell Mountain Trail on the right near the start and the Razorback Trail on the right at 0.2 mile. The trail gradually bears right, taking you toward the Great Notch. At 0.6 mile, pass a junction with a spur to the Sluiceway Trail on the left. Reach the notch and the junction with the Western Trail at 1.2 miles. Here there are four log benches to sit on and take a rest—a nice touch.

The Great Notch is a major four-way intersection on the Western Mountain Trail system. Signs point out the various destinations accessible from here and how far away they are. To reach Mansell Mountain, the closer of the two peaks that make up Western Mountain, turn right (east) at the notch and climb along the ridge. At 1.3 miles, pass a junction with the Razorback Trail, which comes in from the right. Here there's a view south toward the Gulf of Maine. At 1.4 miles, pass a junction with the Mansell Mountain Trail, which also comes in from the right. Reach the wooded Mansell Mountain summit, elevation 949 feet, and the junction with the Perpendicular Trail at 1.5 miles. There are no views here. The only markers are a wooden post and cairn and a flat gray stone with the words "Arlie: Her last mountain" etched on it.

At 1.6 miles, reach a viewpoint just before the Perpendicular Trail starts its steep descent. Here you can look down on Long Pond and see Beech Mountain and its fire tower to the northeast. Also visible to the south are Somes Sound and the Cranberry Isles. Return the way you came.

Options: To do an approximately 3-mile loop from the viewpoint overlooking Long Pond, head down 0.8 mile on the steep Perpendicular Trail. At the pond's shore, turn right and travel 0.2 mile. Just before the Long Pond pumping station parking area, turn right on the 0.4-mile-long Cold Brook Trail to return to the Gilley Field parking area.

---

75 Sluiceway Trail

Highlights:	Steep climb up along creek to Little Notch and Bernard Mountain.
Type of hike:	Day hike; out-and-back.
Total distance:	2.2 miles.
Difficulty:	Strenuous.

Finding the trailhead: From Southwest Harbor, head north 0.5 mile on Maine Highway 102. Turn left (west) at Seal Cove Road and follow the road for 2.9 miles, as it turns from pavement to gravel. Then turn right at a gravel road, where a sign points to Seal Cove Pond and Western Mountain Road. Bear right at the next junction. Turn left, heading toward Mill Field, at the following junction. The trailhead is at the northern edge of the field.

Parking and trailhead facilities: You can park at the Mill Field parking area; there are no facilities.

Sluiceway Trail

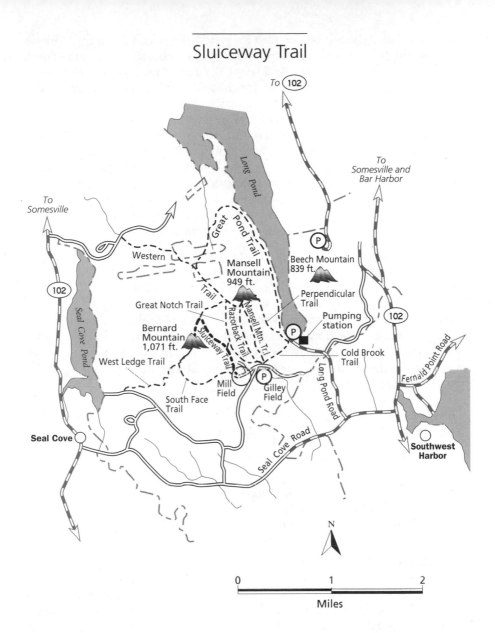

Key points:

- 0.0 Sluiceway Trailhead.
- 0.4 Junction with a spur to the Great Notch Trail, stay straight.
- 0.9 Little Notch; junction with the South Face Trail; turn left.
- 1.1 Bernard Mountain summit.

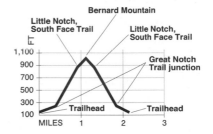

The hike: Called the Sluiceway Trail for good reason, this steep trail follows a fast-moving creek much of its way. Shorter but more difficult than the South Face Trail that also goes to the 1,071-foot Bernard Mountain, the Sluiceway features switchbacks, rough terrain, precipitous sections, and multiple creek crossings.

At 0.4 mile reach a junction with a spur to the Great Notch Trail, which heads off to the right (east). Bear left and continue up the Sluiceway. At 0.9 mile and elevation 890 feet, reach Little Notch and a junction with the South Face Trail. Turn left (southwest) and follow the South Face Trail to the wooded Bernard Mountain summit, elevation 1,071 feet, at 1.1 miles. Look for signs pointing to an overlook, where there is a log bench to sit on and take in the views. Bernard Mountain is the highest peak on Mount Desert Island west of Somes Sound. Return the way you came.

Options: To do a 2.6-mile loop, head off Bernard Mountain by continuing southwest on the South Face Trail. At the junction with the West Ledge Trail 0.5 mile below the summit, bear left to stay on the South Face Trail. In another 1 mile, the trail takes you back to the Mill Field parking area. To add on a 0.2-mile round trip spur to Knight's Nubble and its overlook, when you reach Little Notch at the top of the Sluiceway, turn right (northeast) toward the 930-foot elevation nubble. You can then backtrack to Little Notch and head toward Bernard Mountain and its overlook.

76 South Face Trail

Highlights:	Rugged climb up south face of wooded, 1,071-foot Bernard Mountain.
Type of hike:	Day hike; out-and-back or loop.
Total distance:	3.4 miles out-and-back, or 2.6-mile loop.
Difficulty:	Strenuous.

Finding the trailhead: From Southwest Harbor, head north 0.5 mile on Maine Highway 102. Turn left (west) at Seal Cove Road and follow the road for 2.9 miles as it turns from pavement to gravel. Then turn right at a gravel road, where a sign points to Seal Cove Pond and Western Mountain Road. At the next junction, bear right. Turn left toward Mill Field at the following junction. The trailhead is at the northwestern edge of the field.

Parking and trailhead facilities: You can park at the Mill Field parking area; there are no facilities.

Key points:
- 0.0 South Face Trailhead.
- 1.0 Junction with the West Ledge Trail; bear right.
- 1.5 Bernard Mountain summit.
- 1.7 Little Notch; junction with the Sluiceway Trail.

South Face Trail

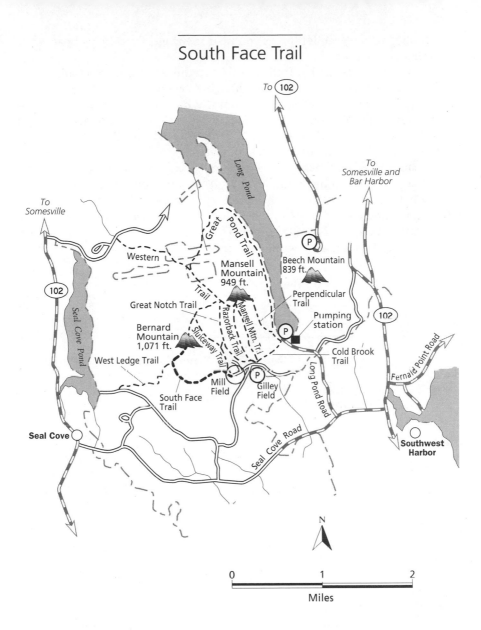

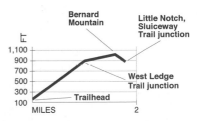

The hike: Taking you over a gorge and cascades on wooden bridges, and up and around the south face of wooded Bernard Mountain, this trail is a rugged one. Heading in a westerly direction first, the trail soon takes you over the first wooden bridge spanning a gorge and its rushing stream. Ascend steeply. The trail becomes a wide, rock-strewn path. Cross another wooden bridge over a bubbly creek and continue on the steep, wide path.

209

The climb gradually moderates as you near the ridge. Cross a log boardwalk through a boggy area.

At 1 mile, the West Ledge Trail comes in on the left. Climb gradually along what is now a shaded path under low-hanging evergreens. At 1.5 miles, reach the wooded summit of Bernard Mountain, which at 1,071 feet elevation is the highest peak on Mount Desert Island west of Somes Sound. Look for the sign that points to the Bernard Mountain overlook. There's a nice log bench to sit on and take in the beautiful views.

You can turn around here for a 3-mile round trip, because the views don't get better than this on the South Face Trail. If you choose to follow the trail to its official end, continue northeast along the rocky, steep ridge, reaching Little Notch and a junction with the Sluiceway Trail at 1.7 miles. Return the same way back for a 3.4-mile round trip, or head down the even steeper Sluiceway Trail for a total 2.6-mile loop back to the parking area at Mill Field.

77 Western Trail

Highlights: Gradual walk up Western Mountain's wooded west face to 949-foot Mansell peak.
Type of hike: Day hike; out-and-back.
Total distance: 3.8 miles.
Difficulty: Moderate.

Finding the trailhead: Head south of Somesville on Maine Highway 102; turn right at the flashing yellow light toward Pretty Marsh. Stay straight, passing the Pretty Marsh picnic area at 4.1 miles, then turn left onto a short paved road at 5.2 miles. Take a quick right onto the gravel Long Pond Fire Road and follow that for another 0.9 mile to the trailhead on the right side of the road.

Parking and trailhead facilities: Park along the gravel Long Pond Fire Road; there are no facilities.

Key points:
0.0   Western Trailhead.
1.1   Junction with the Great Pond Trail; bear right.
1.5   Great Notch; turn left.
1.6   Junction with the Razorback Trail; bear left.
1.7   Junction with the Mansell Mountain Trail; bear left.
1.8   Mansell Mountain summit; junction with the Perpendicular Trail.
1.9   Overlook down to Long Pond, at the top of the Perpendicular Trail.

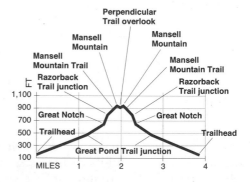

210

Western Trail

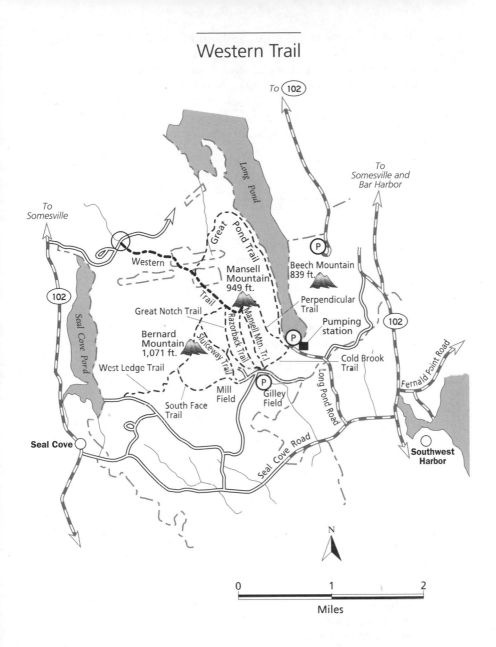

To (102)

To
Somesville and
Bar Harbor

To
Somesville

Long Pond

Great Pond Trail

P

Western Trail

Mansell
Mountain
949 ft.

Beech Mountain
839 ft.

Perpendicular
Trail

Great Notch Trail

Mansell Mtn. Trl.

Razorback Trail

Pumping
station

(102)

Bernard
Mountain
1,071 ft.

Sluiceway Trail

P

Cold Brook
Trail

102

Seal Cove Pond

West Ledge Trail

Fernald Point Road

Mill
Field

P

Gilley
Field

South Face
Trail

Long Pond Road

Seal Cove

Southwest
Harbor

Seal Cove Road

N

0   1   2

Miles

The hike: This is the longest and most gradual way up wooded Mansell Mountain and the least traveled. The trail heads east-southeast from the gravel Long Pond Fire Road, taking you along a fast-moving creek and over split-log bridges through boggy areas. At 1.1 miles, reach a junction with the Great Pond Trail. Bear right to continue on the Western Trail. At 1.5 miles and 640 feet elevation, reach a four-way intersection at the Great Notch. There are a couple of wood benches conveniently placed here. Turn left (east) at this intersection. Bear left at the next two junctions, where the Razorback

Trail comes in on the right at 1.6 miles and the Mansell Mountain Trail at 1.7 miles.

At 1.8 miles, reach 949-foot Mansell Mountain and the junction with the Perpendicular Trail. There is no view at the wooded summit, but if you continue straight (east) you'll reach an overlook at the top of the Perpendicular Trail at 1.9 miles. There are views down to Long Pond, east to Beech Mountain and its fire tower, and south to the Cranberry Isles.

78 West Ledge Trail

Highlights: Steep hike up Bernard Mountain's open western ledges; good views.
Type of hike: Day hike; out-and-back.
Total distance: 3.2 miles.
Difficulty: Strenuous.

Finding the trailhead: Head south of Somesville on Maine Highway 102; and turn right at the flashing yellow light toward Pretty Marsh. Stay straight for 7.6 miles, traveling past Pretty Marsh and Seal Cove. Turn left onto the gravel Seal Cove Road and travel for 0.5 mile, then turn left at the sign pointing to Western Mountain Road. At a four-way inter-

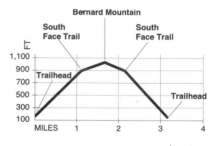

section reached in another 0.4 mile, turn right following the sign to Western Mountain Road. At the junction with Western Mountain Road, reached in another 0.4 mile, take a left toward Seal Cove Pond. The trailhead is on the right in 0.4 mile.

Parking and trailhead facilities: Park in a small pullout along the gravel Western Mountain Road on the left beyond the trailhead.

Key points:
- 0.0　West Ledge Trailhead.
- 1.1　Junction with the South Face Trail.
- 1.6　Bernard Mountain summit.

The hike: This hard-to-reach trail offers some of the best views of all the trails up mostly wooded Bernard Mountain, the highest peak on Mount Desert Island west of Somes Sound. Alternating between steep ascents through vintage Acadia forest and open rock ledges, the West Ledge Trail provides increasingly sweeping views the higher you go.

Begin ascending. At one point along the exposed ledges, you get great vistas of the towns of Bernard and Bass Harbor and the Gulf of Maine to the south. Seal Cove Pond sits off to the west. Next the trail climbs through a

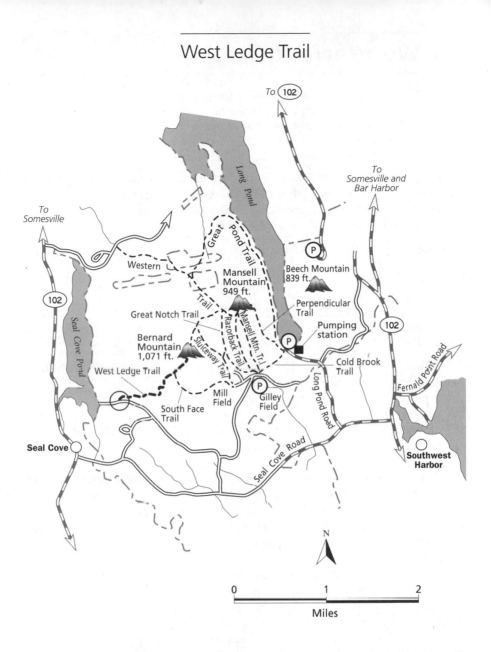

birch grove and takes you through a marshy area. After a bit of level walking along a wooded ridge, you ascend steeply again at a sharp pitch to the right. The climbing is very steep and tough here along an open rock face marked by cairns, but the views behind you are spectacular.

At 1.1 miles, reach a junction with the South Face Trail. Bear left toward Bernard Mountain, reaching the summit at 1.6 miles. The 1,071-foot peak is wooded, but there is an overlook; look for the sign. There's a nice log bench to sit on and take in the beautiful views.

79 Wonderland Trail

Highlights:	Pink granite outcroppings along shore; tide pools for exploring at low tide.
Type of hike:	Day hike; out-and-back.
Total distance:	1.4 miles.
Difficulty:	Easy.

Finding the trailhead: From Southwest Harbor, head south 1 mile on Maine Highway 102. Bear left on ME 102A, passing the town of Manset in 1 mile and the Seawall Campground and picnic area in 3 miles, and reaching the Wonderland Trailhead on the left in 4 miles.

Parking and trailhead facilities: The trailhead parking lot is on the left (south) side of ME 102A.

Key points:
- 0.0   Wonderland Trailhead.
- 0.1   Slight uphill.
- 0.7   Rocky shoreline.

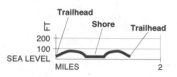

The hike: Once you see the smooth pink granite along the shore, smell the salty sea, and explore the tide pools, you know why they call this the Wonderland Trail. The easy trail along an old gravel road starts by winding through dark woods, but a huge, smooth pink granite rock on the left soon hints at the picture show to come.

At 0.1 mile, walk up a slight hill and make your way carefully among some roots and rocks. This is the toughest part of an otherwise very easy, well-graded trail. Skunk cabbages are found along this section of the trail, with their distinctive purplish red leaves and yellow flower in early spring and huge green foliage in summer. Through the trees you can see the ocean on the right (southeast).

At 0.7 mile, the trail takes you to the shore, where the pink granite dramatically meets the sea. You can spend hours exploring here, especially when low tide exposes tide pools and their diverse marine life, from rockweed to barnacles to green crabs. Be careful of wet rocks, slick seaweed, and sudden waves, however. Return the way you came.

Wonderland Trail

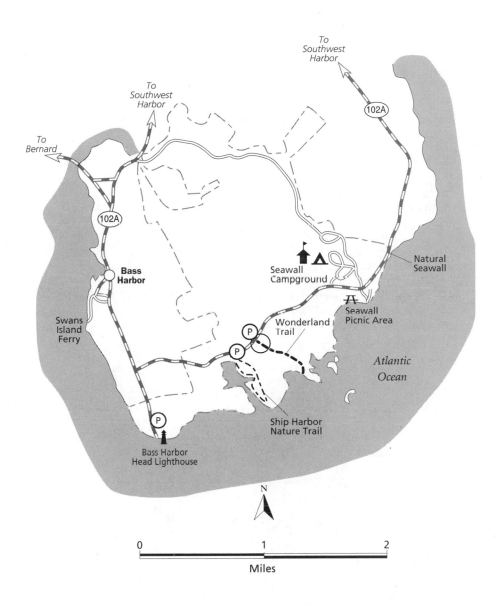

To Southwest Harbor

To Southwest Harbor

To Bernard

102A

102A

Bass Harbor

Swans Island Ferry

Seawall Campground

Natural Seawall

Seawall Picnic Area

Wonderland Trail

Atlantic Ocean

Ship Harbor Nature Trail

Bass Harbor Head Lighthouse

N

0   1   2
Miles

80 Ship Harbor Nature Trail

Highlights: Pink granite cliffs along shoreline.
Type of hike: Day hike; loop.
Total distance: 1.3 miles.
Difficulty: Easy.

Finding the trailhead: From Southwest Harbor, head south 1 mile on Maine Highway 102. Bear left on ME 102A, passing the town of Manset in 1 mile and the Seawall Campground and picnic area in 3 miles, and reaching the Wonderland Trail parking area in 4 miles. The Ship Harbor Trailhead is 0.2 mile after Wonderland.

Parking and trailhead facilities: The trailhead parking lot is on the left (south) side of ME 102A; there is a chemical toilet here.

Key points:
    0.0   Ship Harbor Nature Trailhead.
    0.1   Bear left (southeast) at the first fork.
    0.3   Three-way intersection; bear left (southeast) up a hill.
    0.6   Trail meets the shoreline; bear right (north) along the Ship Harbor channel.
    1.0   Three-way intersection; bear left (northwest) along Ship Harbor.
    1.2   Bear left (northwest) at a fork.
    1.3   Ship Harbor Nature Trailhead.

A birch grows along Bernard Mountain's West Ledge Trail.

Ship Harbor Nature Trail

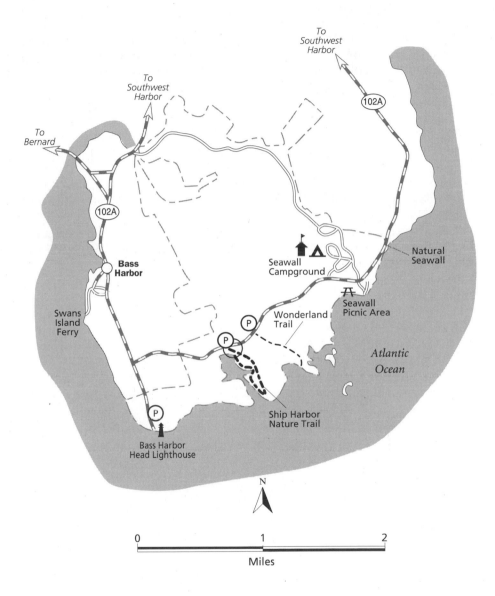

The hike: The drama of the sea crashing against Acadia's pink granite cliffs is this easy trail's greatest reward. But there are also other, smaller pleasures, like seeing ocean ducks known as common eiders floating at the mouth of Ship Harbor. The guided nature trail—the descriptive brochure is available at the park visitor center for 50 cents—takes visitors along 14 different signposts, providing lessons about the glacial action that carved out Mount Desert Island; the spruce and tamarack trees; the pink granite cliffs; and the local legend's explanation for the name Ship Harbor. Although the loop trail is easy, footing is rough with roots and rocks in places, and hilly in others. Wear appropriate footwear.

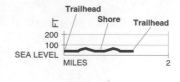

The trail, built in 1957, begins with a view of the harbor in the distance and a sign marking the apple trees of a farm that once stood here. At the first fork at 0.1 mile, bear left (southeast) to follow the numbered signposts through the woods. Soon after signpost No. 4 at 0.3 mile, you'll come to a three-way intersection. Bear left (southeast) up the hill to follow the signposts in order. (If the uphill presents too much of an obstacle, however, take the middle path to the shoreline instead, and backtrack on the return to avoid the hill.)

Whether you climb the hill or take the easier middle path, you'll soon come to the dramatic pink cliffs at 0.6 mile. You can spend hours exploring the shoreline, especially at low tide, when barnacles, rockweed, snails, and other sea life are exposed by the receding waters. Remember to put back tide pool creatures where you found them.

Loop back, heading north along the channel leading to Ship Harbor, until you come back to the three-way intersection again at mile 1. Follow the arrow on the signpost to the left (northwest) to get to the final leg of the loop trail, taking you along Ship Harbor.

Legend says that during the Revolutionary War, an American ship escaping a British gunboat got stuck in the mud here—hence the name Ship Harbor. After the last signpost, No. 14, at 1.2 miles, you'll soon come to another fork in the trail. Bear left (northwest) and you'll be back at the parking lot.

Isle au Haut

A distinctive island of mountains named by French explorer Samuel Champlain in 1604, Isle au Haut, pronounced locally as "Isle a Ho" (High Island), is one of the most remote parts of Acadia National Park. But the views and feeling of being transformed to another place and time make it worth the 1½-hour drive from Bar Harbor to catch the mail boat (not ferry, as locals quickly point out) from Stonington.

First settled in 1792 by farmers, boat builders, fishermen, and their families, Isle au Haut is still home to around 70 year-round residents and scores of summer residents. Part of the island was donated to the park in 1943 by one of the Boston-area families that began summering here in the 1880s.

There's a special quality to the passage of time here, the sense of humor and the way events in the island's history get remembered.

Everyone who lives on the island recalls the year the male moose swam to the island during rutting season. But when he "didn't find any of his kind, he hung around Al Gordon's cow," said Wayne Barter, a descendant of one of the original settlers here and a longtime National Park Service employee. The moose swam off after a couple of weeks.

Another time, Barter recalled, "there were 28 days of straight fog in the summer time." Sometimes, one half of the island will be foggy and the other half sunny, he said.

Barter left the island to work on the mainland for a while, but the pull of the place brought him back. "It's in my blood, ever since I was a kid," he said. And, he wryly added, "You can visit America anytime."

Fellow park employee John Cousins, a relative newcomer, having moved to the island in the late 1980s, shared with us a park display contrasting a vertebra of the humpback whale with a vertebra of a deer, to show how much bigger the whale is. And he pulled out a memo pad with statistics to show us how much visitation to the island has increased. Between 1985 and 1998, the number of visitors nearly quadrupled to 8,822. To protect the island from overuse, day visitors are limited to 50 a day during the height of the season and 25 a day during the off-season. Every day in the off-season, except Sundays and postal holidays, the mailboat named *Miss Lizzie* comes over twice to the island's town landing, dropping off mail and park visitors.

The Duck Harbor Trail is the only park trail near the town landing and leads 3.8 miles south to where many of the other trails begin at Duck Harbor Campground and Landing. The trail serves as the only access off-season to the campground and must be backpacked its entire length by overnight campers that time of year.

At the height of the tourist season, the mail boat makes three trips to the town landing a day, Monday through Saturday, and one on Sundays and holidays. A second boat goes directly from Stonington to Duck Harbor Landing, taking visitors close to many of the island's other trailheads and the Duck Harbor Campground with its five lean-to shelters, available only by reservation. There is no auto ferry.

Isle au Haut

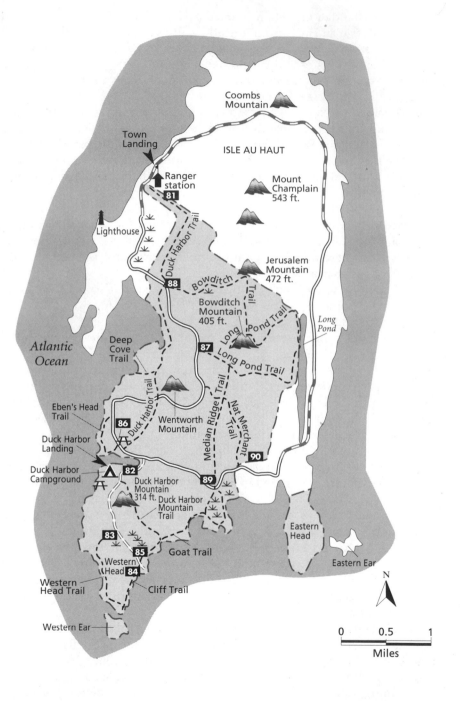

Coombs Mountain

ISLE AU HAUT

Town Landing

Ranger station

81

Lighthouse

Duck Harbor Trail

Mount Champlain 543 ft.

88

Bowditch

Jerusalem Mountain 472 ft.

Bowditch Mountain 405 ft.

Long Pond Trail

Long Pond

Atlantic Ocean

Deep Cove Trail

87

Long Pond Trail

Wentworth Mountain

Eben's Head Trail

86

Duck Harbor Trail

Median Ridge Trail

Nat Merchant Trail

Duck Harbor Landing

Duck Harbor Campground

82

90

Duck Harbor Mountain 314 ft.

89

Duck Harbor Mountain Trail

Eastern Head

83

85

Goat Trail

Eastern Ear

Western Head

84

Western Head Trail

Cliff Trail

Western Ear

N

0   0.5   1
Miles

Summertime day-trippers can have lunch at the picnic tables at Duck Harbor Landing and the nearby Eben's Head Trail. More ambitious hikers and overnight campers can explore some of the approximately 20 miles of trails that crisscross the island, up low mountains, along the rocky shore, and through marshland and bogs. The views can be spectacular, with glimpses of the Camden Hills on the mainland and the island of Vinalhaven—as long as the fog doesn't roll in.

To catch the mail boat out of Stonington, drive north on Maine Highway 3 from Bar Harbor to Ellsworth. Take ME 172 south to Blue Hill, then ME 15 south to Deer Isle and Stonington. Call the Isle au Haut Company at (207) 367-5193 for the boat schedule. Limited parking can be found in town. Advanced reservations for the five lean-to shelters at Duck Harbor Campground, open May 15 through October 15, must be made in person or by mail using a special reservation request form, beginning April 1. No telephone requests are accepted. Reservations can go fast, particularly for summertime and weekend slots.

For fees and other regulations, write: Acadia National Park, Attn: Isle au Haut Reservations, P.O. Box 177, Bar Harbor, ME 04609.

Hop aboard Miss Lizzie *to reach Isle au Haut.*

81 Duck Harbor Trail

Highlights: Woods and bog walk, with some rocky coast; spur trail to Deep Cove.

Type of hike: Day hike; out-and-back.

Total distance: 7.6 miles.

Difficulty: Moderate.

Finding the trailhead: From the town landing, turn right (southwest) and walk on the paved road for 0.3 mile. Turn left at the ranger station and walk past a bench and under an awning to reach the trailhead.

Parking and trailhead facilities: There is no parking and the only facility is a chemical toilet. Don't miss the display that compares a whale vertebra to a deer vertebra.

Key points:

0.0	Duck Harbor Trailhead.
1.4	Junction with the Bowditch Trail.
1.5	Cross the island loop road.
2.1	Goss Beach.
2.4	Eli Creek cascades at an old cabin.
2.7	Junction with the Deep Cove Trail.
3.0	Cross the island loop road.
3.8	Island loop road; Duck Harbor Campground is 0.5 mile to the left (southeast), then right (south) at the next fork.

The hike: This is the only north-south trail that leads from the town landing to Duck Harbor Campground. Off-season campers must plan to backpack

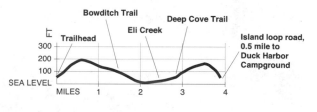

the entire 3.8-mile length of the trail, plus another 0.5 mile on an unpaved road to reach the campground's lean-to shelters.

The blue-blazed trail immediately goes through a boggy area with plentiful skunk cabbage, then enters an evergreen forest. At 1.4 miles, at the junction with the Bowditch Trail, bear right (south) and soon cross the road that circles the island. For day-trippers pressed to catch the mail boat back to the mainland, you can turn right on the road and loop back to town landing in another 1 mile.

At 2.1 miles, the Duck Harbor Trail begins to skirt the rocky shore of Goss Beach. The trail is tricky here, sometimes taking you along the beach over a bed of seaweed and mussel shells and other times swinging inland. Watch

Duck Harbor Trail

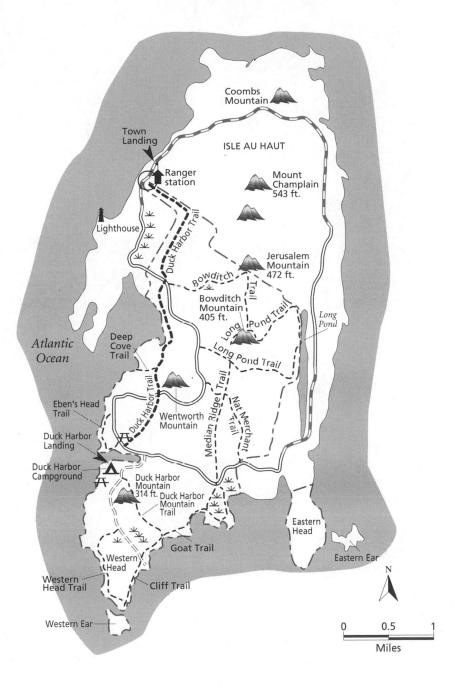

Pink granite shoreline and deep blue sea make for a unique Acadia contrast.

carefully for cairns on the beach and an unusual Isle au Haut trail marker—lobster trap buoys hanging from the trees.

At 2.4 miles, the trail crosses a log bridge by an old cabin, taking you across cascades, where Eli Creek goes into the ocean. You'll soon skirt a small cove where the water appears deep green on calm days. Head inland again.

At 2.7 miles, reach a junction with the Deep Cove Trail, a short spur to the right (west). The spur descends 0.2 mile, crossing a log bridge just before you reach Deep Cove. Continue south on the Duck Harbor Trail, going up and down through the woods and along some log bridges. Cross the island loop road for a second time at 3 miles, and reach the trail's end at the third intersection with the loop road at 3.8 miles.

To continue to the campground, turn left (southeast) on the road, then bear right (south) at the next fork toward Duck Harbor Landing. The trail to the lean-tos leads behind the chemical toilet at the picnic area, just before the boat landing.

82 Duck Harbor Mountain Trail

Highlights:	Strange rocky knobs called the Puddings; panoramic views atop Duck Harbor Mountain.
Type of hike:	Day hike; out-and-back or part of loop.
Total distance:	2.4 miles.
Difficulty:	Strenuous.

Finding the trailhead: From Duck Harbor Landing, turn right (south) on the unpaved Western Head Road. The Duck Harbor Mountain Trailhead is on your left in 0.1 mile.

Parking and trailhead facilities: None.

Key points:

0.0   Duck Harbor
         Mountain Trailhead.
0.3   Duck Harbor Mountain summit.
0.5   Puddings.
1.2   Junction with the Goat Trail.

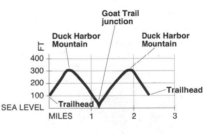

The hike: Duck Harbor Mountain Trail is the most strenuous hike on Isle au Haut, but it also offers some of the most spectacular views. The trail begins steeply through the woods, alternating between switchbacks and brief flat sections on ridges. At 0.2 mile, turn sharp right (south) onto an open ledge. Continue climbing up open ledges and reach the 314-foot summit of Duck Harbor Mountain at 0.3 mile, marked by a USGS metal disk. Views of the rest of Isle au Haut, the island of Vinalhaven, and the mainland can be seen along here.

Follow the trail through a flat wooded area. At 0.5 mile, reach the Puddings, a series of challenging rocky knobs that require scrambling on all fours in some areas. There are no iron rungs here to help you along the smooth rock face, so to climb up you need to find nooks and crannies for handholds and footholds, and to get down you need to slide on your behind. Don't let

Duck Harbor Mountain Trail

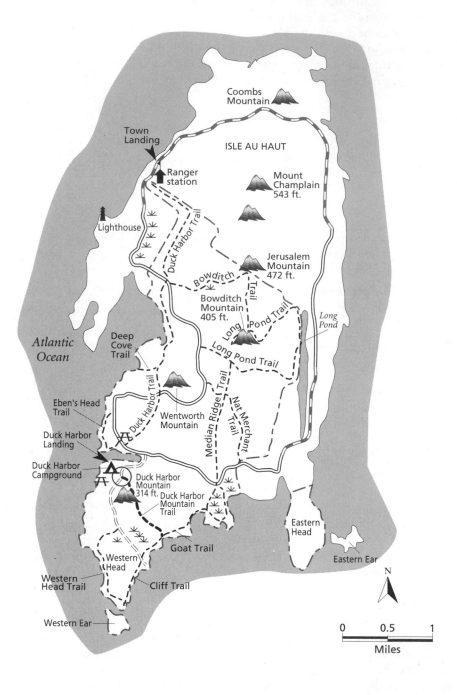

the great views distract you from focusing on the rock climbing you need to do here.

The trail takes you through a narrow rock chasm, then descends a steep rock face. Reach the Goat Trail in 1.2 miles, where the trail ends. If you're a glutton for punishment, or you're dying to see the spectacular views again, you can return the same way, making it a 2.4-mile out-and-back hike. For an easier but slightly longer 2.9-mile loop hike, turn right (west) on the Goat Trail for 0.5 mile. Then turn right (northwest) on the unpaved Western Head Road. Return to the Duck Harbor Trailhead in another 1.2 miles.

83 Western Head Trail

Highlights: Spectacular rocky coast walk; Western Ear accessible at low tide.
Type of hike: Day hike; out-and-back or part of loop.
Total distance: 4.2 miles, including 0.7-mile walk to trailhead.
Difficulty: Moderate.

Finding the trailhead: From Duck Harbor Landing, turn right (south) on the unpaved Western Head Road. Walk 0.7 mile on the road. The Western Head Trailhead is on the right.

Parking and trailhead facilities: None.

Key points:
0.0 Duck Harbor Landing; bear right on the Western Head Road.
0.7 Western Head Trailhead, reached via the Western Head Road.
1.2 Reach the shore.
1.7 Reach cliffs.
2.0 Junction with the Cliff Trail; turn right.
2.1 Western Ear.

The hike: If you time the hike along this rocky coast trail to coincide with low tide, you can cross over to explore the small rocky isle known as Western Ear. If not, you will still get the spectacular views

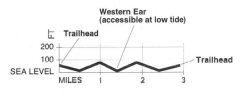

from this part of Isle au Haut known as Western Head. Of the two trails that lead to Western Ear, this is the longer one, while the shorter Cliff Trail has more steep ups and downs.

At 0.7 mile from Duck Harbor Landing, the Western Head Trail heads west from the unpaved road, going over moss-covered roots and rotting logs to start. At 1.1 miles, you get views of the coast and offshore rocky outcroppings. At 1.2 miles, you quickly descend to the shore, where a pile of colorful buoys marks the path. The trail continues up and down along the

Western Head Trail

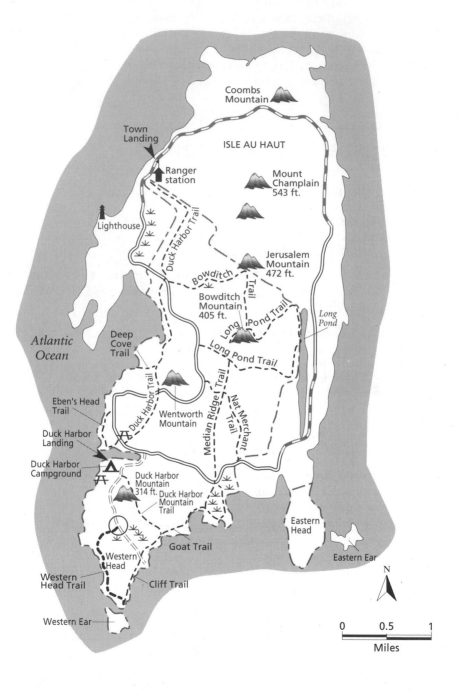

Coombs Mountain

Town Landing

Ranger station

ISLE AU HAUT

Lighthouse

Mount Champlain 543 ft.

Duck Harbor Trail

Bowditch Trail

Jerusalem Mountain 472 ft.

Long Pond Trail

Bowditch Mountain 405 ft.

Long Pond

Atlantic Ocean

Deep Cove Trail

Long Pond Trail

Duck Harbor Trail

Eben's Head Trail

Wentworth Mountain

Median Ridge Trail

Nat Merchant Trail

Duck Harbor Landing

Duck Harbor Campground

Duck Harbor Mountain 314 ft.

Duck Harbor Mountain Trail

Goat Trail

Eastern Head

Western Head

Eastern Ear

Western Head Trail

Cliff Trail

Western Ear

N

0   0.5   1
Miles

A unique guidepost on Western Head Trail.

craggy coast, passing a cove and a distinctive pink granite formation. It's easy to lose the trail as it gets tricky here, weaving inland at times through woods and coming back out to the rocky beach again. Just keep paralleling the shore until you pick up the path again.

At 1.7 miles, the trail climbs steeply to cliffs, then continues through a rugged stretch of woods coming out at a cove. Although the trail appears to follow the granite along the shore here, it actually heads inland a bit, ending at 2 miles at the junction with the Cliff Trail. Turn right (southwest) onto a 0.1-mile spur to the tip of Western Head, the jumping-off point for the low-tide walk across to Western Ear. Remember not to get stranded by the incoming tide if you do explore the rocky isle. Return the way you came, on the 0.1-mile spur back to the junction and then left (northwest) onto the Western Head Trail.

Options: For a 4.2-mile loop, on the return from the tip of Western Head, go straight (northeast) on the 0.7-mile-long Cliff Trail rather than turning left at the junction back onto the Western Head Trail. At the end of the Cliff Trail, turn left (northwest) on the unpaved Western Head Road, looping back to the Western Head Trailhead in another 0.6 mile. Duck Harbor Landing is another 0.7 mile down the road.

84 Cliff Trail

Highlights: Dramatic cliff views; low-tide walk to Western Ear.
Type of hike: Day hike; out-and-back or part of loop.
Total distance: 4.2 miles, including 1.4 miles to reach trailhead.
Difficulty: Moderate.

Finding the trailhead: From Duck Harbor Landing, turn right (south) on the unpaved Western Head Road. Walk 1.4 miles on the road, until it nears the shore. The Cliff Trailhead is on the right.

Parking and trailhead facilities: None.

Key points:
- 0.0 Duck Harbor Landing; bear right on the Western Head Road.
- 1.4 Cliff Trailhead, reached via the Western Head Road.
- 2.0 Junction with the Western Head Trail.
- 2.1 Tip of the Western Head.

The hike: If you're hurrying to catch low tide to cross over to the rocky island of Western Ear, this is the shorter of two trails to get you there. But the Cliff Trail has more ups and downs along the cliffs than

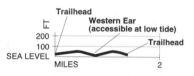

the Western Head Trail and requires a longer walk on the unpaved Western Head Road to reach the trailhead.

Starting in a level grassy area at the end of the road, the Cliff Trail heads southwest and quickly climbs along the craggy coast. Soon, a deep chasm in the cliff walls along the trail allows the ocean spray to spit through and the sound of the waves to thunder in, especially on a windy or stormy day.

At 2 miles from Duck Harbor Landing, the Western Head Trail comes in from the right. Continue straight (southwest) and reach the tip of Western Head at 2.1 miles. If it's low tide, you can cross over and explore Western Ear, but be mindful of the time so you don't get stranded. Return the way you came.

Options: To do a loop, backtrack 0.1 mile from the end of the trail at the tip of Western Head and turn left (northwest) onto the Western Head Trail. Walk 1.3 miles, then turn left (northwest) on the unpaved Western Head Road. Duck Harbor Landing is 0.7 mile down the road.

Cliff Trail

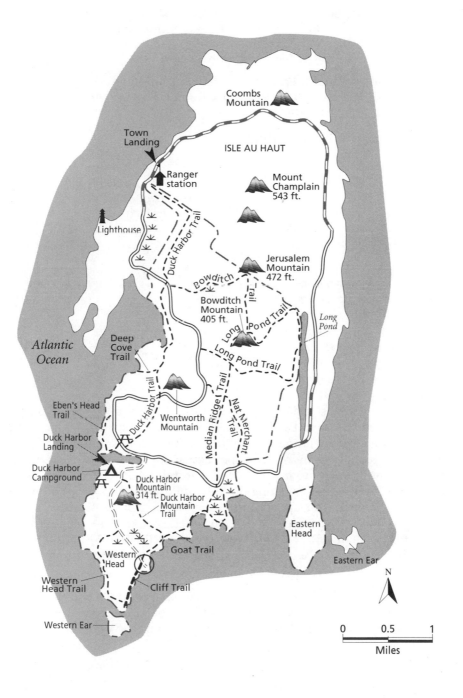

Coombs
Mountain

Town
Landing

Ranger
station

ISLE AU HAUT

Mount
Champlain
543 ft.

Lighthouse

Duck Harbor Trail

Bowditch

Jerusalem
Mountain
472 ft.

Bowditch
Mountain
405 ft.

Long Pond Trail

Long
Pond

*Atlantic
Ocean*

Deep
Cove
Trail

Long Pond Trail

Eben's Head
Trail

Duck Harbor Trail

Median Ridge Trail

Nat Merchant Trail

Wentworth
Mountain

Duck Harbor
Landing

Duck Harbor
Campground

Duck Harbor
Mountain
314 ft.

Duck Harbor
Mountain
Trail

Eastern
Head

Eastern Ear

Western
Head

Goat Trail

N

Western
Head Trail

Cliff Trail

Western Ear

0   0.5   1
Miles

85 Goat Trail

Highlights: Rugged hike with coastal views.
Type of hike: Day hike; out-and-back or part of loop.
Total distance: 6.8 miles, including 1.3 miles to reach trailhead.
Difficulty: Moderate to strenuous.

Finding the trailhead: From Duck Harbor Landing, turn right (south) on the unpaved Western Head Road. Walk 1.3 miles on the road, until it nears the shore. The Goat Trailhead is on the left.

Parking and trailhead facilities: None.

Key points:
    0.0   Duck Harbor Landing; bear right on the Western Head Road.
    1.3   Goat Trailhead, reached via the Western Head Road.
    1.6   Junction with the Duck Harbor Mountain Trail.
    2.5   Junction with the Median Ridge Trail.
    3.4   Island loop road.

The hike: This trail is rugged enough for a mountain goat, and it offers spectacular coastal scenery as a reward. If you're lucky you may also spot evidence of the elusive mink, a semiaquatic weasel, along the way as well.

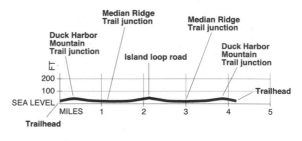

At the outset, the trail skirts Deep Cove (where a 45-foot humpback whale washed ashore in February 1983), crosses a small creek (dry in summer), and reaches the junction with the Duck Harbor Mountain Trail. Here the ocean knifes in to shore, with spectacular spirelike cliffs. Next the trail climbs up and down mountain goat–like terrain, over creeks, along cliffs, and on rocky beaches. All along the way are dramatic views of ocean and coves, including an especially picturesque scene of Barred Harbor.

At 2.5 miles, at the eastern end of Barred Harbor, the trail reaches a junction with the Median Ridge Trail. From here the Cliff Trail heads into marshland that may be too wet to hike after rain. It ends at 3.4 miles at the unpaved island loop road. Return the way you came.

Options: To loop back to Duck Harbor Landing, at trail's end turn left on the unpaved island loop road and walk 1 mile. Then turn left on the unpaved Western Head Road, reaching Duck Harbor Landing in another 0.3 mile.

Goat Trail

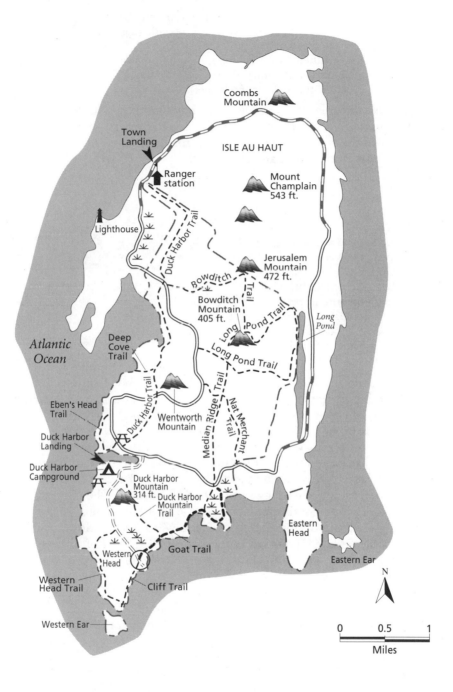

Coombs Mountain

Town Landing

Ranger station

ISLE AU HAUT

Mount Champlain 543 ft.

Lighthouse

Duck Harbor Trail

Bowditch Trail

Jerusalem Mountain 472 ft.

Bowditch Mountain 405 ft.

Long Pond Trail

Long Pond

Long Pond Trail

Atlantic Ocean

Deep Cove Trail

Eben's Head Trail

Duck Harbor Trail

Wentworth Mountain

Median Ridge Trail

Nat Merchant Trail

Duck Harbor Landing

Duck Harbor Campground

Duck Harbor Mountain 314 ft.

Duck Harbor Mountain Trail

Eastern Head

Goat Trail

Eastern Ear

Western Head

Western Head Trail

Cliff Trail

Western Ear

N

0   0.5   1
Miles

86 Eben's Head Trail

Highlights: Distinctive rock outcropping known as Eben's Head; open grassy area for picnicking and shoreline for exploring.
Type of hike: Day hike; loop.
Total distance: 2.9 miles, including 0.8 mile to reach trailhead.
Difficulty: Easy to moderate.

Finding the trailhead: From Duck Harbor Landing, bear left on the unpaved Western Head Road and go around the harbor. At 0.3 mile, turn left (northwest) onto the unpaved island loop road. Reach the trailhead on the left side of the loop road in another 0.5 mile.

Parking and trailhead facilities: No parking is available; there is a picnic table, but no other facilities.

Key points:

0.0 Duck Harbor Landing; bear left on the Western Head Road.
0.3 Unpaved island loop road; turn left.
0.8 Eben's Head Trailhead.
1.1 Junction with a spur trail to Eben's Head.
1.6 Unpaved island loop road; turn right to loop back.
2.1 Eben's Head Trailhead.
2.9 Duck Harbor Landing.

The hike: The Eben's Head Trail is an easy to moderate hike for day-trippers and picnickers who arrive at nearby Duck Harbor Landing. It doesn't provide mountaintop views, but does offer a picnic table and an open grassy area, and gives you an opportunity to explore the rocky shore and the distinctive outcropping known as Eben's Head.

The trail starts easily through the woods, then skirts the shore, with a view across Duck Harbor to the boat landing. The trail curves right (northwest). A spur trail leads left (west) to a grassy area at the base of Eben's Head, a nice spot for a picnic, with views of the rocky coastline. The main trail then gets a little rougher, continuing northwest across a stretch of rocky beach, marked by cairns and lobster trap buoys, toward a set of low rocky cliffs marked by blue blazes. Look behind you for a good view of Eben's Head.

Scramble up the low cliffs and follow the trail through the woods. The trail goes sharply left and takes you onto the rocky shore again and up another series of low cliffs. The trail continues to weave in and out along the shore, up and down rocky outcroppings. It turns inland (northeast) for the last time at a bright blue wooden arrow nailed to a tree. Turn right (southwest) along the well-graded unpaved road, returning to the trailhead in another 0.5 mile.

If you're catching the boat back to the mainland, remember to factor in the extra 0.8 mile walk along unpaved roads from the trailhead back to Duck Harbor Landing.

Eben's Head Trail

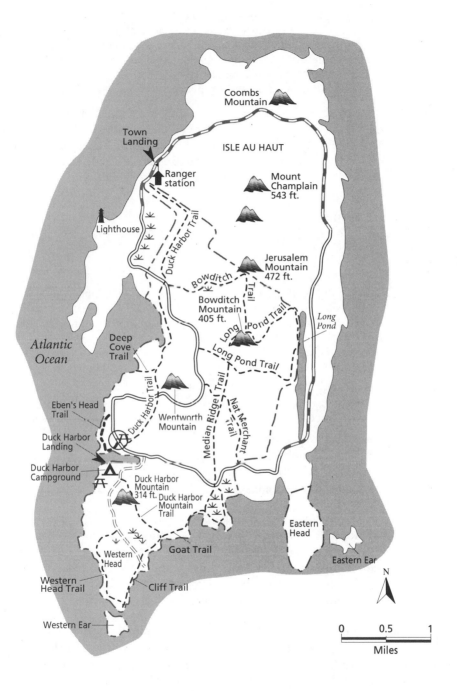

Coombs
Mountain

ISLE AU HAUT

Town
Landing

Ranger
station

Mount
Champlain
543 ft.

Lighthouse

Duck Harbor Trail

Bowditch

Trail

Jerusalem
Mountain
472 ft.

Bowditch
Mountain
405 ft.

Long Pond Trail

Long
Pond

Deep
Cove
Trail

Atlantic
Ocean

Long Pond Trail

Eben's Head
Trail

Duck Harbor Trail

Wentworth
Mountain

Median Ridge Trail

Nat Merchant
Trail

Duck Harbor
Landing

Duck Harbor
Campground

Duck Harbor
Mountain
314 ft.

Duck Harbor
Mountain
Trail

Eastern
Head

Goat Trail

Western
Head

Eastern Ear

Western
Head Trail

Cliff Trail

N

Western Ear

0   0.5   1

Miles

87 Long Pond Trail

Highlights:	Views of mile-long freshwater pond; wooded Bowditch Mountain; uncrowded.
Type of hike:	Day hike; loop; or part of overnight camping trip.
Total distance:	9.0 miles, including 3 miles to reach trailhead from the town landing.
Difficulty:	Moderate to strenuous.

Finding the trailhead: From the town landing, turn right on a paved road and walk 3 miles, following the road as it becomes unpaved. The Long Pond Trailhead is on the left (east) or to reach the trailhead from Duck Harbor Landing, turn left on the unpaved Western Head Road and walk 0.3 mile. Then turn left on the island loop road, unpaved here, and walk 2.5 miles. The Long Pond Trailhead is on the right (east).

Parking and trailhead facilities: None.

Key points:
0.0 Town landing; turn right on the paved road.
3.0 Long Pond Trailhead.
3.4 Junction with the Median Ridge Trail; begin the Long Pond Trail loop.
4.5 Reach the shore of Long Pond.
5.3 Junction with the Bowditch Trail; wooded summit of Bowditch Mountain.
5.6 Junction with the Median Ridge Trail again; bear right.
6.0 Long Pond Trailhead.
9.0 Town landing.

The hike: Because the trailhead is about a 3-mile walk on the island loop road from either the town landing or Duck Harbor Landing, Long Pond Trail is the most difficult to reach on Isle au Haut.

The trail begins easily enough, along a level stretch of woods, and over log bridges through a skunk cabbage–filled bog. At 0.4 mile from the trailhead, the trail reaches a four-way intersection, with the Median Ridge Trail coming in from the right, the southern part of the Long Pond Trail loop straight ahead, and the northern part of the Long Pond Trail loop coming in from the left. Go straight on the southern part of the loop and head across the ridge through stands of cedar and birch, then down steeply at times, toward Long Pond.

At 1 mile from the trailhead, bear sharply left along a creek, where two blue blazes on a tree mark a change in trail direction. The trail then crosses over an old stone wall and parallels it. The going gets rather rough here, and some boulder hopping might be necessary. You'll reach a sign pointing

Long Pond Trail

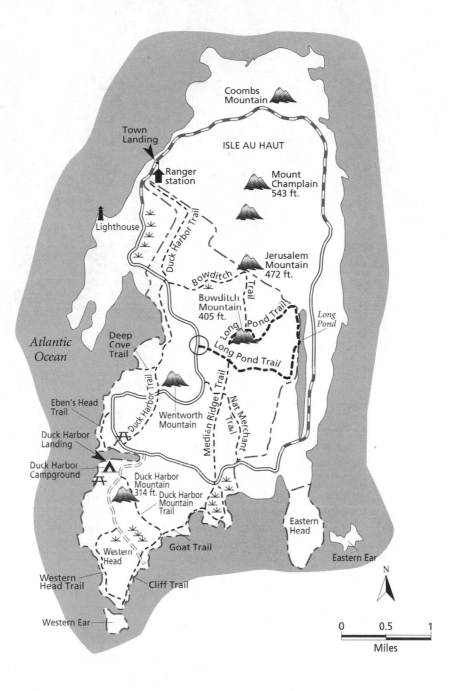

Coombs
Mountain

Town
Landing

Ranger
station

ISLE AU HAUT

Mount
Champlain
543 ft.

Lighthouse

Duck Harbor Trail

Bowditch

Jerusalem
Mountain
472 ft.

Trail

Bowditch
Mountain
405 ft.

Long Pond Trail

Long
Pond

Atlantic
Ocean

Deep
Cove
Trail

Long

Long Pond Trail

Eben's Head
Trail

Duck Harbor Trail

Duck Harbor
Landing

Wentworth
Mountain

Median Ridge Trail

Nat Merchant
Trail

Duck Harbor
Campground

Duck Harbor
Mountain
314 ft. Duck Harbor
Mountain
Trail

Eastern
Head

Western
Head

Goat Trail

Eastern Ear

Western
Head Trail

Cliff Trail

N

Western Ear

0   0.5   1

Miles

A log bridge through marsh on the Long Pond Trail.

to Long Pond and leave the distinctive stone wall behind. The trail takes some tricky turns across creek beds and along granite faces, so watch for small cairns and blue blazes that mark the way.

Shortly after the trail goes by a cascade, Long Pond comes into view through the trees. When the trail finally reaches the shore at 4.5 miles from the town landing, be sure to savor the views. The path follows the pond for less than 100 yards before it heads steeply back up the ridge via switchbacks. The trail takes you over a deep crevice on a small wooden bridge and continues its upward course, steeply and then more gently.

At 5.3 miles from the town landing, reach Bowditch Mountain's wooded summit, elevation 405 feet, and the junction with the Bowditch Trail. Bear left (southwest) to continue on the Long Pond Trail, closing the loop in another 0.3 mile when you reach the junction with the Median Ridge Trail again. Turn right (northwest) at this four-way intersection and return to the trailhead at the island loop road again in another 0.4 mile. Turn right onto the island loop road to return to the town landing, or left to return to Duck Harbor Landing.

Options: To avoid the long hike back on the island loop road when returning to the town landing, you can take the Bowditch Trail rather than closing the Long Pond loop. At the junction with the Bowditch Trail, bear right (north) and walk about 2 miles until you reach the intersection with the Duck Harbor Trail. Turn right (northwest) on the Duck Harbor Trail and reach the island loop road close to the town landing in another 1.4 miles. Turn right (northeast) on the paved road to reach the town landing in another 0.3 mile.

To avoid the long hike back on the island loop road when returning to Duck Harbor Landing, you can take the Median Ridge Trail on the return instead. After closing the Long Pond Trail loop at the four-way intersection, head straight across and south on the Median Ridge Trail. After 1.5 miles, the Median Ridge Trail reaches the island loop road. Turn right, or northwest on the unpaved road, and walk 1 mile. Then turn left (southwest) on the unpaved Western Head Road, reaching Duck Harbor Landing in another 0.3 mile.

88 Bowditch Trail

Highlights:	Climb up wooded summit of Bowditch Mountain, highest peak within island's park boundary; little traveled.
Type of hike:	Day hike; out-and-back or loop.
Total distance:	7.4 miles, including 1.7 miles to reach trailhead.
Difficulty:	Moderate.

Finding the trailhead: From the town landing, turn right on the paved road. Walk 0.3 mile, turn left at the ranger station, and hike Duck Harbor Trail for 1.4 miles to Bowditch Trailhead on the left.

Parking and trailhead facilities: None.

Key points:
- 0.0 Town landing; turn right on the paved road.
- 0.3 Duck Harbor Trail.
- 1.7 Bowditch Trailhead.
- 2.8 Take a sharp right (south).
- 3.7 Bowditch Mountain summit.

The hike: The Bowditch Trail offers no expansive mountaintop views, but it blooms with rhodora, sheep laurel, and tiny white star flowers in spring. It is useful as a connector to the Long Pond Trail, or as part of an extended inland hike along the spine of the island.

From the junction with the Duck Harbor Trail, head east toward Bowditch Mountain. Cross a long series of log bridges, through a marshy area with huge skunk cabbages. The trail now begins a long gradual ascent toward Isle

Bowditch Trail

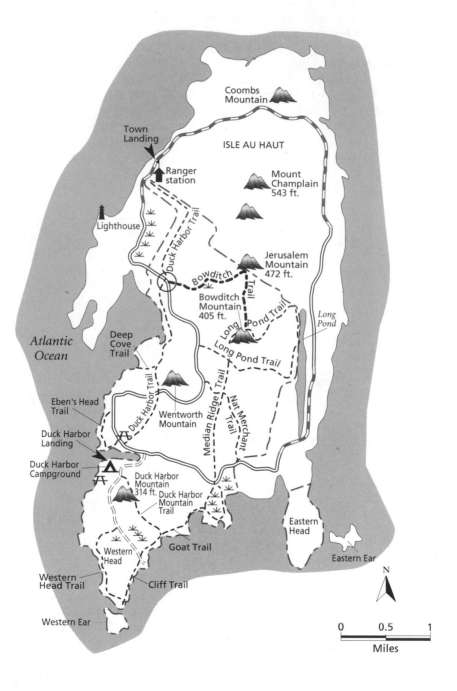

au Haut's north-south ridge. Behind you, you can catch views of the ocean between the trees.

At 2.8 miles from the town landing, after attaining the ridge, the trail makes a sharp right turn at a junction at the park boundary. Follow the sign that says "South." The trail goes up and down the rocky ridge, through rhodora and sheep laurel, fiddlehead ferns, and mature spruce stands. You can catch glimpses of the ocean between the trees here, too.

At 3.2 miles from the town landing, the trail jogs right and climbs a bit, then curves left to an open area with limited views west toward some of Isle au Haut's wooded hills. The trail winds along the ridge; be careful because it can be wet and slippery. After you pass a field of ferns, you'll reach the unmarked and wooded summit of Bowditch Mountain at 3.7 miles at the junction with the Long Pond Trail. There are no views here. You can return to the trailhead the way you came or do a loop back to the town landing using the Long Pond Trail and the island road. To loop back from the summit, bear right (southwest) on the Long Pond Trail, and turn right (northwest) at the next trail junction, in 0.5 mile. Reach the island loop road in another 0.4 mile. Turn right onto the road and reach the town landing in another 3 miles.

89 Median Ridge Trail—North and South Spurs

Highlights:	Rock garden; old-growth woods; cedar swamp; little traveled.
Type of hike:	Day hike; out-and-back; best done as part of overnight camping trip.
Total distance:	5.6 miles north spur; 3.2 miles south spur, including 1.3 miles to reach trailhead.
Difficulty:	Moderate.

Finding the trailhead: From Duck Harbor Landing, turn left on the unpaved Western Head Road and walk 0.3 mile. Turn right on the unpaved island loop road and walk another 1 mile. The trailhead for the Median Ridge north spur is on the left, for the south spur, it's on the right.

Parking and trailhead facilities: None.

Key points North Spur:
- 0.0 Duck Harbor Landing; bear left on the Western Head Road, then right on the island loop road.
- 1.3 Median Ridge Trailhead, north spur, reached via the Western Head and island loop roads.
- 2.4 Junction with the Nat Merchant Trail.
- 2.8 Junction with the Long Pond Trail.

Median Ridge Trail—North and South

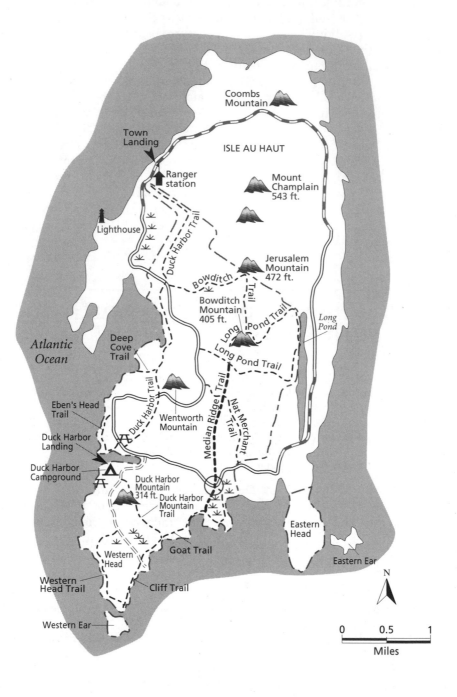

Coombs
Mountain

Town
Landing

ISLE AU HAUT

Ranger
station

Mount
Champlain
543 ft.

Lighthouse

Duck Harbor Trail

Jerusalem
Mountain
472 ft.

Bowditch
Trail

Bowditch
Mountain
405 ft.

Long Pond Trail

Long
Pond

Atlantic
Ocean

Deep
Cove
Trail

Long Pond Trail

Eben's Head
Trail

Duck Harbor Trail

Wentworth
Mountain

Median Ridge Trail

Nat Merchant
Trail

Duck Harbor
Landing

Duck Harbor
Campground

Duck Harbor
Mountain
314 ft. Duck Harbor
Mountain
Trail

Eastern
Head

Western
Head

Goat Trail

Eastern Ear

Western
Head Trail

Cliff Trail

N

Western Ear

0   0.5   1

Miles

Key points South Spur:

   0.0   Duck Harbor Landing; bear left on the Western Head Road, then right on the island loop road.

   1.3   Median Ridge Trailhead, south spur, reached via the Western Head and island loop roads.

   1.6   Junction with the Goat Trail.

The hike: North spur: Out of the way and with few coastal views, the 1.5-mile-long north spur of the Median Ridge Trail is most useful for overnight campers, as part of long day hikes traversing the island. The trail provides access to Isle au Haut's central ridge and other in-

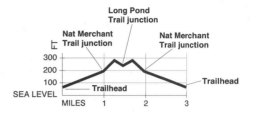

land paths like the Long Pond and Bowditch trails, while also taking you by a rock garden, towering old-growth trees, and cedar swamps.

From the island loop road, the north spur quickly ascends the median ridge, crosses a creek, and goes through a rock garden. After a bit of up and down, the trail takes you by boggy areas with lots of skunk cabbage. Be careful on the slick tree roots along the trail here. Reach the intersection with the Nat Merchant Trail at 2.4 miles.

Next the trail ascends through sheep laurel and fiddlehead ferns, and takes you past huge cedars. Leveling off, the trail comes to a clearing and ends at the intersection with the Long Pond Trail at 2.8 miles. Return the way you came.

Options: To loop back to Duck Harbor Landing, backtrack from the trail's end to the junction with the Nat Merchant Trail. Turn left (southeast) onto the Nat Merchant Trail, reaching the unpaved island loop road in another 1 mile. Turn right (west) on the road and head back to Duck Harbor Landing.

South spur: The 0.3-mile south spur heads southwest from the island loop road, goes through marshland, and ends at the Goat Trail, on the eastern end of scenic Barred Harbor. Return the way you came.

Options: At the junction with the Goat Trail, turn right (west) and follow the rugged shoreline trail for 1.2 miles to the unpaved Western Head Road. Turn right on Western Head Road and reach Duck Harbor Landing in another 1.3 miles.

90 Nat Merchant Trail

> **Highlights:** Boggy woods walk near Merchant Brook; little
> traveled.
> **Type of hike:** Day hike; out-and-back or loop as part of overnight
> trip.
> **Total distance:** 5.6 miles, including 1.7 miles to reach trailhead.
> **Difficulty:** Easy.

Finding the trailhead: From Duck Harbor Landing, bear left on the unpaved Western Head Road and skirt the harbor. At 0.3 mile, turn right (southeast) onto the unpaved island loop road. Reach the trailhead in another 1.4 miles, the second trailhead on the left, at the park boundary.

Parking and trailhead facilities: None.

Key points:

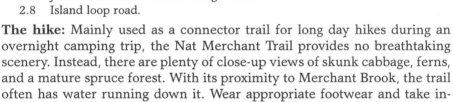

0.0 Duck Harbor Landing; bear left on Western Head Road, then right on the island loop road.
1.7 Nat Merchant Trailhead, reached via the Western Head and island loop roads.
2.4 Slight uphill to rocky knobs.
2.5 Junction with the Median Ridge Trail.
2.8 Island loop road.

The hike: Mainly used as a connector trail for long day hikes during an overnight camping trip, the Nat Merchant Trail provides no breathtaking scenery. Instead, there are plenty of close-up views of skunk cabbage, ferns, and a mature spruce forest. With its proximity to Merchant Brook, the trail often has water running down it. Wear appropriate footwear and take insect repellent during the buggy season.

The trail heads north from the unpaved island loop road and soon hits a series of log bridges with gigantic skunk cabbage growing right through the gaps between the logs. The boggy woods are finally left behind, with a slight elevation gain to some rocky knobs at 2.4 miles. Even though there is no view here, you can hear the sound of the surf crashing if you're hiking on a particularly windy or stormy day. At 2.5 miles, reach the junction with the Median Ridge Trail, where there is a big old birch. One hand-carved sign nailed to a tree says "Nat Merchant," and another says "To Road." Cross the Median Ridge Trail and follow

Skunk cabbage is luxuriant in the moist earth of Isle au Haut.

Nat Merchant Trail

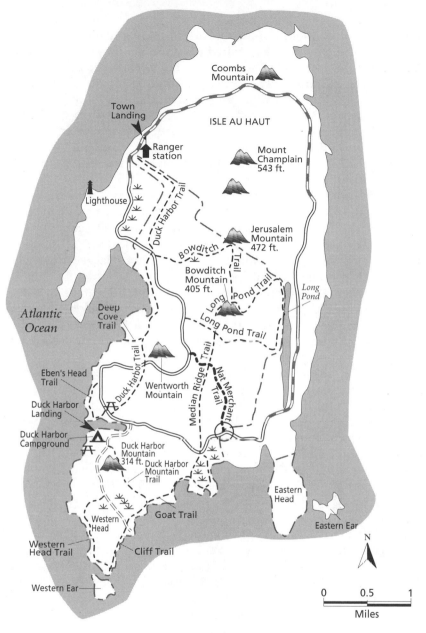

the sign to the road. The trail ends at 2.8 miles at the unpaved island loop road, 4 miles south of the town landing.

You can return to the trailhead the way you came or loop back by turning left (south) onto the island loop road. If you stay on the road, you will reach Duck Harbor Campground in another 2.5 miles, but if you take a shortcut via the Duck Harbor Trail, you'll reach the campground in 2 miles.

Schoodic Peninsula

The only section of Acadia National Park on the mainland, Schoodic Peninsula is one of the park's least visited parts. There aren't many hikes here, and the longest one is only 0.9 mile long, but what Schoodic lacks in trails, it makes up for in solitude. The closest most visitors to Acadia get to Schoodic is atop Cadillac Mountain, when they look southeast from the summit parking lot and see the distinctive Schoodic Head in the distance, across Frenchman Bay. Schoodic is also a magnificent place to see the forces of nature up close, with its rocky coast jutting into the Atlantic. But don't get too close, especially during stormy weather. People have been swept away by waves violently crashing against the shore.

The rocky coast here also includes prime examples of what geologists call dikes—prominent black bands of basalt in between the granite. Years ago, under great pressure, magma intruded into underground fractures in the granite, then cooled and hardened into the black basaltic dikes. Erosion exposed the dikes at the surface and wore them down to form jagged crevices. Some dikes measure more than 150 feet wide.

Schoodic Peninsula is an hour away from Mount Desert Island, due east of Ellsworth on U.S. Highway 1, then south of West Gouldsboro off Maine Highway 186. The closest town to the Schoodic park entrance is a little hamlet called Winter Harbor. There's limited lodging and dining available there, testimony to the nontouristy nature of the area.

There's only one way in and one way out of the Schoodic section of Acadia, along the one-way paved Park Loop Road that parallels the coast around the peninsula. One hike—the Schoodic Head Trail—begins off a gravel road that heads left and inland from the paved Park Loop Road, 2.5 miles south of the park entrance and before the U.S. Naval Reservation. The three other hikes—the Alder, Anvil, and East trails—begin directly from the paved Park Loop Road, after it passes the naval reservation and Schoodic Point.

Although the Anvil and East trails are described here as heading uphill from the paved Park Loop Road toward Schoodic Head, it's possible to drive the gravel road inland to the Schoodic Head parking area and walk them downhill first. But this steep gravel road is closed when it is wet or icy.

For those who want the Schoodic Peninsula views with a minimum of climbing, there are plenty of points along the Park Loop Road to park and take a walk along the rocky coast. And it's possible to get the view atop Schoodic Head with only a short, easy walk from the gravel Schoodic Head parking area, via the Anvil and Schoodic Head trails.

Schoodic Peninsula

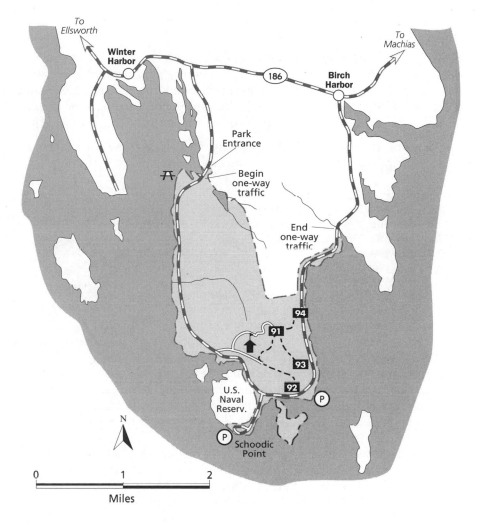

91 Schoodic Head Trail

Highlights:	Expansive views from atop Schoodic Head; elevation 440 feet.
Type of hike:	Day hike; out-and-back.
Total distance:	1.2 miles, including 0.1 mile to reach trailhead.
Difficulty:	Moderate.

Finding the trailhead: From the Schoodic park entrance, head south on the one-way paved Park Loop Road for 2.5 miles and turn left onto gravel road. At the fork in the gravel road, bear left toward the Schoodic Head parking area. Follow the Anvil Trail from the south end of the parking area for 0.1 mile. The Schoodic Head Trailhead is on the right.

Parking and trailhead facilities: Parking is available at the gravel Schoodic Head parking area, but there are no facilities.

Key points:
- 0.0 Schoodic Head parking area.
- 0.1 Schoodic Head Trailhead, reached via the Anvil Trail.
- 0.2 Schoodic Head viewpoint.
- 0.6 Gravel road.

The hike: This trail provides a fresh perspective on Acadia National Park, taking you along Schoodic Head, the distinctive knob that most park visitors see only from a distance, from atop Cadillac Mountain.

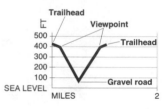

In 0.2 mile from the Schoodic Head parking area, reach the Schoodic Head viewpoint. Here you can get dramatic vistas west to faraway Mount Desert Island and Cadillac Mountain, Frenchman Bay, the Porcupine Islands, and Egg Rock and its lighthouse. Closer by, to the right (northeast) are Ned Island and Turtle Island. To the left (southeast) is Pond Island. These are the best views on the trail, although the path continues downhill to a gravel road.

If you choose to hike on, be careful because the trail descends steeply, then goes through a wet area on log bridges. The blue metal trail markers here are shaped like woodpeckers and are hard to miss. The trail continues down through lush woods and reaches the gravel road at 0.6 mile. Return the way you came.

Options: For a 2.3-mile loop, rather than returning the way you came, turn left at the gravel road for 0.1 mile and pick up the 0.6-mile-long Alder Trail. Take the Alder Trail to the paved Park Loop Road along the coast and turn left for 0.1 mile, to the Anvil Trail. Turn left and ascend the 0.9-mile Anvil Trail back to the gravel Schoodic Head parking area.

Schoodic Head Trail

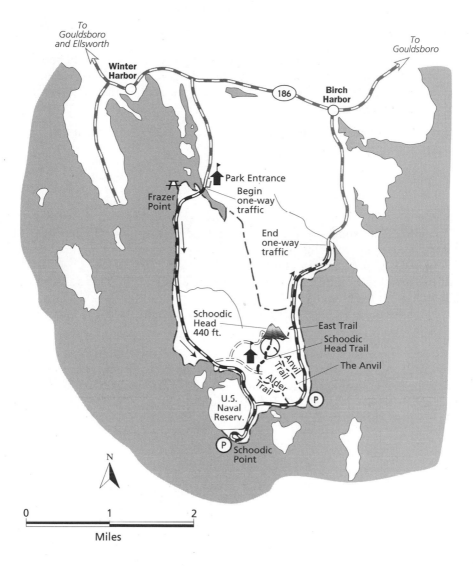

92 Alder Trail

Highlights:	Pleasant walk through old farmland.
Type of hike:	Day hike; out-and-back.
Total distance:	1.2 miles.
Difficulty:	Easy.

Finding the trailhead: From the Schoodic park entrance, head south on the one-way paved Park Loop Road past the U.S. Naval Reservation and Schoodic Point, to the Blueberry Hill parking area. The trailhead is on the left (north) side of the road.

Parking and trailhead facilities: Parking is available at the Blueberry Hill parking area; there are no facilities.

Key points:
    0.0   Alder Trailhead.
    0.6   Gravel road.

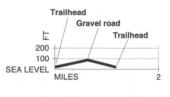

The hike: This short, easy walk goes inland from the rocky shore along a grassy path among overgrown fruit trees and alder bushes. Butterflies are common here, as are pitch pines, cedars, birches, and ash trees. This pleasant trail highlights the contrast between ocean and old farmland. At 0.6 mile, the trail ends at a gravel road. Return the way you came.

Options: To do an approximately 2.2-mile loop rather than returning the way you came, turn left at the gravel road for 0.1 mile, then right onto the 0.5-mile Schoodic Head Trail. Climb the Schoodic Head Trail to the junction with the Anvil Trail. Turn right onto the 0.9-mile Anvil Trail and head down to the paved Park Loop Road. Turn right on the Park Loop Road for 0.1 mile back to the Blueberry Hill parking area.

Alder Trail

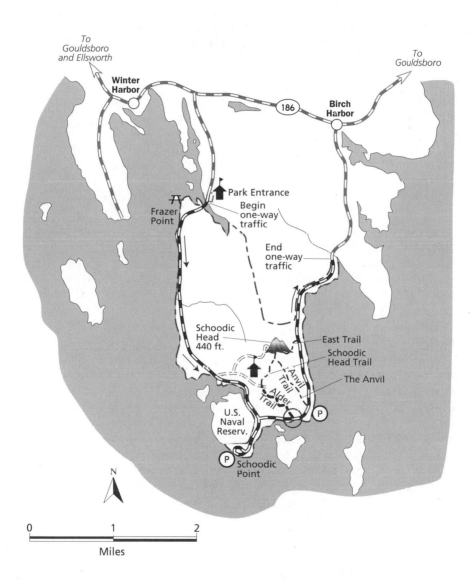

93 Anvil Trail

Highlights: Hike up the Anvil and Schoodic Head; great views.
Type of hike: Day hike; out-and-back.
Total distance: 1.8 miles.
Difficulty: Moderate.

Finding the trailhead: From the Schoodic park entrance, head south on the one-way paved Park Loop Road past the U.S. Naval Reservation and Schoodic Point, to the first pullout 0.1 mile beyond the Blueberry Hill parking area. The trailhead is across the road.

Parking and trailhead facilities: Park at the first pullout along the paved Park Loop Road after the Blueberry Hill parking area.

Key points:

0.0   Anvil Trailhead.
0.3   The Anvil.
0.8   Junction with the Schoodic Head Trail, turn left.
0.9   Schoodic Head viewpoint.

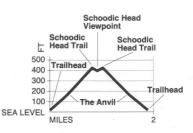

The hike: The longest hike on Schoodic Peninsula, the Anvil Trail provides access to views from both the rocky knob known as the Anvil and the 440-foot Schoodic Head. The trail starts by climbing through woods of ash, birch, and spruce.

At 0.1 mile, it takes a sharp right and goes uphill steeply. Then it zigzags up a cliff and squeezes between rock faces. At 0.3 mile, reach the Anvil overlook with its views of Mount Desert Island and Cadillac Mountain across the ocean to the west and Schoodic Head immediately to the right (northwest). The trail dips down and crosses a smooth rock face with limited views of Schoodic Head ahead. Entering the woods again, the trail stays relatively level until the final assault up Schoodic Head. Go up some loose rock, a series of stone steps over a cliff, and switchbacks. As the trail nears the summit, it levels off a bit and takes you over a wet area on a log bridge.

At 0.8 mile, turn left at a junction with the Schoodic Head Trail. At 0.9 mile, reach the Schoodic Head viewpoint, with a vista straight ahead (west) to Cadillac Mountain, Frenchman Bay, the Porcupine Islands, and Egg Rock and its lighthouse. To the right (northeast) is Ned Island and Turtle Island; to the left (southeast), Pond Island. Return the way you came.

Options: For a 2.2-mile loop rather than returning the way you came, continue downhill on the Schoodic Head Trail for another 0.4 mile. Turn left at the gravel road and reach the Alder Trail in another 0.1 mile. Continue on the 0.6-mile Alder Trail to the paved Park Loop Road. Turn left on the Park Loop Road and return to the Anvil Trailhead in another 0.1 mile.

Anvil Trail

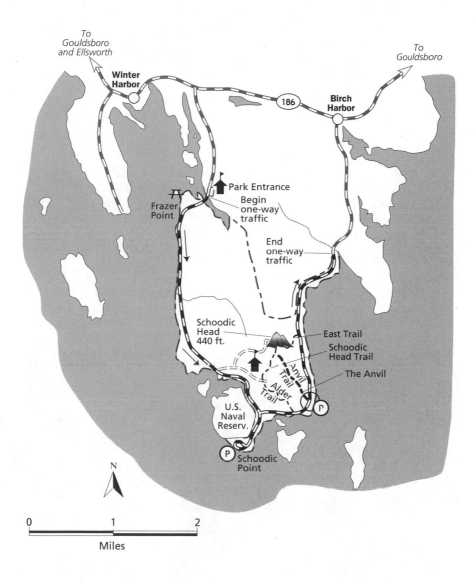

To
Gouldsboro
and Ellsworth

To
Gouldsboro

**Winter
Harbor**

186

**Birch
Harbor**

Park Entrance

Begin
one-way
traffic

Frazer
Point

End
one-way
traffic

Schoodic
Head
440 ft.

East Trail

Schoodic
Head Trail

The Anvil

Anvil
Trail

Alder
Trail

U.S.
Naval
Reserv.

P

P Schoodic
Point

N

0   1   2

Miles

94 East Trail

Highlights: Short, steep climb to Schoodic Head viewpoint.
Type of hike: Day hike; out-and-back.
Total distance: 1.4 miles.
Difficulty: Moderate.

Finding the trailhead: From the Schoodic park entrance, head south on the one-way paved Park Loop Road past the U.S. Naval Reservation and Schoodic Point and 1 mile beyond the Blueberry Hill parking area. The trailhead is on the left (west) side of the road.

Parking and trailhead facilities: Park in the pullout on the right side of the road 1 mile after the Blueberry Hill parking area across from Spruce Point.

Key points:
- 0.0 East Trailhead.
- 0.5 Cross the gravel Schoodic Head parking area to the Anvil Trail.
- 0.6 Junction with the Schoodic Head Trail; turn right.
- 0.7 Schoodic Head viewpoint.

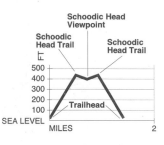

The hike: This short but steep trail goes up the eastern side of Schoodic Head, with views along the way of Schoodic Point to the southwest and Spruce Point to the northeast. The trail begins as a level woods walk, then rises quickly via switchbacks. In the spring, Canada dogwood, also known as bunchberry, and tiny

A tuft of lichen on the trail.

East Trail

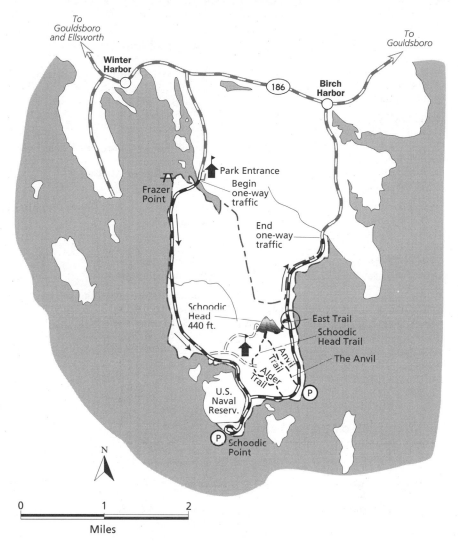

To Gouldsboro and Ellsworth

To Gouldsboro

Winter Harbor

186

Birch Harbor

Park Entrance

Begin one-way traffic

End one-way traffic

Frazer Point

Schoodic Head 440 ft.

East Trail

Schoodic Head Trail

The Anvil

Anvil Trail

Alder Trail

U.S. Naval Reserv.

P

P

Schoodic Point

N

0   1   2

Miles

white starflowers bloom along the trail. There are also lots of gnarled pitch pines, cedars, and sea-green lichen here.

At 0.5 mile, after you've risen above treeline, the trail reaches the gravel Schoodic Head parking area. Cross the parking area to the Anvil Trail, and at 0.6 mile turn right onto the Schoodic Head Trail. Reach the Schoodic Head viewpoint at 0.7 mile, with a great view straight ahead (west) to Mount Desert Island and Cadillac Mountain, Frenchman Bay, the Porcupine Islands, and Egg Rock and its lighthouse. To the right (northeast) is Ned Island and Turtle Island, and to the left (southeast) is Pond Island. Return the way you came.

Appendix A: For More Information

Acadia National Park
P.O. Box 177
Bar Harbor, ME 04609
(207) 288-3338
www.nps.gov/acad/

Hulls Cove Visitor Center
Maine Highway 3, northwest of Bar Harbor
Open 8 A.M. to 4 P.M. daily, mid-April
through June, and October
Open 8 A.M. to 6 P.M. daily, July and August
Hours vary daily in September

Winter Visitor Center
Acadia National Park headquarters
Maine Highway 233, west of Bar Harbor
Open 8 A.M. to 4:30 P.M. daily, November
through mid-April
Closed Thanksgiving Day, December 24 and
25, and January 1

FOR INFORMATION ON CONSERVATION AND
HISTORIC PRESERVATION PROJECTS IN THE
PARK AND MEMBERSHIP:
Friends of Acadia
P.O. Box 45
Bar Harbor, ME 04609
1-800-625-0321
www.friendsofacadia.org

FOR INFORMATION ON NATIVE AMERICAN
HERITAGE AND HISTORY:
Abbe Museum
P.O. Box 286
Bar Harbor, ME 04609
(207) 288-3519
www.abbemuseum.org

FOR THE MAIL BOAT SCHEDULE FROM
STONINGTON TO ISLE AU HAUT:
Isle au Haut Co.
P.O. Box 709
Stonington, ME 04681
(207) 367-5193

FOR A SCHEDULE, ROUTE MAPS, AND
OTHER INFORMATION FOR THE FREE
ISLAND EXPLORER BUS SHUTTLE:
www.exploreacadia.com

FOR LODGING AND SERVICES
INFORMATION:
Bar Harbor Chamber of Commerce
P.O. Box 158
Bar Harbor, ME 04609
(207) 288-5103
www.barharbor.org

Mount Desert Chamber of Commerce
P.O. Box 675
Northeast Harbor, ME 04662
(207) 276-5040

**Southwest Harbor/Tremont Chamber of
Commerce**
P.O. Box 1143
Southwest Harbor, ME 04679
1-800-423-9264
www.acadia.net/swhtrcoc

**Schoodic Peninsula Chamber of
Commerce**
P.O. Box 381
Winter Harbor, ME 04693
1-800-231-3008 (outside Maine)
(207) 963-7658
www.acadia-schoodic.org

**Deer Isle–Stonington Chamber of
Commerce**
P.O. Box 459
Stonington, ME 04681
(207) 348-6124
www.deerislemaine.com

Ellsworth Area Chamber of Commerce
P.O. Box 267
Ellsworth, ME 04605
(207) 667-5584
w2.downeast.net/eacc/

FOR INFORMATION ON LEAVE NO TRACE
PRINCIPLES:
LNT Inc.
P.O. Box 997
Boulder, CO 80306
1-800-332-4100
www.lnt.org

Appendix B: Further Reading

Many of these helpful books can be found at the bookstores run by Eastern National at the park's Hulls Cove Visitor Center and the Nature Center at the Sieur de Monts entrance. Local bookstores and libraries and the gift shops atop Cadillac Mountain, at the Jordan Pond House, and along the Park Loop Road near Thunder Hole may also have many of these volumes.

Appalachian Mountain Club. *AMC Guide to Mount Desert Island and Acadia National Park.* Boston: Appalachian Mountain Club Books, 1993.

Coffin, Margie and Jim Vekasi. *Historic Hiking Trail System of Mount Desert Island: Cultural Landscape Report for Acadia National Park, Maine, Volume 1.* Bar Harbor, Maine: National Park Service, 1999.

Dorr, George B. *The Story of Acadia National Park.* Bar Harbor, Maine: Acadia Press, 1991.

Gillmore, Robert. *Great Walks of Acadia National Park & Mount Desert Island.* Goffstown, N.H.: Great Walks, 1994.

Grierson, Ruth Gortner. *Wildlife Watcher's Guide: Acadia National Park.* Minocqua, Wisc.: NorthWord Press Inc., 1995.

Harmon, Will. *Leave No Trace.* Helena, Mont.: Falcon Press, 1997.

Harmon, Will. *Wild Country Companion.* Helena, Mont.: Falcon Press, 1994.

Nyiri, Alan. *Acadia National Park: Maine's Intimate Parkland.* Camden, Maine: Down East Books, 1986.

Rothe, Robert. *Acadia: The Story Behind the Scenery.* Las Vegas: KC Publications, 1987.

St. Germain, Tom and Jay Saunders. *Trails of History.* Bar Harbor, Maine: Parkman Publications, 1993.

St. Germain, Tom. *A Walk in the Park: Acadia's Hiking Guide.* Bar Harbor, Maine: Parkman Publications, 2000.

Appendix C: Hiker's Checklist

With limited backpacking allowed only on Isle au Haut, packing for a hike in Acadia is relatively simple. Use this list to make sure you have everything you need.

☐ Day pack
☐ Drinking water
☐ High-energy snacks
☐ Insect repellent
☐ Hiking boots (recommended) or at least sneakers
☐ Tissue
☐ Small flashlight or headlamp
☐ Maps and field guides
☐ Compass
☐ Watch
☐ Sunscreen
☐ Sunglasses

☐ Cap or hat with brim
☐ Fleece jacket or woolen sweater
☐ Rain gear
☐ Small first-aid kit, with bandages and antibacterial ointment for cuts, moleskin for blisters, and aspirin or anti-inflammatory for aches and pains
☐ Small scissors or Swiss Army knife with scissors
☐ Camera and film
☐ Notebook and pencils
☐ Binoculars

Index

About the Authors

Dolores Kong and Dan Ring backpacked all 270 miles of the Appalachian Trail in Maine and have been hiking and backpacking together for years in New England and elsewhere. Dolores is a reporter at the *Boston Globe* and Dan is statehouse bureau chief in Boston for the *Union-News* of Springfield, Massachusetts. They are married and live outside Boston.

Dolores Kong and Dan Ring on the Razorback Trail in Acadia National Park.